Stuar...
of Weste...

<small>UNIVERSITY OF
THE PACIFIC</small>

HORSE WRANGLER

Sixty Years in the Saddle
in Wyoming and Montana

HORSE
WRANGLER

SIXTY YEARS IN THE SADDLE
IN WYOMING AND MONTANA

By Floyd C. Bard
As told to Agnes Wright Spring

UNIVERSITY OF OKLAHOMA PRESS : NORMAN

LIBRARY OF CONGRESS CATALOG CARD NUMBER: 60-13477

Copyright 1960 by the University of Oklahoma Press,
Publishing Division of the University.
Composed and printed at Norman, Oklahoma, U.S.A.,
by the University of Oklahoma Press.
First edition.

FOREWORD

My INTENSE INTEREST IN THE Johnson County War, called the Cattlemen's Invasion of Wyoming, began when I was asked to "stand up" at the wedding, some years ago, of Frances Davis, daughter of "Hard Winter" Davis, a big cattleman, and Mart Tisdale, the son of Johnnie Tisdale, a homesteader or nester, whose death at the hands of an assailant was one of the incidents leading up to the war. I went with Frances and Mart to Omaha on a cattle train for the wedding.

For years I have collected data pertaining to the participants in this so-called war. I was engaged by the Wyoming Stock Growers Association to write their "70 Years Cow Country"; I knew personally Governor Joseph M. Carey, Senator Francis E. Warren, Governor Amos Barber, and Billy Irvine.

In 1957, when I learned that Floyd Bard of Big Horn, Wyoming, had worked on the roundup with some of the most prominent "nesters" in Johnson County, including Johnnie Tisdale, Jack Flagg, and Al Allison, I began a correspondence with him to urge him to write his autobiography. I hoped to get some unpublished data on the Johnson County War.

Because some of my old classmates at the University of Wyoming were his neighbors in Big Horn, Floyd Bard and his wife,

Mabel, accepted me as their friend and said they would try to send me his story.

As the installments reached me, I realized that here was the story of a man who had lived on the fringe of the frontier, who had seen the Old West, and who had really lived in it as few men now living have done. My interest in the story of the war became secondary. My interest in Floyd Bard increased with each installment. His sincerity, his absolute knowledge of the things he wrote about, and his ability to picture vividly the life he knew were most unusual.

At the age of seventy-eight years, Floyd Bard began to write down his experiences. He finished the work just before his seventy-ninth birthday in April, 1958.

He has pulled no punches. He has written just what he remembered, and his memory for detail is truly remarkable. He has ridden the roundup with nesters, roped wild horses and longhorn cattle on the open range, busted broncs, bought war horses, shot rattlesnakes and prairie dogs, trapped bears and coyotes and wolves. And he remembers every horse he ever wrangled!

From Wyoming, Mr. and Mrs. Bard followed the frontier up to middle Canada and beyond to British Columbia. Then they came back to their beloved homeland in the shadow of the Big Horns, the one-time hunting grounds of the Sioux.

Because of his integrity and "know-how," Floyd Bard has held positions of great trust as foreman for wealthy livestock men. He played polo with them and rode on a championship team with world champion Tommy Hitchcock.

In telling his story, Floyd Bard has used "no high falutin' words." Because, as he says, he was "afraid of spreadin' it on a little too thick." He did not tell that William Moncrieffe said he was the "best cowman I've ever seen."

Up to the time he was nearly twenty, most everyone called Floyd "Kid" or "Pistol." Sometimes they called him "Uncle," because, in his words, "I took my time in gettin' up to a bronc." Yes, he took his time, and he never hitched his horse on the wrong side of the tongue.

In placing his story in my hands for "brushin' up like an old saddle horse after a hard winter," his instructions were—"You're the boss. Tell me which circle to ride."

Agnes Wright Spring

Denver, Colorado
April 20, 1960

CONTENTS

ILLUSTRATIONS

xi

HORSE WRANGLER

Sixty Years in the Saddle in Wyoming and Montana

THE NESTER KID

I WAS BORN ON A HOMESTEAD some forty or fifty miles north of Cheyenne, Wyoming on Little Horse Creek, on April 21, 1879. There was nothing much there but cowboys and long-horned cattle that were being trailed in from Texas.

Like a lot of young men, my father, Charles Warren Bard, headed west when he was sixteen and became a cowboy. His father had died in the trenches in the Civil War. His mother had taken him, when he was very young, from his birthplace, Whiteville, New Jersey, to Mankato, Minnesota to live with her parents. She had died soon afterwards, and his grandmother had raised him.

From Minnesota my father went to Colorado, then drifted into Nebraska. In the summer of 1876, he went to Cheyenne, Wyoming, where he hired out to two men as a buffalo hunter. The wages were forty dollars per month with everything furnished. The camp where he stayed was forty miles out from Cheyenne. One day after he had killed two buffalo cows and a big bull, he was overtaken by a bad blizzard. He dragged the hides over against a small brush thicket, rolled up in the freshly killed bull hide and stayed there until the following morning.

He said he had quite a lot of difficulty getting out of the half-frozen buffalo hide, which he knew had saved his life.

The following spring, my father, then twenty-five years old, hired out to a cow outfit as a roundup cook. There for the first time he met Frank Canton, a lanky cowboy who had drifted in from the southwest. When Frank went to work for the outfit, he didn't have any bed, so my dad shared his bed with him.

During the summer of 1877, Jim Goodrich, the horse wrangler of the outfit, and Dad became very good friends. Late that fall after the roundup wagon had moved into the home ranch, Jim Goodrich and Charley Bard drew up their wages and headed for Fort Dodge, Iowa where Jim's folks lived on a farm. As my dad had been writing letters to Jim's sister, he was kind of anxious to see her. Here at the Goodrich farm Dad and Minerva Emily Goodrich were married. Not long after the wedding Dad headed back for Wyoming and his homestead on Little Horse Creek.

There during the next three months he worked like a beaver building a comfortable log cabin and getting things fixed up for Mother who was due in Cheyenne about the first of April. Dad was Johnnie-on-the-spot to meet her. After a couple days shopping they headed for mother's new home—the homestead. Here they lived during the next four years. A year after Mother arrived in Wyoming I was born. In the fall of 1880, Mother went back to her old home in Iowa where my brother Charles Albert (Tode) Bard was born.

In the spring of 1882, my folks sold the homestead and what cattle they had on hand. Dad rigged up two covered wagons, loaded them with household goods, a mowing machine, and a small hay rake. Dad had got acquainted with a young man named B. F. Perkins who had come out west for his health. As my Mother was to drive one team, a two-horse outfit, Perkins could relieve her. She and us kids could ride with my dad with

4

his four-horse team outfit. The only extra stock was one saddle
pony. As a teamster Perkins wasn't worth a dime. He let the
team wander around the hillsides and once, while crossing a
creek, he tipped the wagon over and broke Mother's sewing
machine. She sure was sore as a sewing machine was a luxury
in those days.

We were a month making the trip from Horse Creek to Buffalo, Wyoming, a distance of about eighty-five miles. We would
stop for a day or two on the road. Mother would wash. She had
a few chickens in a box, and they would be let out for exercise.
At Buffalo the only person the folks knew was Frank Canton,
who at this time was sheriff of Johnson County.

My folks rented a house near the court house where Mother,
Tode, and I made our home. Mother did the cooking for Canton
and some other county officials, while Dad and Perkins went on
farther north looking for a location.

One day as Tode and I were playing alongside of the jail,
digging in the sand by the foundation, along came Canton. He
sure looked mad. He said, "If you boys don't quit that digging,
I'm going to put you both in jail." After that we were both scared
of Canton.

On Mead Creek, about ten miles south of Sheridan, Dad
pitched camp and found what he wanted. He filed a pre-emp-
tion claim on a hundred and sixty acres, while my mother filed
a desert claim on a hundred and twenty acres.

While Dad and Perkins were putting up some prairie hay
and building a good-sized one-room dugout on the bank of
Mead Creek, Mother and us boys continued on at Canton's
place. Just before winter set in we moved into our new home.
The walls were about eight feet high. The lower half of the walls
were dirt, the upper half was jack-pine logs. The roof was poles,
covered with brush, prairie hay, and clay dirt. The floor was dirt,

5

which wasn't too bad after it once got packed down. There in the dugout the five of us lived all through the winter. Dad made regular trips up into the foothills with a team and bobsled to cut jack pines to build a two-room cabin.

That spring of '83, just before the cabin was finished, there came some hot days, melting the snow so fast that the creek went out of its banks and into our dugout. Mother and us boys went to a neighbor over on Prairie Dog Creek, while Perkins and Dad finished our cabin. After the cabin was done the two men drove into Sheridan. Dad came back alone. He said that Perkins got a job working in the J. D. Loucks General Store and Post Office in Sheridan.

It was just one year later, the spring of '84, that Dad went to Big Horn after the mail. There on the stagecoach was Perkins, headin' back for his home in Philadelphia, where his father was a doctor. Dad asked Perkins what he was doing on the stagecoach. He said, "I'll tell you, Charley, it's no go. I am on my way back to my old home to die."

After the two men talked things over for a while, Dad convinced Perkins that the best thing for him to do was to come home with him and file a homestead on a piece of land two miles upstream from the Bard place. And that's what he did. He then went back to Sheridan where he worked at various things during the next few years. This is the same B. F. Perkins who built up the Bank of Commerce, and later became one of Sheridan's most wealthy men.

The year of 1883 was a very busy year for the Bards, Mother and Dad. The first thing was a fencing of a strip of valley land on the west side of Mead Creek. This strip was a quarter-mile wide and three-quarters-mile long. Dad got Jack Dow, a surveyor from over near Big Horn, to come and survey a ditch covering the land. Two or three years earlier Dow had surveyed and helped to map out the town of Big Horn. In 1882 he did the same for Sheridan.

After the survey was done on our place, Mother drove the team and followed the survey stakes while Dad held the plow handles. After the first furrow or two were busted loose, the dirt was pushed over a little by using an A-shaped go-devil made of heavy two-inch plank. After five furrows had been plowed and go-deviled out, there was a pretty good lower ditch-bank made. After a few months time the little ditch was completed. A dam was made across this small stream of Mead Creek, and the water was turned into the ditch. From the ditch the water was spread out over the rich bottomland where there was town after town of prairie dogs.

Now with that irrigation water, Dad had one sure way of getting rid of prairie dogs. There were hundreds of them. He would drown them out. When they started leaving their homes for higher ground, Dad would kill them with his shovel. It seemed as if the country was literally alive with rattlesnakes. There was one sure way of destroying these poison reptiles. In the fall of the year when they were denning up for the winter, the devils were usually found on a red shale hill where there had been a blowout some time during the Dark Ages.

On warm sun shiny days when there was no snow on the ground, the snakes would leave their dens for some fresh air and a snooze in the sunshine. It was a common thing to find two or three dozen rattlers coiled up and asleep only a few feet from the entrance of the den. Most any kind of noise would wake them and they would start crawling over each other towards the den. That was the time to start blasting them with the old shotgun. What were not killed were badly crippled. The snakes were so numerous it wasn't a good policy to go away and leave the cabin door open. The chance was that upon your return there would be a rattler coiled up on the cabin floor sound asleep. Out on the range, it was a common sight to see some cow brute with a head twice its natural size, that had been bitten by a rattlesnake. Sometimes they died. Not so with the horses. They were as shy of the rattlesnake as they were of the big grey wolf, which was taking a heavy toll of range stock.

That summer of 1883, Dad cut enough prairie hay to winter all of our horses. The hay was put up in two separate stacks. One stack served the purpose as a roof for a bank stable that would shelter six head of horses. We had no cattle, not even a milk cow. One day when some Flying E cowboys stopped at the ranch and found we had no milk, Tom Kazee, the wagon boss or foreman, told Dad to take up one of their heifers. These were long-horned, wild heifers and to break one to milk was almost impossible. After we got a good, stout round corral built, Dad corralled one of those heifers that had just come fresh. Mother and us kids were on hand to see the milking of this wild heifer.

When Dad went into the corral with a rope and pail, the heifer charged him. Not having time to climb the corral fence, he dropped flat on the ground and the heifer jumped over him and went on around the corral. Dad yelled to Mother to "open the gate and let that damn cow out."

There were a lot of prairie chickens and they were quite tame. During the winter months they lived mostly on rose buds and chaparral berries, quite often called bull berries or buffalo berries. Down around the stable and on the haystack there were always prairie chickens looking for grass or weed seed.

One of the only two guns on the ranch was a ten-gauge shotgun which Dad had bought from a fellow who got drunk and jammed the barrel in the mud, then tried to fire it. That cracked the barrel nearly half-way up. After the barrels were sawed off it made a dandy prairie-chicken gun, but kicked like a mule.

8

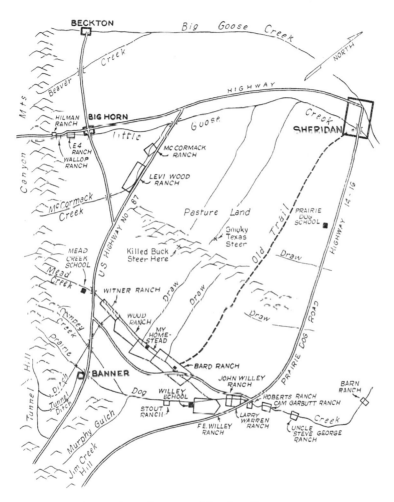

The Bard Ranch and its neighborhood.
Redrawn from a sketch by Floyd Bard.

Dad called the gun Old Betsy. It was the real thing when it came to shooting into a flock of chickens and killing two or three at a shot.

One day while Dad was doing some hunting, just below the buildings, us kids were tagging along. While we were following a path through a wild plum thicket, we came upon a very good saddle, bridle and blanket and a throw rope lying a few feet away from the saddle. Why this outfit was cached in the thicket will always remain a mystery.

Just prior to the Bard's locating on Mead Creek, a man by the name of Iden had a band of sheep on the land. That spring of 1883, one of the old bedgrounds was plowed up and put into garden, where we raised a lot of spuds and vegetables. That winter the Bards had nothing much to worry about. There was a big coal pile only a few feet from the cabin door, mined from a surface coal bank only about a half-mile from the cabin. Mother had put up quite a lot of wild plum preserves and plum butter. As to jelly, there were three kinds: bull berry, wild currant, and choke cherry. As to meat, Dad and another man, with a four-horse outfit, went over into the Powder River country. Up near Hazelton they got a wagonload of mostly elk and some deer. There were plenty of antelope near the ranch. Here at the ranch we were not molested or bothered with Indians. The only Indians we seen was when we went to Sheridan or Big Horn where a few Crows were camped nearby.

One thing we had plenty of was cowboys and long-horned cattle that were trailing in mostly from Texas. The Flying E outfit over on Piney was running about 50,000 head of long horns out on the big open range. Two miles down stream where Mead Creek empties into Prairie Dog was the FE outfit, which had a lot of cattle on the range. Just about every day there would be a cowboy or two ride into the Bard ranch at noon for a bite to eat and a feed for his cowpony. When these cowboys seen Mother making little suits for Tode and me out of discarded clothing, they started saving up their California pants, which were worn only in the seat. Mother sure did make some nice little suits from that discarded clothing.

That winter of 1883 and 1884, there were enough logs hauled from the foothills to build another room on our cabin. The cracks in between the logs were daubed with clay mud. The floor was of rough boards sawed at a little sawmill near the head of Prairie Dog Creek.

Out in front of the cabin there was a hitch rack for horses. Nearby there was a stile or step for the women who rode sidesaddles.

Mother would tie her Polly saddle mare to the hitch rack while she changed into her riding habit. The skirt was about two feet too long. There was a jacket made of the same kind of material. After Mother was ready to go she would mount old Polly, reach down and pick me up off the stile. I rode on behind Mother, while Tode rode on her lap. This is the way we would go to visit some of our neighbors.

The best of the land was taken by the real pioneers such as government scouts, beaver trappers, bull whackers, and mule skinners who were hauling freight into the country. There were times when a road agent would take time off to file a claim on some choice piece of land. I knew one old trapper who swapped off a hundred and sixty acres of good valley land for a team and wagon.

SETTLERS ROLL IN

As THE COVERED WAGON KEPT ROLLING into the country, a part of the real old pioneers would sell off their relinquishment or squatter's right, then move on farther west. Most of these early-day settlers were called nesters. Then came the dirt farmers mostly from Iowa, Missouri, Illinois, and Arkansas. They were called grangers. The nesters had a roundup wagon out on the range working right along with the big cow outfit. The grangers only had a roundup wagon out on the range in late fall to gather their cattle for winter feeding. There were times when the granger and some cow outfit would consolidate, with the cowman furnishing a mess wagon, a cook, and a foreman. The cowman only gathered what stock that really needed feeding, such as cows with fall calves and some old bulls.

In the spring of 1884, the grangers were plowing up sagebrush land and planting it to grain, mostly wheat, which could be ground into flour at the Beckton mill. It was then that Dad plowed up the old prairie-dog town on Mother's desert claim and put it into wheat and oats. With a scarcity of grain binders, Dad and George Griffin cradled or scythed the crop and bound it by hand. Fat Jack Hardy, from over near Buffalo, came with a small horse-power machine and did the threshing for our neighborhood. The next spring the folks leased out our place to a crop-renter for a three-year term. With a team and wagon and a good camp outfit we moved over into the Monkers' and Mathers' big pasture some four miles north of Buffalo. Here we lived in a tent while Dad helped to build the Monkers' and Mathers' irrigation ditch. Late that fall we headed for Big Horn, going by way of the Flying E cow ranch. Here we spent the night. With the roundup over for the season there were quite a lot of cowboys at the ranch. Even if I was not quite six years old, I remember some of the cowboys. There was Jumbo Mc-Kenzie; Bill Cameron; Jim Swisher, one of the wagon bosses; Tom Kazee, another boss; and Fay Parker, the manager. Joe LeFors, a fuzzy-faced kid, was hobbling around on crutches with a broken leg. There were Jim Simpson and Joe Proctor, two colored gentlemen, who had come from Texas with one of the trail herds. The next morning after leaving the cow ranch I was riding my old Jennie burro in the lead of the wagon. While going down a steep hill, old Jennie balked. It was then the team and wagon ran into Jennie knocking her nearly down. After that I rode behind the outfit. Tode and I each had a burro to ride. Tode's burro was a two-year-old, one of Jennie's colts. He rode bareback. I rode an old army saddle. Wherever I went Tode's burro would tag along.

At Big Horn we moved into a house about a hundred feet south of the C. W. Skinner Store. In Big Horn we attended our first term of school. The place wasn't very large, but plenty wild at times. One day when Mother sent me to the store for something there was a fight in progress in front of the store. A big old man with long white whiskers was fighting with a young man. They were rolling and tumbling around on the plank sidewalk. When the old man let the young fellow up, the young one spit a part of the old man's little finger out onto the walk. This I picked up and put on top of a hitch post. I sure felt sorry for the old man. I can yet see him bathing his hand in the water of the ditch that ran by the store.

It was only a few days after this that the young man got what was coming to him. Upon passing by in front of a saloon I heard some loud talk. Upon peeping through the window I saw an older man bring a chair down across the head of the young

13

fellow. I was scared. I thought the young fellow was done for. Well, he wasn't, but it sure broke him of picking fights.

For a small pioneer town, Big Horn had quite a good-sized school. In every family in and around town there were from three to a half-dozen kids. The fall of 1886, Mother rented the Big Horn Hotel just across Main Street from the store. Dad had a saloon about two hundred feet south of the hotel. The school house wasn't more than two hundred yards to the south of the hotel. That winter of 1886–87, with all that deep snow and bitter cold weather, us kids had some difficulty in going and coming from school. This winter of 1886 and 1887 has always been remembered. When winter set in, there were possibly a million cattle out on the big open range of Wyoming where there was free grass and water for all. With that deep snow, bitter cold weather, and one blizzard after another, more than half the range stock died. The spring of 1887 found the cattlemen just about whipped. Some were flat broke with scarcely enough left to pay off their cowboys. Some of the outfits were so badly bent that they only retained a part of their range men.

With a surplus of cowboys, some drifted back down into Texas. Some drifted into the small, pioneer towns and started into some kind of business of their own. But the largest per cent stayed. They took land by a squatter's right or some kind of right, and became nesters starting up a cattle business of their own. When they started to branding a few slicks or mavericks they were called rustlers. These nesters or rustlers pooled together and ran a roundup wagon of their own.

I can remember seeing old Gidley, the superintendent of the stage line, come into the office of the hotel during that winter. After discarding his buffalo overcoat he went and stood beside the old pot-bellied heater. There he went to taking the icicles from his long, sandy mustache. Big Horn might be called the end of a division of the stage line. Here is where the stage horses were changed and a new driver took over. There on the bank of Little Goose Creek was a stable that would shelter several spans of driving stock, mostly horses that were raised by Gidley. All of the stage horses were branded GID on the left thigh. Among the stage drivers I can only remember two that boarded at the hotel. Bill Eckerson and a nephew of Gidley named Harry Cochran. One day when Harry was laying over in town, he went to the Skinner and Sackett pond just east of town. He didn't return for supper. His clothing was found near the pond. After several attempts, it was Lee Sackett who dove into the pond and brought Harry to the surface. He was among the first to be buried in the Big Horn cemetery.

That spring and summer of 1887, both Mother and Dad were doing a very good business. They were investing their money in livestock, both cattle and horses. Whenever they found a bargain they snapped it up. They would take the stock to the ranch, where the renter took over.

Quite a few people came in by stage, and after stopping a while at the hotel, would move on somewhere else looking for a location. The larger per cent of them stopped at Sheridan. Among those I remember were J. F. (Judge) Hoop and his young wife, a Miss Ivy, Tom Tynan, Tom Green, Fay Summers and a newspaperman, Joe Debarth, who rode a grey Indian pony over from Lander. He was the man who wrote up the life of Frank Grouard, one of the greatest Indian scouts among them all. There was Andy Eads, who landed in Big Horn with a small bunch of Durham cattle. After boarding some time at the hotel, he paid his board bill with two red milk cows, then moved onto Prairie Dog Creek, two miles east of Sheridan. It wasn't long until he set up a harness and saddle shop in Sheridan. Why more men did not locate in Big Horn was probably due to the fact that Sheridan would get the railroad when it was built into the country.

Johnson County's first and second annual fairs were held over across Little Goose Creek, just to the east and south of Big Horn. There on some good bottomland of the Jack Sackett place the race track and fair grounds were located. The trustees of the fair voted "to furnish every convenience for those who bring their families and pitch their tents at Big Horn during the fair. Free wood and clean straw, good camping ground near one of the finest streams of water in Wyoming and feed and provisions at reasonable rates. Good beds and restaurant facilities can be had." During the second fair, in one of the races, a beautiful bay or brown thoroughbred stud fell and broke a front leg at the knee. Levi Woods on McCormack Creek bought this stud and bred him to some Missouri mares and a few mustangs. It was only a few years until the Woods ranch had some of the best saddle stock in the country.

When the renter's lease was up in the spring of 1888, my folks sold out their interests in Big Horn. We were sure happy to be back on the ranch. During the past three years, the folks had bought up about fifty head of cattle and some horses, among them several good, gentle saddle ponies. We nester's kids, Tode and I, sure made good use of some of those ponies. The renter hadn't been idle. The ranch was all fenced. The meadows were mostly seeded down to alfalfa and timothy. There were several new neighbors. One of them had about thirty head of Indian ponies. He spent one winter on the Jack Burnsides ranch just down stream from the Bard ranch.

During the next two years, Tode and I put in part time on the range looking after our stock. The other half was spent in school. In the summer of 1889, we rode horseback four miles to the Banner school. Our teacher, Bill Brown, boarded at our place and rode with us to school.

In the fall of 1889, the folks leased out the ranch and stock against Mother's wishes. Mother was the real rancher. Dad was the town guy. We moved into Buffalo, where Dad got a job as day cook in the American Restaurant. That winter we kids attended the Buffalo school and lived in a house near the bank of Clear Creek just down back of the Brick livery stable. That spring of 1890, just after school had let out Mother asked me to run over to Mrs. Taylor, one of our neighbors, and borrow her shears to cut my hair. That's where I first met Jack Flagg. He offered me a job wrangling horses at thirty dollars per month and take my wages in yearling heifers at eleven dollars per head. The folks said it would be O.K. with them, if I wanted to go with Flagg.

It was only a few days prior to the meeting with Flagg that I was up at Red Angus' place, watching Red groom his rangy-built brown gelding that was wearing the US brand. This top-notch saddle horse Red probably bought off of some army officer at Fort McKinney, two miles southwest of Buffalo. One day while I was at Red's place playing with his bloodhound puppies, Red gave me one. When I took the pup home, Mother said, "No." A day or two later I swapped the pup to Bill Foster for a cream-colored saddle pony. The pony was small but gentle and well broke, just the right size for a kid. The only saddle that I owned was the old army saddle. Tode had a new saddle that Dad had bought from old man Lynn, who had a saddle shop next door to the American Restaurant. This was the first saddle that was put together by Percy Wilkerson, a boy learning the saddle trade. In later years the Wilkerson saddles became quite famous among the cowboys.

Now with this cream-colored pony and Tode's new saddle, I was all set to go with Flagg. Early one morning, Mother tied my little war bag (sack of clothing) on back of my saddle, told me to be a good boy, then kissed me good-bye. It was then that Flagg and I rode out of Buffalo heading for Powder River. Our first stop was at the Hank Devoe horse ranch, where we had lunch with the Devoe family, and Sig Donahue and Ranger Jones, who were breaking horses there at the Bar 5 (5̄) horse ranch. That night we rode up to the nester wagon, which was camped on the bank of Powder River. Here I met Flagg's four partners in the cattle business, Lew Webb, Tom Gardner, Billie Hill, and Al Allison, and the cook, who was a German called Dutchie. He was a poor roundup cook. The only meat we had then was beef, and it was good beef—yearling heifer, the best on the range. We cowboys liked the steaks fried, but with Dutchie it was different. Everything was boiled. I never did know what Dutchie's name was. Maybe he didn't have one over here in the United States.

A HORSE WRANGLER FOR NESTERS

THE MORNING AFTER I REACHED the nester wagon, I took over the job as a horse wrangler. There were about forty head of good saddle horses in the cavvy, or remuda. Each partner had his own string of cow horses. In my string there were three ponies, a rather tall flea bitten bay, a little old bench-kneed brown that wasn't worth a damn, and a small strawberry roan that was a real saddle pony. At first I was a little homesick and some disappointed. When I hired out I supposed it to be herding horses on some ranch. At first I was a little spooky, with the cowboys all having some sort of a gun in a holster on their cartridge belt. Some of the tough-looking guys were wearing two six-shooters. With most everyone being nice to me, it was only a few days 'till I felt right at home among the cowboys. These five men of the nester wagon were using the hat ⌂ brand on their cattle. They were all top cow hands who knew the cow business and range conditions. When the winter of 1886-87 hit the country, they probably were among those who were out of a job. They pooled their wages, located a claim on the Red Fork of Powder River, and started up in the cattle business. They were not cattle thieves. They were just small cattlemen or nesters, no different than 80 per cent of the nesters and grangers. They probably would brand a maverick or slick when one crossed their path. The HAT wagon worked right along with the cow outfits. They were, though, not allowed to work the roundup until the cowmen were through. There were always nesters at the HAT wagon, gathering up their own cattle, branding up their calves. The cowboys and nesters were quite friendly. It was the foremen or managers of the cow outfits who were bitter towards the nester. They were all in the maverick game. Some of the managers or foremen for the cow outfits had their own private brands, and in one way or another were building up their herd with mavericks. It was the big cowmen who were caught in the squeeze, which led up to the cattle war.

That summer of 1890, during the spring or general roundup, there were, at one time, nine roundups working the range together. There were sure some big roundups. The big-jawed steers were cut from the roundup and were shot down like buffalo. With their jawbone full of pus, probably caused from a bruise or snakebite, the meat was no good. One day when the gunmen failed in stopping one of these big jaws, it came into our camp. Was sure on the prod. Nearly wrecked our camp. There were nesters in the mess wagon and nesters under the wagon. When the steer saw me riding into camp—well, I just had to do some fast riding to outrun that big old long horn.

Out on that big open range along with many other roundup wagons the "76" outfit had two wagons. Jim Drummond was the wagon boss of one wagon and Blue Osborn was boss of the other wagon. Blue was a lanky cowboy. He wore a red mustache and had red hair. Was sure a good cowman. One day while my cavvy was grazing along a little valley, I rode over to where the roundup was being worked. Blue put me on his top cut horse, Hornet, and told me to ride into the roundup and cut out a white cow. It was Hornet that cut out the cow. When the cow went into the cut, Hornet made for a small knoll about two hundred yards away. On top of the knoll he quit running, began to snort and wave his tail in the air, just like an old ridge-running gelding. Just before he took off again, a cowboy caught old Hornet and pulled me from the saddle. Hornet was a top cutting horse, but he was no kid horse. Working for the "76," Blue had two men that I remember quite well. One had the nickname of Red Shirt. He most always wore a red shirt. The other man was a lanky, good-looking cowboy called Curly Vest. The vest he wore looked like it might be the hide from some poodle dog's back. One day when there was calf branding going at the big roundup corral, Curly Vest along with other calf wrastlers unbuckled his six-shooter belt and hung it on the corral fence. After the branding was over, Curly Vest forgot his six-shooter and belt. He hadn't gone far 'til I overtook him. Together we rode back to the corral where he gave me ninety cents, mostly in nickles and dimes. It was only a short time after this that Curly Vest was drowned in the North Fork of Powder River, while trying to swim his horse across the stream when it was

Floyd Bard, 10, and Tode Bard, 9,
as "town kids" and scholars.
"The next year, Floyd became a full-fledged horse wrangler."

Cinchin' up tight.
"With a bronc on cold mornings, a cowboy usually had to
tie up a hind foot, kick the bronc in the belly a few times,
before it could be saddled."
Courtesy the Library, State Historical Society of Colorado

running bank full, at the old One Hand Smithie place, now the place called Mayoworth. It was Smithie who, about two weeks later, found Curly Vest's body tangled up in a pile of drift wood.

This man Red Shirt I think was a cowpoke, wasn't worth a damn for nothing. Couldn't even catch his saddle horse. When Blue offered to trade Red Shirt for me, Flagg told him, "Nothing doing." I can well remember while the HAT wagon was camped right where Kaycee is now located, I had the cavvy grazing on the south side of the river. While I was in camp for something, my pony slipped away and was heading across the bridge to the cavvy, when Johnny Pierce, the EK foreman, caught him. When I crossed the bridge, Pierce was at the John Nolan cabin talking with Mrs. Nolan. Pierce said I owed him a dollar for catching my pony. When I offered him the ninety cents that Curly Vest had given me, he said, "No. You'll have to dig deeper."

Well, he just kept teasing me until I started to cry. Then Mrs. Nolan came to my rescue and gave Johnny Pierce a good bawling out. I have always remembered Mrs. Nolan and the cabin that two years later was burned to the ground when Nate Champion and Nick Ray were murdered by the White Caps.

One evening while we were camping there, sitting around the campfire, Dutchie, the cook, was teasing me about something. When I told him to shut up, he picked up a handful of sand and threw it in my face. For this I hit him over the back of the neck with a stick of firewood. With Dutchie after me I started to run around the campfire. Al Allison put Dutchie down on the ground and told him to sit there and "leave that kid alone." Dutchie and I were never very friendly after this.

With the spring roundup over the HAT or nester wagon pulled into the ranch on the Red Fork of Powder River. Jack Flagg, Dutchie, and I stayed here and lived with the Johnny

Tisdale family. Johnny and Kate had three young children. Gardner, Hill, Webb, and Allison, with a pack outfit, went into the rough country to round up cattle. Every few days they would come to the ranch with some HAT cattle. These cattle were turned loose up above the ranch. I was much happier living with the Tisdales on the ranch than I was out on the roundup where all hands were up by four in the morning. My job as horse wrangler was easy enough. The only thing was that I couldn't get enough sleep. The HAT cavvy was easy to look after with plenty of grass and water. They were right at home wherever we made camp. At the ranch Dutchie and Johnny Tisdale were busy cutting and stacking hay for winter feeding of the winter saddle stock and a milk cow or two. Flagg and I did quite a bit of riding out on the range north from the ranch. One day while riding out there we came upon two grizzly bears feasting on a fresh-killed cow. The bears didn't run away. Instead, they began to growl and show fight. We beat it. Rode to the Jones cabin and told Johnnie Jones about the bears. Jones was the official trapper for that foothills area. That was plainly seen. There on the end of the cabin hung a number six bear trap. Inside the cabin where we stayed for lunch there was about thirty gallons of bear grease or lard in five-gallon coal-oil cans. Why Jones was saving all this bear grease, I don't know. Probably he was going to make up a lot of pie crust. One day while out on the range, we headed up a little canyon away from Red Fork. Up near the head of the canyon the going was pretty rough. In one place it was nothing but stairsteps of rock. After crossing over the little divide and headin' down another canyon we came out on to some more open country. Somewhere over there we stopped at the Carr ranch for lunch. After lunch when we went to the stable, we found that Flagg's horse had colic. The men said it was lampas, a congestion of mucous membrane of the hard palate. The horse was cut across the roof of the mouth with a sharp knife, which caused the blood to run freely.

Flagg borrowed an old pony from Carr for me to ride while he took my little Roanie pony, a top cow horse. Before we got back to the little canyon, we had gathered up about thirty head of HAT cattle. Among them there were two or three slicks or mavericks and a big, wild, ornery roan steer which got on the fight when we tried heading the bunch up into the canyon. Every time the steer would break back, Flagg would shoot him through the nose to stop him or bend him back into the bunch, where I was trying to hold them in the mouth of the canyon. This was a tough job on that old pot-bellied pony that I was riding. After the steer was shot through the nose or head a few times and knocked down a time or two he got back into the bunch and stayed there. It was then that I noticed I had lost the blanket out from under my saddle. This I blamed on to the pony. He had no business swelling so big while I was tightening the cinch. Among the cattle there was a good-looking slick, a yearling bull that Flagg said I should have to go with yearling heifers that I was buying with my wages.

After a little argument as to whether I should pay eleven or fifteen dollars for the slick, it was agreed that I was to get the bull at twelve-fifty. When we got back to the ranch, I took little Roanie and held the cattle up in a fence corner while Johnny Tisdale took Ratler, his top cow horse, and did the roping. Flagg did the branding. My bull was left 'till the last to be branded. Johnny dragged him up to the branding fire by one hind foot. When Flagg went to tail the bull down, he got horned in the belly, knocking the wind out of him. That sure made Flagg mad. He stamped my U up and ∩ down brand good and deep on the bull's ribs and turned him loose into the horse pasture, where he'd be handy to gather along with heifers that I was

23

to have. While holding the cattle in the fence corner, I noticed one big, old blue roan cow that was belching and swelling up. Tisdale said she probably had eaten poison weed or larkspur. And the best thing to do was to stick her. When we got to the outside of the horse-pasture fence, we cut the old cow and her calf away from the other cattle, which we drove farther up Red Fork. Upon our return we didn't see the old cow, but the calf was standing at the edge of a willow thicket. Tisdale said the cow was probably down, and that he and Flagg would go in and stick her to let the gas escape from the stomach. The two went on foot into the willows. The cow was yet on her feet. When she saw Tisdale coming in on that old cowpath, she rushed him. To keep from getting horned he fell over backwards into the willows and yelled, "Look out, Flagg."

Well, Flagg wasn't so lucky, but did dodge the good horn. And she, the old cow, came out of the willow patch with Flagg up across her head. About all the damage done was the stub horn nearly tore the flap from Flagg's stiff-bosomed white shirt. The cow headed around a bend of the stream and went out of sight.

Tisdale said, "Come on, Flagg, let's go around there and see where she is."

Flagg said, "To hell with that damn old cow. I don't want to see no more of her."

A couple of days later I was up around the bend in the stream, and there was the cow lying on her belly, as if she might have dropped dead while running. It was only a few days 'til Flagg says, "Kid, you take Roanie and go to the EK ranch and get the mail."

It was about ten miles to the EK. There had been a red bull that had strayed away from the ranch. Tisdale rode part way with me looking for the bull. As we were headin' up a dry wash or little draw, we rode up on an old bitch coyote and her pups. Tisdale pulled his six-shooter from the shoulder scabbard from under his vest and began shooting coyotes.

It was only a few days after this that I heard Tisdale tell Flagg how he had met Nate Champion out on the range. There they agreed that the next time either one of them met up with old Mike Shonsey, they were to hold him with their six-shooter and try to find out what he knew about the big cow outfits—what kind of medicine they were mixing up for the nesters and most anyone else that crossed their path. That day before the two men separated, they saw Mike riding towards the EK cow ranch, where he was the general manager, and here is where they held up Mike. As I remember, Flagg and Tisdale had quite an argument about this. Flagg seemed to think that Mike would be out for revenge. He was right as was proven during the next two years.

During that summer of 1890, just for an eleven-year-old kid I saw a lot and heard a lot. One day while the HAT men were bringing some of their cattle to the ranch, Flagg and I rode out to meet them. In among the cattle there were three or four of the steers that were hobbled on the hind legs. For some reason one of those hobbled steers took in after my little brown bench-kneed pony. With a lot of whipping and spurring, I finally won the race. After that I was spooky about those steers.

There was a lot of speculation out on the range among the cowboys and nesters that summer as to who were the guilty ones in the hanging of Jim Averill and Cattle Kate down on the Sweetwater the previous year. As I remember, here is about the way it was discussed. Some seemed to think the only reason for the lynching was that Kate and Jim had each taken claims on some land that the cattlemen prized quite

highly as some of their best range. The majority of the rangemen thought that Jim Averill and Ella Watson (Cattle Kate)
had filed a homestead each on some rich bottomland. Here
Jim ran the post office and sold whiskey. Just over across the
line on the Ella Watson claim, Cattle Kate had a dance hall,
where there was always a few girls on hand. This being the
most popular place of entertainment of the big open range,
there were always men of the range coming to the post office
for their mail and a little fun at the dance hall. When a cowboy went broke and wanted more fun, Ella would extend
him credit up to about ten dollars. To pay his debt when he
got back on the range the cowboy branded mavericks or slicks
at five dollars per head. Jim or Ella seldom ever rode the
range, but there were a lot of fresh-branded yearlings showing up with their brand. If the big cowmen had of hanged some
of their own cowboys it probably would have had more effect
out on the range.

One night Flagg informed Dutchie and me that he was going
into Buffalo to get married. He said he would probably be away
for a week or ten days. Dutchie was to help Johnny Tisdale with
the ranch work. I was to look after a few extra saddle horses
that were ranging just outside of the ranch up along Red Fork.
At this time Mart Tisdale, Johnny's son, was only about six years
old. He would put his saddle on his old sorrel pony and ride
with me. As I remember we two kids had a lot of fun fishing for
Red Horse suckers there in the Red Fork of Powder River. The
morning Flagg left for Buffalo I saw him put a sack of Bull Durham in the pocket of his bearskin overcoat that was hanging on
the bunkhouse wall. About a week later Flagg rode into the
ranch just in time for supper. After supper when we went into
the bunkhouse, Flagg went to the overcoat for his smoking tobacco. The tobacco wasn't there. When he asked Dutchie about

it, he said he didn't know anything about it. When he asked me, I said, "Yes, I saw Dutchie take it from your coat." Which I had. Flagg didn't say anything, just kept on looking, until he came to where Dutchie was sitting just under a clock shelf. Then Flagg took a forty-five from off the shelf and jammed it into Dutchie's ribs, saying, "You Dutch So-and-So. Dig up that tobacco." After a little argument Flagg shoved the Dutchman out of the bunkhouse door. And that's the last we saw of him. Not long after that Flagg met him in Buffalo and paid him his wages. It was only a few days after that that Tom Gardner took me back to Buffalo, a mighty happy kid, who was to get four yearling heifers and the yearling bull for his wages. Later while the HAT outfit were delivering some steers to the butcher at Buffalo they brought along my heifers. The bull they couldn't find. It was three years later that the bull showed up on a roundup at the double crossing on Clear Creek, about a hundred miles from the HAT ranch. The bull I never did get home. I sold him to Bob Foote, Jr., who was running a butcher shop in Buffalo. The price paid was fifteen dollars. Thus I made a two-dollar-and-a-half profit.

Not having a saddle horse at Buffalo, I borrowed one from Frank Smith, who was the delivery man for Bob Foote, Sr., at that time. (In later years he was elected sheriff of Johnson County.) That was a good cow horse. The heifers were wild and spooky, but I made good time in taking them to the Bard ranch on Mead Creek, a distance of about thirty miles.

NIGHTHAWKIN' AT TWELVE

THE SUMMER OF 1890 WHILE I WAS AWAY with the HAT outfit, Mother moved from Buffalo to the ranch on Mead Creek. With the aid of a hired man named George Rexford, she relieved the renter, whose time had expired. I was only at the ranch a few days. Tode and my little sister started to school at the Willey school house, while I went back to Buffalo to stay with Dad at the American Restaurant. He was still day cook there. Why it was so arranged I don't know. It was all right, but I would rather have been at the ranch with Mother. That winter I learned a lot both in school and out of school. The teacher who taught the fifth and sixth grades was a wonderful teacher, a Miss Manley. (She later became the wife of Judge Parmalee.) Bowser, a small man who wore a taffy-colored beard, was the professor. He was hell on wheels. Just like a stick of dynamite ready to explode at all times. One day he came dragging Byron Foote into our room by the shirt collar and beating him up. He would slam Byron onto a desk and hammer his head up against the back of the seat. By the time he ran out of wind, Byron was more dead than alive. He was out of school three days, and when he came back he still had a black eye. It was only a few days after this that Bowser overmatched himself when he tied into Joe Todd. It was then he sent for one of the school board, who was a big, slow-gaited fellow. After he had given Joe a black eye, he turned to Frank Hopkins, a husky young man and a clever boxer, asking him if he wanted some of it. When Frank said that he would go him a few rounds, it was then that the town marshal stepped in and broke up the fight.

The American Restaurant had a good trade, not only town trade but county trade for miles around. It was here where you heard all the news. One morning I heard the men talking about Hill Ruff, a saloonman, being accidentally shot the previous night in Maggie Jesse's dance hall. The men said he was now on a bed in a shack just back of the saloon. Being sort of curious to see a dead man, I beat it out the back door of the restaurant, up to the little one-room shack, tiptoed to a window and peeped in. As if asleep, Hill was lying on top of the bed. He had on one of those long swallowtail coats, a fancy vest, a big gold watch chain and striped pants. On a little stand was his silk hat. He wore a dark mustache and sideburns. He was a typical, old-time saloonman and gambler. He was accidentally shot while a dance-hall girl was sitting on his lap, shot by Dan, a friend who was sort of scuffling with another girl. When Dan's gun dropped from the waistband of his pants, it fell on the floor and discharged, killing Hill instantly. Kidlike, I never missed out on what was going on. I knew most of the dance-hall girls who took a part of their meals in a private dining room at the American Restaurant.

Generally on Saturday afternoon, when the coasting was good, I would take my sled, go up the hill near the dance hall, and coast down the alley or street in back of the restaurant. Sometimes the girls would give me two bits a ride to coast them down the hill. One time when the sled sorta jackknifed and spilled us off in the snow, we took it belly buster from then on. The girl would lie down on her stomach full length, and I would lie on top and away we would go. There were quite a lot of Saturday afternoons that I would get from a dollar to two dollars from these sled rides.

What interested me most of all was seeing the freighting outfits coming into town. Those old bullwhackers would sometimes have three wagons coupled together, with seven or eight yoke of oxen pulling the outfit. Some of the freighters used mules or horses. They were called mule skinners. One Saturday afternoon there was a bullwhacker unloading freight at the J. H. Conrad store at the south side of Main Street. At the north end of the street a mule skinner was unloading freight at Bob Foote's general store. On the old plank sidewalk there were nine Negro soldiers from Fort McKinney that were about half drunk. They were taking the sidewalk as they came. When they met an old, white, whiskered man, they forced him from the walk into the gutter. When the old gentleman got back onto the sidewalk he was crying. It was then that Jumbo McKenzie, a big Flying E cowpuncher, showed up. When he saw the old man crying he said, "Uncle, what's the trouble?"

When the old gentleman told Jum what had happened, Jum overtook the soldiers and the fight was on. Jum just backed up against a building. Every time a Negro got within reaching distance Jum would floor him. He had down six Negroes before the fight was stopped. Not long after this there came Maggie Jess down the walk with a wheelbarrow. Riding on it was one of her dance hall girls. Mag wheeled her cargo into a saloon. I slipped in to see what was going on, and got there in time to hear Mag say, "A free bus for the Astor house. . . . The drinks are on me."

Back in those days most every saloon had some sort of music. In here the two Crews brothers, Clate and Cliff, twins, were furnishing the music. Claton, the larger twin, played the fiddle, Cliff, the mandolin. They sure made good music even if they were just cowboys off the range and out of a job.

During the winter before I went to school each day, Dad would make up the pie dough and set out the filling, and I had to do the rest. There were usually about eight pies to get ready for the oven. When Sunday came Dad saw to it that I shined up my shoes, scrubbed my neck and ears and got ready for Sunday school. Usually after Sunday school I went to the home of some friend to spend the rest of the day.

That spring of 1891, instead of going to the ranch after school, I hired out as night-hawk or night herder to a large survey party. Every night I was up herding or looking after the work and saddle stock, about twenty-five head in all. This was a mighty tough job for a twelve-year-old kid. That civil engineer Shannon really had a good outfit. He had two four-horse outfits, a bed wagon, and a mess wagon just the same as the cow outfits were using. The mess box set on the tail end of the wagon, something like a kitchen cabinet. There was a big door that closed up the cabinet. It had hinges at the lower end. At the top end there was a leg fastened with a hinge. When the door was let down even with the bed of the wagon, it made a very good cook table. Bolted to the side of the mess box was an old coffee grinder. This was strictly a Dutch-oven outfit. Frank Fuller was a Dutch-oven cook. Most all food was cooked in three ovens even to pie, cake, and bread. In the survey party there were two engineers. Each had two chain men, a flag man, and a corner builder. Then there were a bookkeeper, the cook, and Harry Ward, the teamster who drove the bed wagon and who was horse wrangler while in camp. There were fourteen of us in the party that were heading for the Red Desert. Shannon had some sort of contract to sectionize the country in between Big Sandy Creek and the Green River. As I remember this scope of country was about fifty miles wide with very little water. After leaving Buffalo we went out by the way of the Bar C ranch, only a few miles from the Hole-in-the-wall country. There, within a short distance of the Hole-in-the-wall, we made camp one night. That night, while I was out looking after the horses, one of the work horses got a broken leg just above the hock joint, caused from a kick of a newly shod horse. We laid over at this camp while Shannon went back to the Bar C and bought a work horse for $100.

31

It was along in the afternoon that two cowboys rode into our camp. One was Ross Gilbertson. The other was Nate Champion. They were no strangers to me. I knew them from down in the Powder River country. Nate and Harry Ward were old friends. After they had visited for an hour or more the two cowboys headed for what was called the old Hall place on Powder River. Nate was making his home at that place at the time. Ross was staying with him. We were about two weeks in making the trip from Buffalo to Big Sandy stream, where there was but very little settlement at that time. There was, however, lots of wild game.

In our crew there was a tall, raw-boned fellow by the name of Big Hank, who claimed that he came from the lapover country, that is, where Missouri laps over on to Arkansas, in the Ozark Mountains. Hank being the best hunter in our outfit, he was paid fifteen dollars per month to keep the camp supplied with fresh meat. With that old single-shot 45–90 Sharps rifle, Hank lived up to the agreement. He saved all the empty shells and did the reloading. The powder was bought by the keg or flask; the lead, for bullets, by the bar. One of the men had along a double-barrel shotgun which came in handy for small game which was mostly young sage chickens and ducks. They were quite plentiful. Both Big and Little Sandy were alive with trout. No one had thought to bring along any fishing tackle. Harry Ward tied together several lengths of wrapping twine or string for a fish line. He then took a safety pin and worked it over into a fish hook. For a pole he used a green willow. The bait was either a small piece of fresh meat or a grasshopper. With this outfit Harry would catch enough fish for a mess. When I tried it, I would just about get the fish to the top of the water when he would flop off the hook. Hank was not only a good hunter and fisherman, he also was a topnotch hillbilly fiddler. In camp there were two fiddles, a guitar, and mandolin. Of evenings we had plenty of music. I didn't get to hear much of it as I was out night herding the horses.

Over in this Green River country where we were camped a part of the time, the nights were quite chilly. One of the men had a bearskin overcoat which he loaned me. It was much too large for me, but I would roll up the sleeves about half-way. Getting into this coat was about like getting into bed. With it on I had some little trouble in mounting my pony. Most nights I sat on the pony and sort of dozed while my pony would graze over on the north and east side of the desert. Along the Big Sandy it was much warmer and I didn't wear the coat so much. Up and down the Big and Little Sandy the grass was knee high everywhere. There were only two ranches anywhere near where we camped. An old man by the name of Pipper had a horse ranch. He branded the ILL brand on the left thigh. Two of our crew each bought a saddle horse from him. Our nearest neighbor on the Big Sandy hadn't lived here long. He and his family were busy clearing the big sagebrush off some bottomland, where that very spring they had taken a homestead. From the stream it was only a short distance, probably a quarter of a mile to the old Oregon Trail, which was quite famous back in pioneer days.

The boss was always bawling me out because I didn't take the horses back a mile or so from camp to herd them, when there was plenty of grass near camp. He said the big bell on one of the horses kept him awake. One moonlight night I was grazing the horses in along Big Sandy only about a quarter of a mile from camp. It was about eleven o'clock. Everything was perfectly quiet. Most of the horses were asleep. Some were stretched out on the ground. Others were on their feet dozing. I was about half asleep sitting on my pony, when he let out a snort or whistle. Upon opening my eyes I saw something white coming in my

33

direction. It looked like a man in a night shirt and probably was the boss coming to bawl me out for herding too close to camp. After my pony began to snort, most of the other horses did the same. Right then is when my small cavvy stampeded up out of that creek bottom with my pony running in the lead. The bell on that work horse was making plenty of noise! When we hit that old Oregon Trail or wide road it was like a race track. Up the trail we went with me still in the lead. We must have gone up the trail for about half a mile before I got the outfit under control. After this the cavvy was a little spooky about night herding. This little incident I kept under my hat, the same as the boss did. The next morning the boss took the bell off the work horse. Nothing more was said about me herding too close to camp.

Rock Springs on Bitter Creek, a branch of the Green River, a small coal-mining town, was where we got our mail and supplies. I well remember one time while we were camped out about ten miles from Rock Springs that we heard a terrible blast, just a big boom. The next day two men rode out from Rock Springs and told us what had happened. There were two coal miners who went on a little spree. With their single horse and buggy they drove out past the powder house. Just for a little fun they shot into the house, which touched off the whole works. The big blast broke most of the window lights in town and caused considerable damage. These two men said that when they left town most of the population was out with baskets gathering up the remains of the two coal miners.[1]

[1] According to the *Wyoming Guide* (New York, Oxford University Press, 1941), 350, about a quarter of a mile from Killpecker Creek "is the site of No. 6 Powder House, where, on July 17, 1891, two men on a drunken lark fired into 1,200 kegs of blasting powder and 700 pounds of dynamite. The building disappeared, leaving a great ragged hole. Four men were killed."

The two surveying crews all had saddle horses which they rode a part of the time while out in the field. The four chain men had to take it on foot. Once the engineers located an old established corner, they would work out from it into the desert. After the engineer had set up his instrument directly over a corner stone, he would line the flag man up for some little knoll or some high spot a quarter to a half-mile distant. The flag man would get off his horse and stand up the elevation rod or stick which was about ten feet long. It usually was painted black with all kinds of numbers on it. After the engineer got the flag man lined up on the right spot, he would begin reading some of the numbers on the rod. The flag man with some sort of sliding gauge on the rod would give the engineer the right elevation, or something, I'm not just sure what. Anyway when that gauge stopped on the right number the engineer would put both hands above his head, then drop them to his side. This meant "O.K." After jotting down some numbers the engineer would mount his horse with the tripod and instrument and ride over to the flag man, while the two chain men chained off the distance. This chain was, I should think, about four rods in length. The lead chain man carried, I think, ten small metal pins with red rags tied to the tops. The pin was made of wire with six-inch joints. The measuring started at the established corner. When the head chain man dragged the chain out full length the rod man would yell, "Stick." The lead man would stick a peg in the ground and yell, "Stuck." When the rear man came to the peg, he would pick it up and yell, "Stick." All day long it was stick and stuck with those chain men. Along with the chain men came the corner builder or the marker of different corners. These corner stones were oblong and about the size of a small water pail, with two or more smooth sides where some numbers were chiseled on. In a square out a few feet from the stone there would be four small pits dug, some places, only two. And that's something like the way the survey was being made.

I do not remember seeing any sheep on the desert that whole summer. There were only a few horses which mostly belonged to Mr. Pipper. There was only one cow outfit that I remember, and that belonged to a small, black-whiskered man by the name of Loomis or Luman.

I remember one day when Shannon had camped our party in a small hay meadow where there was a line camp belonging to the cowman, we hadn't been in camp long until this old cowman and some of his cowboys came riding up. I never heard such a bawling out as Loomis gave to Shannon. When Shannon saw that the old cowman and his cowboys all were packing six-shooters, he moved out on double quick. Big Hank didn't like the way that Loomis had threatened our outfit. From then on out Hank wasn't particular as to what kind of meat he brought into camp.

Whenever we had to cross over the desert from Big Sandy to Green River, our outfit shortly after noon would fill up the water barrels, gather up some firewood, pull out onto the desert about twenty miles and make a dry camp. The horses didn't get any water. Before we got to Green River next day the horses were mighty thirsty. The last mile out before reaching the river, the horses would scent the water and would begin to travel faster. At a half-mile the teams were pulling on the bridle bits and wanting to go faster. Already the loose horses were far in the lead. The last quarter-mile the loose horses made on high. It was all the teamsters could do to hold their four-horse outfit down to a steady trot. Some of the horses could have developed lockjaw, but they didn't. At the upper end of the desert, up towards the mountains, the country was quite rough. There were large groups of sand rock. Quite often in around these sand

Four in the morning on the roundup.
"The night-hawk had the cavvy in the rope corral,
and we were eating breakfast . . . ."
Courtesy the Library, State Historical Society of Colorado

Open country, big appetites.
"We cowboys liked the steaks fried,
but with Dutchie it was different.
Everything was boiled."

rocks we would find elk carcasses where there was nothing much only some old dry hide and bones. These elk probably had frozen or starved to death during the hard winter of 1886 and 1887. Here it would have been easy to have gotten a lot of elk teeth, but at that time there was no market for them except to the Indians.

I don't remember seeing any large bands or herds of wild horses on the Red Desert that summer of 1891. They were probably built up in later years, probably in the 1890's when horses were so cheap that the horsemen wouldn't bother to brand up their increase or castrate the young studs.

It was now nearing the time when I would be leaving the survey party and heading back to Buffalo and home. It had been a tough summer on a twelve-year-old nester's kid. There wasn't much that I was afraid of except lightning and thunder, but I was dead on my feet for the want of sleep. It was about August 20 when Frank Wilderson, one of the flag men, and I tied a bed on a horse, and with two saddle horses we rode out of camp heading for Buffalo. We didn't carry any camp outfit or any provisions. We just took our chances on making road houses or ranches for our meals.

One day we had made a long, dry ride. At the approach of night we were planning on making a dry camp, when in the far distance we heard the tiny tinkle of a bell. We continued on down the old freight road for about a mile. There on a small stream we rode into the camp of two bull whackers, who were frying bacon and getting their evening meal. Here we were made welcome. We rolled out our bed and spent the night. The next morning it was a wonderful sight to see the bullwhackers round up their oxen and get them yoked together and placed on either side of that long chain fastened to the front axle of the lead wagon. Their three wagons were coupled together. All were loaded with freight. As I remember, each whacker had six yoke of oxen and one Indian pony. We were nine days in making this trip, with a one-day stopover at the Gus Coleman ranch on Nowood Creek. Here we spent the day with Mrs. Coleman and her son George, who was a kid about my own age. Gus Coleman was one of the engineers of our surveying party. Upon reaching Buffalo I learned that Dad and Charley Olson, a Swede cowboy, had a restaurant of their own. It was a short-order joint. Dad was day cook and Charley was night cook, and I was to be a part-time dish washer before and after school.

CATTLE WAR IN JOHNSON COUNTY

AFTER A FEW DAYS AT THE RANCH with Mother, I went back to Buffalo to the short-order joint and the dish washing. None of it I liked. I should have been at the ranch with Mother. She was the one who needed me most. Well, here at Charley's short-order joint or restaurant the two Charleys had a good trade which was mostly cowboys and nesters. I remember one day two young cowboys or nesters came to Dad and offered him thirty head of yearling heifers for his Quarter Circle Box brand and what cattle were wearing the brand, which were not more than six head—just enough to hold the brand. Dad told them, "It's a trade."

The two cowboy nesters went back down into the Powder River country and started gathering the heifers. They had until the following spring to deliver the heifers at the Bard ranch. About the time they were to deliver the heifers the cattle war broke loose, which knocked the deal in the head. Afterward one of these nesters told Dad why they wanted this ⊓ brand. Out south of Buffalo there was a manager for a cow outfit who branded ⌐⌐. These two cowboy nesters didn't like this old bird, as they called him. They had the big idea that they could work his ⌐⌐ brand over into the Quarter Circle Box ⊓ and put him out of business.

One day when I came from school men were standing around in small groups talking about how four gunmen had raided the Hall cabin on Powder River where Nate Champion and Ross Gilbertson were staying. Here is about the way Nate told of the raid. "Ross and me were asleep in the Hall cabin. It was about four o'clock, just breaking day when someone kicked open the door and some men rushed in and told me to throw up my hands, that they had me this time. I don't know who fired the first shot. I guess we all started shooting about at the same time. Soon the room was filled with gun-powder smoke. I had the advantage shooting towards the open door which furnished some light. I am sure that I drilled one of the birds through the middle. He sorta doubled up and groaned. As they went out through the open door I was still shooting. I then put on my clothes and went to the outside of the cabin. The gunmen were now mounted on their horses and beating it for a cottonwood grove down near the river. There were four of them. One of them must have been badly hit for two of them were trying to hold him in the saddle. Just as they went into the grove I took two shots at them with my six-shooter, which was just a little too far. There stacked up against the end of the cabin were four Winchester rifles, among them was a 30–30 carbine." I don't remember what else Nate had to say. Later in the day there was a burned-out campfire found in the cottonwood grove. In among the ashes there was a blood-soaked bandage that didn't burn. Shortly after this when the Regulators or cowmen

39

made a check on their so-called hired gunmen, they were one short. He was probably buried in the sand somewhere along Powder River.

It was near the end of November when I came for my lunch one day, and Johnnie Tisdale was at the restaurant having his lunch before he left town that afternoon. He and Dad were in deep conversation, so I didn't say anything. Just ate my lunch in the kitchen and beat it back to school.

The next day when I came for my lunch, there was plenty of excitement everywhere. Charley Basch had just ridden into Buffalo with the news that his neighbor had just murdered Johnnie Tisdale out in the sand draw near the Cross H ranch. When someone asked Basch how he knew that it was his neighbor, he said, "I knew the big sorrel horse that he was riding and the bearskin overcoat he had on."

Basch said just as he rode up on the bank of the draw he heard a shot, then another one. Then he saw Tisdale fall back on the loaded wagon as if dead. His neighbor then mounted the big sorrel and caught the team. Basch said when his neighbor saw him sitting on his horse taking it all in, he yelled to Basch to get back up that road and keep his damn mouth shut. While Basch was making a detour he heard two more shots. That afternoon Red Angus, the sheriff, and a posse went to investigate and bring the body into Buffalo. Here is what they found. Down in the sand draw about two hundred yards below where the old stage road crossed the draw there was Johnnie Tisdale lying back among some Christmas toys and supplies. Johnnie was dead with a bullet hole between his shoulder blades. The bullet after passing through Johnnie's body lodged in the neck of Eagle, the big white work horse, causing the loss of a lot of blood. There side by side lay Coalie and Eagle, the team, shot between the eyes, yet hitched to the wagon. That afternoon another team was hitched to the wagon to bring it into Buffalo. The loaded wagon was left in the wagon and buggy shed at the Brick livery stable. Tisdale's body was taken to a little one-room log building not far from the court house. This was at four o'clock just as school was dismissed. Kidlike, I beat it across to this little building where the sheriff was going through the pockets of Johnnie's coat. Here he found a large-sized bill fold which had in it some paper money along with some papers. The sheriff then took off the vest and the shoulder scabbard with Johnnie's six-shooter yet in the scabbard. The hard wood handle of the gun had a fresh-made dent where a bullet had hit. The vest had a bullet hole through from the front of the vest and one from the back of the vest. What else was found I don't know as I had to beat it for the restaurant.

The next day must have been Saturday for I got a pony and rode out to the big sand draw which was not far from Buffalo. I didn't have any trouble in finding the place where Johnnie was murdered in cold blood. Just a little way across the draw there was a large spot of dried blood where old Eagle had nearly bled to death from the bullet wound in the neck. Down along the sand draw were Coalie and Eagle. And right here is where I got off my pony and had a big cry. It was just about like a part of my own family being murdered. Just the year before this Tisdales had been so good to me. Mrs. Tisdale had even done my washing along with the family wash. While I sat there crying I thought of what Flagg had said about the old Irishman would be out for revenge. It looked as if this was true. It wasn't a month since the gunmen had tried to get Nate and had failed. When I got back to Buffalo it was a little after noon. There at the restaurant there was a cowboy or nester who was getting ready to leave town for Powder River. I heard one of the men say to Rinker, "Ranger has been missing the last three or four days. Better keep a close lookout for the buckboard tracks."

Just as Jim Ricker crossed over the Muddy Bridge he saw where the buckboard tracks had left the main road. He followed these tracks for about a hundred yards down along Muddy Creek. And there he found Jones shot to death, with three bullet holes through his body. The team had been turned loose and the harness lay in a pile. Ranger was yet in the seat of the buckboard. With a part of the body over the back of the seat, his head was resting on the floor of the buckboard. This was the second or third of December and the body was stiff as a board. He was left this way while the rig was trailed behind another rig into Buffalo and up to the rear of the undertaker's place of business.

Well, I was there to see what was going on. When some of the men lifted Ranger's stiff, half-frozen body from the rig his hair, which he wore rather long, was matted with blood and stuck to the floor of the rig. It was yet there when they lifted Ranger out of the rig. This was the third cold-blooded murder during the past six months. It was during the month of June that four gunmen went to the Wagoner horse ranch and took Tom Wagoner away from his wife and two or three small children. They took the man a mile or so from home up a small canyon and hung him to the limb of a tree. Tom only had about four hundred head of horses, but it was said they were eating too much free grass away from the cowmen's long horns. Then someone tried to poison Pumpkin Butte Smith, who had a small horse ranch. One day while Smith was out on the ranch, a good neighbor dropped by and left some fresh beef on the table. Later while Smith was building a fire in the cook stove, his dog got the meat off the table and ate a part of it. The big dog died almost instantly. With all of this dirty work going on the sentiment of most of the people of northern Wyoming was very bitter towards the hired killers and the men who were backing them. After the cold-blooded murder of Johnnie Tisdale people became bewildered and confused. They didn't know what to expect next. Most everyone was in for taking up arms against these men that it seemed were running the State of Wyoming.

At Christmas time I said good-bye to my many young friends and classmates of Buffalo and went home to Mother and the ranch. Here, after the holidays, I started to attend the Willey school along with my brother and young sister. It was on a Saturday, about the twelfth of April, that Mother told me to hitch a team on the spring wagon, go over to Buffalo and take a message to Dad, and get some supplies. The latter was mostly garden seeds. This was the year the railroad was built into Sheridan. Mother had a gardner already hired, and was raising vegetables for the grading camps. I hadn't much more than hit the old stage road between Sheridan and Buffalo until it looked like everybody was heading for Buffalo. There were men in rigs with a bedroll and some sort of gun, men on horseback— all heading for Buffalo and the TA ranch, where the nesters and grangers had about thirty cowmen and about twenty hired gunmen bottled up or corraled in the TA ranch buildings.

The nesters already had established a camp about a half a mile upstream from the TA building. The battle was on with nester recruits coming to the nester camp, both day and night. The only ones left at home were the women folks and the kids under fifteen. From our neighborhood there were several teenage boys at the nesters' camp. When I saw Chate Price and Bill Edwards, two neighbor boys, one fifteen and one sixteen, headin' through Buffalo for the TA, I wanted to take one of our teams and go along. Since I was just thirteen, Dad said I was too young to go.

43

During the battle between the nesters and White Caps, as the cowmen and their hired gunmen were called, Jumbo Mc-Kenzie, a cowboy nester, come near getting killed when the White Caps shot his horse out from under him. To even the score Jum took a work horse from off one of the White Caps' supply wagons, which was in the hands of the nesters. For safekeeping, Jum brought this fresh-branded gray gelding to the Bard ranch on Mead Creek and turned him loose with our horses until that fall. Then Jum came and got him.

Among the White Caps there were two hired Texas gunmen who were buried in a lonely grave. One of them got accidentally shot in the leg when his horse bucked him off. He died of blood poisoning. The other one got shot in the belly while standing near a window in the TA ranch house. As I remember it was the morning of the third day that Uncle Sam stepped in and saved that White Cap gang.

I got to see all of them as they were being marched from the TA to Fort McKinney, two miles south of Buffalo. All told there were fifty of them. They rode horseback in pairs, with a Negro soldier riding on either side. First in this parade were the cowmen. Then came about ten of their seasoned killers. Bringing up the rear were the hired Texans. They were a sorry-looking lot with their stubble beards, and eyes that looked like burned holes in a blanket. They hadn't shaved for a week, had had very little sleep and nothing much to eat while bottled up in the TA ranch house. Some of these men I knew personally, others, just on sight out on the range or in Buffalo. A part of them I had never seen before.

While the invaders were being marched on to the fort, Red Cranson, Ab Grant, and I got saddle horses and rode out to have a look at the ranch. At the ranch there were two cowboys or ranch hands with a team of horses dragging away dead horses, saddle stock of the White Caps, which had been penned up in a feed lot. These horses had been killed by stray bullets. I noticed cattle crippling around on three legs. Things were badly shot up. Out two or three hundred yards from the buildings there were piles of rock and rifle pits used by the nesters during the day time. I just don't remember what all I did see. About the only cheerful thing I saw was a little cottontail rabbit with a pink ribbon around its neck, lying beside a log pile sunning itself.

In Buffalo I attended the funeral of Nate Champion and Nick Ray, the two men who had recently been murdered at the John Nolan place at the crossing of Powder River where Kaycee now stands. This was the work of the White Caps. While waiting in Buffalo for the TA fight to end I got to see Nate Champion's body while it was being taken into the funeral home. Nate was pretty well shot up. His hands were tried across his breast with some sort of cord or small rope. He was dressed in a black suit of clothes. He was in his stocking feet. The black hat was pulled well down over his forehead. Nick Ray was burned up in the Nolan cabin. There wasn't much left of him, only a part of his hips. It was sure a big funeral, with lots of flowers. Behind the hearse Jack Flagg led the top saddle horses of Nate and Ray. Nate's was a whitefaced buckskin. Nick Ray's was a rangy bay or brown, as I remember.

Now with the war over, and the revengeful old Irishman at the fort in the bull pen with the rest of the White Caps, and with Negro soldiers riding herd on them both day and night, the big cowman who stayed neutral was probably happy.

It was now about April 20. The new grass was getting a good start. It was time for the nesters and grangers to brand up the fall and winter calves, dehorn the yearlings, and turn their small herd out on the big open range to roam at will until the granger

45

roundup wagon started to gathering in the cattle for winter feeding. The horse man now could start his spring horse round-up, with no danger of being hung, shot in the back, or poisoned. The mavericker would go out on the range, brand up every slick that he thought belonged to the range hog. Of course the cow thief would help himself to whatever he thought he could get away with. There have always been cattle thieves, and there always will be. Now, however, with their rubber-tired outfit they can work much faster.

During those four days that Dad kept me in Buffalo, it was sure a wild town. For a thirteen-year-old kid I got to see a lot and to hear a lot. On the fourth day when I hitched the team and headed for home, I had plenty of company. They were our neighbors and men from all parts of Sheridan County. They were weary from the loss of sleep, but their spirits were high. Now they could go home and start in where they left off. There would be no hired gunmen telling them to pull up stakes and move on to somewhere else where the climate might be more healthy. Down at the mouth of Mead Creek about two miles from the Bard ranch, there was the FE cow outfit that hired several cowboys and run a roundup wagon on the range. This was a good little outfit, with Dave Dunnick as the manager and part-owner of the outfit. Along in the late eighties Dunnick saw the way things were shaping, with the possibility of Sheridan getting a railway. He closed out the FE cattle and moved into Sheridan. Most of his cowboys went with him.[2]

[2] In Sheridan most all of these cowboys went into businesses of their own. Dave Dunnick, with a part of his cash, got Perkins by the seat of the pants and boosted him farther up the ladder in the banking business. Then along came H. C. Alger, another big man of those early days. He also gave the Bank of Commerce a boost. George Griffin, another FE cowboy, went to work for E. A. Whitney of the First National, where he worked for about fifty years. Jim Enoch, another FE cowboy or wagon boss, was elected second sheriff of Sheridan County—Author's note.

The Flying E, another neighboring cow outfit less than twenty miles from the Bard ranch, with Fay Parker as its manager, was looking at the range situation through colored glasses. They teamed up with the White Caps, with Parker as their representative. Soon after the invasion, the Flying E or Murphy Cattle Company was quitting business. After the company had gathered all of the cattle it could find, there still were some cattle on the range. There were a few old wild cows that never went into a roundup. Every year they raised a calf and every year there was a maverick or slick for someone to brand.

Not far out on our ranges there were two old outlaw steers. They were Texas steers with long horns. They were big, ornery, and wild, and never went into a roundup. Most always they beat it for some rough country whenever a rider would show up. One was a cream-colored buckskin; the other was a smoky buckskin with a beautiful set of horns. We nester kids named these steers Smoky and Buck. A lot of nesters wanted smoky's horns, but they didn't know how to get them. When we kids saw Buck alone out on the range, we just supposed that some nester had killed Smoky for his horns. An old mossback who was one of our neighbors claimed that he had bought these two steers of the Flying E. Smoky wasn't to be found, so he slipped up on Buck and shot him down, butchered him up like a buffalo, and took the meat home.

One day while I was out riding the range, I was just going to cross a small draw. There in the bottom of the draw laid old Smoky, with one of those long horns jammed into the ground. It evidently had held him there until he died of thirst. He had fought an awful battle in trying to regain his feet. The more he struggled, the deeper the horn went into the earth. There were mounds of dirt that he had piled up with his hoofs. All that was left of the steer was hide and bones, and those long horns, and one of them was augured into the earth until it was impossible for me to pull it out with my saddle pony. Two weeks later when I took a pick and shovel and went for the horns, someone had beat me to them. What became of Smoky's horns always remained a mystery.

NESTER KIDS KEEP BUSY

THIS YEAR OF 1892 WAS AN UNUSUAL YEAR and a busy year at the Bard ranch. It was along in February that my kid brother was born. Mother had a hired girl who did most of the cooking and house work, while Mother supervised the raising of a big garden. The garden produce was for the railroad grading camp over on Dutch Creek, about twenty miles from our place. Mother's gardener was old Dan Snyder, a saloon bum in the winter time, but a darned good ranch hand and gardener during the summer and fall, a hard-working man, who never went to town during the summer months. He saved his wages, patched his own clothing. Sometimes when the knees of his coveralls became worn, he would turn them around and wear the backside in front. Once he hit town, his wages were soon gone. Then he would get a job as swamper at the Nelson brothers' saloon. Dan worked at the Bard ranch about four seasons. The crop land of the place was leased or rented out to a fellow about like Dan, a bachelor by the name of Mackey, who boarded with us.

Along about the first of May, Dad bought some more horses. There were two studs. One was a draft stud; the other was a Hambletonian stud, trotting horse or harness horse. This stud weighed about thirteen hundred pounds. For color he was

48

like the draft horse. He was black with a brown nose and brown flanks. Along with these horses came a fellow named George Saxton, to take care of the studs.

With both Mother and Dad buying a few head of stock now and then, and with what increase we raised, we now had a nice little herd of both cattle and horses. With Tode and I being the cowboys that summer of 1892, we were two busy kids. When we were not driving the vegetable rig to and from the Mike Elmore grading camp, we were out on the range riding after stock. When we had to make our regular trips to the grading camp, the vegetables were got ready the day before and loaded onto a heavy spring wagon shortly after daylight. As a driver of the rig, Mother had Tode or myself. She had to take the baby along to nurse him. As I remember there were three grading camps. They were doing the grading by the mile. Each one of these contractors had his own tent camp, with a kitchen, a dining room, bed tents and a commissary tent with most all kinds of supplies for both the kitchen and the teamsters, keeping pace along with the camps, there were tent saloons. One night a tent saloon was held up and robbed. The two proprietors were killed and a by-stander was wounded.

These trips of ours were about forty miles. How Mother and the baby ever stood them, I don't know. One morning Mother said, "You boys go over to Mr. Dow's place on Dutch Creek and get those horses that he was to gather for us."

When we got to the A. P. Dow horse ranch, he hadn't yet made his horse roundup. Mr. Dow wasn't at home, but Mrs. Dow fixed a nice lunch for us. On our way home we had just crossed over the Dutch Creek Divide and were headin' down along one prong of Cat Creek, when a man on foot came runnin' from a grove of trees along the creek bank. He came right towards us kids. He was yelling, "My God, man, don't shoot me any more. Don't shoot."

49

About that time another man came up from the trees with a six-shooter in his hand shooting towards the first man. When the first man fell, I said to Tode, "Come on, let's get out of here." We sure left there on high. Just as we had topped a ridge, I looked back to see if anyone was chasing us. Tode yelled, "Look out! Don't run over that dead cow."

Right at the edge of some scrub brush there was a maverick tied down. After taking one look at this red yearling heifer, we were one our way as fast as our ponies could run. When we did finally slow down to a walk we had the whole thing figured out. Those two men were out after mavericks, and their little "act" was just one way of getting rid of us kids.

One time during that summer George Saxton, who was a good bronc rider, thought he would ride Jum's big gray White Cap horse which was yet at our place. The horse, being a work horse, was a little spooky about the saddle, and more spooky about a man riding him. When George mounted that big gray, the horse sure blew up. He bucked around the corner of the house and out of sight. When the short latigo broke, off came the saddle with George yet sitting in the seat.

The next time, George rode the gray to a finish. This was back in the good old horse and buggy days when most of the folks owned a horse of some kind. Some only owned a kid pony. Some had a single driving horse. There were others, including doctors, that had their matched driving teams. The livery stables always had a few good driving teams for hire, with or without a driver. There were times when these town horses would make their escape out into the hills. With Tode and me ridin' the range a part of the time, we knew where most of these stray horses ranged. Whenever there would be a five or ten dollar reward offered for the capture of some certain horse, that's when us kids would go out on the range, corral the horse, take it into town and claim the reward. This reward money was mostly spent for clothing, which was quite cheap. From the Nebraska Clothing Company of Omaha, a mail order house, we could buy a good all wool suit anywhere from eight to sixteen dollars. There were three styles to choose from: the double-breasted, square-tailed coat, the single-breasted coat with rounding corners, and the swallow-tailed coat, more of a dress coat.

Most all grocery stores handled some dry goods, especially foot wear, which came in big wooden boxes about four or five feet square. In one of these boxes there would be about fifty pairs of foot wear. For the men there was the granger boot, made from bull leather with broad toe and flat heels. There was the Congress shoe with an elastic instep for a dress shoe. It was a lace shoe with a long peaked toe. These were called "tooth-pick" shoes. The women's shoes had tops that came a little above the ankle, buttoned on the side and with a flat heel. The kids' boots were made granger style. This kind of footwear sold anywhere from two to four dollars.

In this fall of 1892, when grading was done and the rails were laid, we were all there to see the first train come into Sheridan. As I remember, the depot was nothing more than a section house with a freight shed. I don't remember just where it was located, probably near the present depot. It was about this time that the two Charlies sold out their restaurant in Buffalo. Dad came to the ranch for a short stay, then moved into Sheridan to run a restaurant for John and Oscar Nelson. These two Nelsons had a saloon about where the Edleman Drug Company is now located. The restaurant was next door south. Charley Olson moved into Sheridan and became night marshal. One night he got into some sort of gunplay with two young nesters. No one got hurt only Charley, who got a thumb shot off.

That winter of 1892, we kids were back in school at the Willey school along with about a dozen other nester or granger kids. The first thing on the program of the spring of 1893, was to help our neighbors up and down Prairie Dog Creek to brand their fall and winter calves and dehorn their yearlings. Prairie Dog and Mead Creeks were two of the richest little valleys to be found anywhere. Each granger or nester had anywhere from a hundred up to three or four hundred head of Durham cattle, which ranged out on the open range about six months out of each year. The remainder of the year they were at the ranch and were fed hay when needed. Now with the coming of the railroad everyone felt more secure. There were no more long drives to the end of the track with beef cattle. But there was one great hazard with the coming of the railway. The right of way wasn't fenced, and quite a lot of stock, both cattle and horses, were hit by the engine and were killed or crippled. This stock was paid for by the railroad. The section crews buried or burned the dead stock. The section foremen made a report of all stock killed on the right of way but were not allowed any of the meat as beef. I remember one time when Joe Rebman, my brother-in-law, a railway engineer, was out on his run, there came quite a blizzard. For protection from the storm a bunch of range horses, twenty head or more, drifted into a cut. Here Joe said his engine killed and crippled about half of the herd. With a lot of damage suits on their hands, the railroad got busy and fenced the right-of-way, leaving crossings every mile or so, so that the stock could cross back and forth at will.

Being shipped into the country now were windows and doors, lumber, and a lot of modern machinery. There was the portable steam engine and the self-feeding grain separator that put the old horse-power outfit out of business. With lumber being shipped in and more being sawed along the face of the mountain, the pioneers were building two-story houses. The old log cabin of two or three rooms with a dirt roof and a rough, uneven floor was being torn down or used as a storeroom, a granary, or stable for horses.

During 1893, my folks sold off a part of our cattle with my HAT heifers or cows and their increase included. This money was used to build a nice two-story ranch home. In less than a year, through a faulty chimney, this new home caught on fire and burned to the ground. From the first floor we saved almost everything, even to the range. This was getting mighty hot by the time we had the side of the kitchen chopped away, and a log chain around the range. Two cowboys and their saddle horses pulled the range from the building. This blow fell the heaviest on Mother, who during the last fifteen years had gone up against a lot of hardships, without complaining. Now it was all to do over again.

It was near winter and our good neighbors came to our res-cue. Mother and the younger children went to stay with some neighbors. This time Dad said it would be a rock house, some-thing that wouldn't burn to the ground. With the help of our neighbors it didn't take long to haul in enough cinder rock from the red shale hills for a two-room house, 16 x 32 feet. Two stone masons laid the wall, which was about two feet thick. Instead of lime mortar, the rock was laid up in clay mud. It was freezing weather. The water was heated in a big iron butchering kettle. When the house was finished the walls were white with frost about two inches thick. With a couple of stoves going both day and night, it took about a week to dry out the walls. I was the night fireman, and had to sleep in the frosty house. I got rheuma-tism in one hip, until I walked backwards and sorta dragged that leg. Here is where we put in a few years pioneering until we could get a better house built.

It was late spring of 1893 that the "71" cow outfit of South

Dakota trailed into the Dutch Creek country. Just a little way up above the Dow horse ranch they set up a permanent camp. In among these two thousand head of "71" cattle there were about five hundred head of mixed cattle branded with the Quarter Circle Block brand on the left hip same as my folks were using. Soon these cattle were scattered all over the range. Along early that fall when the cattle got some "taller" on their ribs, the "71" started gathering and shipping them to market. Some of ours were included. One day over in back of our place the "71" was making a roundup, and they were driving off most of our cattle. Four of our milk cows, one with a bell on her neck, were among those rounded up. With Dad away from home, it was sorta up to me to find out what was going on.

After galloping my horse over to the roundup, I asked old Rack Thornton what he was up to. He said the cattle belonged to the Block outfit and he was looking after them, and was going to ship them. I told him I guess he wouldn't ship those cattle that they were our cattle and the brand was registered in the Bard name. When I asked Rack what was the Block ear mark, he said, "A hole punched through the left ear."

When I told him that our ear mark was crop or cut away half of the left ear, he said, "Well, we probably have some of your cattle. I told him not only some but just about all of them. While the cowboys held the roundup, Rack and I cut out what cattle belonged to the Block outfit. We got along all right up to the last steer, which he claimed. It had our ear mark all right, crop off the left ear. But Rack said it was a Block steer and the ear had been frozen off where the hole had been made. I didn't say anything. Just thought all right, old boy, that's a game that two can play at. Not long after this Neri Wood, a neighbor, came to our place and said that Rack had some of our cattle gathered and was going to ship them the following day from

54

Verona. That night Neri spent at our place. Real early the following morning Neri and I were headin' for the Verona stock yards. With the help of a good neighbor we got the Bard cattle back on our Mead Creek range. From there on it was root hog or die. Mother was worried about our cattle. She said that the "71" would be shippin' some of them. I told her not to worry, that I thought we could keep even. During that summer and fall there were quite a lot of Block cattle that had their left ear froze off.

That fall when the "71" made its last shipment and closed out the outfit, we had our full amount of cattle. Some of them had changed color quite a bit, and we kids, Tode and I, had some trained rope ponies.

One day when I tied onto a big four-year-old steer it looked for a while as if I was going to lose my outfit. When I did get that steer roped, I ran my pony around him three or four times, then took off the opposite way. This pulled the steer's legs together, and the steer went down. The pony was yet pulling on the rope until the feet were up near the neck. Now the steer was pretty well hog tied. With a sharp pocket knife it didn't take long to freeze off that left ear, cut the hunda of the throw rope and make a run for my rope horse. When that steer got onto his feet, he was sure to be on the prod.

That fall when the "71" sold out their horse cavvy and paid off their cowboys, some of them went back to South Dakota. Among those who stayed were the two Kitchel brothers, Ben and Ollie, and the two Scott brothers, Lee and Walter. Lee got appointed stock inspector. Walter went to California and became famous as Death Valley Scottie. Norm Garton, another "71" cowboy, brought the first automobile to Sheridan in 1894 or 1895, I don't remember which. This car looked very much like a single-seat buggy or carriage. It was painted red and had

55

a chain drive about like the old Plano mowing machine. If you had plenty of open links in the jockey box, well that would help a lot where the pulling was heavy. Norm made the Willis Peak livery stable his headquarters. He tried carrying the mail from Sheridan to Buffalo. There were a few times the mail came through O.K. But usually it was a day or two late. When Norm found out that he needed a team hitched to this horseless buggy, he disposed of the outfit and went back to his old home in New York City.

When this "71" outfit quit business there were yet a few old "71" cows on the range. There were yet Quarter Circle Block cattle on the range. That was a point in our favor. One time when Dad got a letter stating that the railroad had killed one of our bulls on the right-of-way down by Powder River and they were willing to settle for fifty dollars if that was agreeable, Dad said that would be O.K., just to send along the fifty bucks.

The "71" had grazed off our horse range to such an extent that old Honest John McCormack, the Levi Woods and the Bards gathered what horses were ranging in between Little Goose Creek and Mead Creek. The Woods had about fifty head, the same as Honest John. The Bards had about a hundred head. These horses were moved over across Dutch Creek to the Willow Springs not far from the head of Little Badger Creek, about forty miles from our place. Here we rode line on the horses for a few days until they were pretty well located. While we were locating the horses, we made the Uncle Johnnie Patton ranch our headquarters.

Uncle Johnnie was an old bachelor who had come from Arkansas along in the 1880's. He was a good cook, neat and clean, and he made the best salt-rising bread. Baked it in a Dutch oven. They were big loaves just the size of the oven. Tasted mighty good but smelled something like old dirty socks. Uncle

Johnnie was pretty well off. He had a good ranch and about four hundred head of cattle. He had shipped part of them up from Arkansas. One day he said to me, "I want to adopt you. I am getting old and need some young feller like you that can rope and ride, that knows something about handling stock. I'll make it worth your while if you'll stay with me."

I thanked the old man and told him how much I appreciated his offer, but that my folks would never consent to a deal of that kind.[3] When I got back home Dad had traded off his restaurant to Andy Neilson. In trade he got a lot on Neilson Heights, not far from the high school, a gold watch and chain valued at fifty dollars, and four head of Arabian horses, unbroken. They were five or six years old and nearly white. They were the orneriest damn horses that I have ever seen. When we tried to work them in harness they would balk. When we tried to ride them they would buck. The first chance we got, we swapped three of them off. The best one we kept as a brood mare.

This winter of 1893–94, we kids went to the Willey school. Part of the time we went on horseback. The other part we went to school in what is called a "jumper sled." It was just about like the front bob of a bobsled, only the runners were longer. There was quite a lot of snow up to about the middle of March. There came a few warm days that were sure melting the snow in a hurry. The draws and the creeks were full of slush snow. In midafternoon on March 20, it began to snow. By supper time it was one of the old-time Wyoming blizzards. The snow was

[3] Uncle Johnnie did make some sort of a deal with a young fellow by the name of Al Hilliger, who came from the Southwest. I am not sure but I think Al stayed with the old man until he died. Al didn't realize much out of the estate. The old man had sunk his life savings in a big stone house built up on top of a small knoll overlooking the Dutch Creek Valley. This place is now owned by Walter Peters, a Sheridan County commissioner, and one of the best sheepmen to be found anywhere.—Author's note.

piling up fast, with a strong northerly wind. The snow found all the cracks in the buildings. In a little hog shed where there were three fat hogs about ready for butchering and a six-months-old calf, the calf froze to death. The hogs were partly frozen. There was just enough life left that all they could do was to grunt a little. They couldn't get up on their feet. When we tried butchering one of them we found that the meat was in such shape we couldn't use any of it.

After two days and three nights, the big storm was over. The sun came out nice and warm. With the snow belly-deep to a horse in most places, Dad started to shoveling paths to the out buildings and feeding some of the stock. Tode and I took a couple of saddle horses and a shovel and headed for the back side of our place to get some cattle that were snowbound in a brush thicket. With that snow belly-deep to our ponies a part of the way, it was plenty tough traveling. We had to shovel through some of the drifts. Just before we came to the cattle, there was one big drift on the north side of a draw to shovel through. After we had the path made, we rounded up about twenty head of cattle. They followed the path down through the big drift all right but when they started climbing the bank on the opposite side of the draw, one of the two-year-old heifers that was heavy with calf, slipped down and came sliding into the draw. When she got up she was on the fight and went back the way we had brought her out. We then had to take the cattle back through the drift to her. The second try at crossing the big draw the cattle once again tried climbing the bank, instead of following our horse trail. All made it but the two-year-old heifer. When she came sliding backwards into the bottom of the draw, before she could get to her feet, I had her tailed down and kept her there. Tode shoveled the entrance to the path full of snow. Now we had her. The only thing the heifer could do was to follow our horse trails, which she did after looking the thing over for about thirty minutes. From there on we had no trouble.

During the next few days there were nesters, grangers, and cowboys out on the range shoveling paths to marooned cattle that were snowbound in some brush thicket. There was a heavy loss in cattle during the storm and afterwards, on the ranches and out on the range. Some of the ranchmen were out of hay. We had plenty of hay, but even at that we lost some cattle. Over near Buffalo two ranch women lost their lives in the storm, trying to make it from Buffalo to their ranch home on French Creek, only four miles north and west of Buffalo. I knew these two women personally. When they were found, they were sitting in the seat of the rig locked in each others' arms, frozen to death. Near Buffalo a man by the name of West was badly frozen. He lost both feet. A lot of rangemen had their feet, hands, and ears frost bitten.

When the frost started coming out of my hands, the pain was worse than a bad dose of toothache. I tried rubbing them with snow and put them in a pan of ice water. Nothing helped much until I gave them a bath in some coal oil. This did the trick without any bad effect.

Our next problem was our horses over on the head of Little Badger Creek where the range country was plenty rough. Upon the rocky knolls or red shale knobs the stock did not graze much during the summer months. That was where the good bunch grass grew. And on these high spots the wind kept the snow blown off. It was along about the first of May when Tode and I packed a roundup bed and a little camp outfit on a horse and headed for Willow Springs and the Badger Creek country. Already some of the old mares were back on the home range to foal their colts. Up at the head of Little Badger near a spring, we made camp. While Tode hobbled our two saddle horses and put the pack horse on a stake rope, I cooked up some supper. Then we rolled out our bed and crawled in. The night was clear and bright. Along about midnight there came an awful rain storm which soon wet through our tarp. To keep dry we crawled in under the bed and lay on the ground. It wasn't too bad. We were sleeping in most of our clothing. About the time the rain storm was over, we heard an awful scream like a woman in distress. We knew it wasn't the howl of a wolf. The wolf's howl is more like the old-time fire whistle. By the time we heard that scream a couple more times we knew what it was. It was the scream of a mountain lion. We didn't have a gun, so we just lay quiet and waited for daylight, hoping that our saddle horses would be all right. For a lion there is no better meat than horse meat. As soon as day light came we crawled out from under the bed. Tode went for the saddle stock while I cooked some breakfast. When Tode came back with the horses, he was a little nervous and quite a bit excited. He had seen the lion in some sand rock. As soon as breakfast was over, we packed our outfit and moved camp to Willow Spring.

From here we started riding the range and bunching our horses. In a couple of days we had most of our horses in one bunch. We then packed our camp outfit and headed for home with all the horses we could find. We were short about fifteen head.

About a week later, Thompson (Tomp) Wood came by our place and said there were some of our horses grazing near his place on Dutch Creek. I went home with Tomp and stayed over night. I had no trouble in finding the horses but had a hell of a time in gettin' them home. In the bunch there was a young four- or five-year-old stud that gave me a lot of trouble. This stud would get in the lead of the horses. With his mouth open and his head lowered nearly to the ground, he would drive the horses back a hundred yards or more, until I could get him whipped out with my throw rope. This kind of business was kept up most of the way home. I couldn't get near enough to rope him. All I could do was to cuss and cry and wish I had a gun.

After the stud was corralled at the ranch, Tode helped me rope him by both front feet. We had quite a time in bustin' or throwin' him and hogtiein' him. It didn't take me long though to change him into a gelding. On the left hip there was the pitcher brand ꝗ that belonged to the McCrea outfit about four miles from Buffalo on Rock Creek.

The McCreas had three boys, Johnnie, Jeff, and Howard. The cowboys called the oldest one "Johnnie Pitcher." Johnnie Pitcher came to our place for the horse. After looking at the brand, he couldn't remember the horse which had strayed about fifty miles from the McCrea range, but he was glad to get this four-year-old, good-looking gelding.

After having three experiences with range studs, my folks agreed that I could have a six-shooter like most all of the rangemen carried. It was along in June of 1894 that Doc Tanner, an old-time cowboy, came to our place and sold Dad his squatter's right or homestead filing down on Young's Creek right near the Montana line. In the deal Dad got a dugout cabin and most all of Doc's personal belongings. Soon Doc was on his way for Alaska. Among Doc's belongings there was a good forty-five caliber six-shooter which was given to me. After we had made the spring horse roundup, Tode and I divided up our horse herd. Now we each had about twenty head of trading horses. Same as Dad we became right handy at swapping horses, whenever anyone showed up and wanted a horse trade.

BUSTIN' BRONCS

THIS SUMMER OF 1894, we two nester kids broke out ten or more head of three- and four-year-old geldings to ride. I being fifteen and Tode not quite fourteen, it was up to me to take the wiry edge off of these broncs. Tode did his part in riding the more gentle ones. I got bucked off only once, and that was by a hot-blooded, three-year-old gelding that I got in a trade from Levi Wood. Among these young geldings there were several head of three-year-olds that were from mustang mares and old Starr, the trotting stud. They were ornery about bucking. Some of them we matched up and made driving teams of them. These matched teams, which were mostly blacks, sold for a very good figure.

Among these young geldings there was one blue gray that we called Blue Dog. He was a barnyard-raised colt from one of Mother's driving mares. Blue Dog we rode for two years. He never did quit bucking. When Buffalo Bill Cody came to Sheridan to buy bucking horses and to hire some bucking-horse riders, several of us nester kids went into town to see the fun. Cody was there at the Sheridan Inn standing on the porch where he could best see the riding. The riding took place on the territory between the inn and Little Goose Creek, which was unsettled at that time.

That day Cody bought some good bucking horses and hired several good riders. Two of the riders were nester kids from our neighborhood, Jim Jennings and George Gardener, who became the best rider and all-round showman to be found anywhere.

Among the riders there was a stranger who had drifted in from Idaho. He was a small man. Had yellow, curly hair. He was a pure nester. Had on a pair of granger boots. He wanted a job riding with Cody's wild west show. Gardener and Jennings thought they would job this young granger. They asked him if he could ride Black Diamond. They said if he could he would be sure of a job with the show.

He said, "Bring on that Diamond horse, I can ride him."

Well, we all felt sure that this fellow couldn't ride Black Diamond, a big black gelding weighing about thirteen hundred and the worst bucker of the lot.

Gardener could ride him but it was doubtful about Jennings. When this granger-looking fellow mounted Diamond, he let out a war whoop, hooked his spurs into the black's ribs, threw away both bridle reins and rode that big black devil to a standstill. Cody didn't hesitate any when it came to hiring this young granger or nester or whatever he might be.

Ed Hughes, foreman of the Wrench ranch, an ex-Buffalo Bill rider, was there with some bucking horses for the boys to ride and to sell to Cody. Among these bucking horses there was a good-looking bay gelding, a little sway back. When Jennings rode this horse he was a little leary about riding him. He didn't hang the spurs in like he should have. Ed Hughes saw that. When Cody rejected the horse, Ed said, "Colonel, that sway-backed one you turned down is one of the best buckers from the Wrench range."

Cody said, "I turned that horse down because he wasn't much of a bucker."

"I'll show you," said Ed, "that the horse is a good bucker."

When Ed mounted the horse, he didn't try to ride straight up. Got the horn with his right hand, eased over a little to the left, and hooked his right spur into the bay's shoulder. After Ed had climbed down off the horse, Cody said, "Ed, I'll buy that horse. He's one of the worst buckers I've ever seen."

63

Sam Glen was there from the Dan Harris horse ranch with a good-looking white-faced bay that was supposed to be a bucking horse. When Sam mounted this gelding, it just sorta ran and fought its head. The horse was about half broke when Sam rode up to where some of us nesters' kids were sitting on our horses. He said, "Any of you fellers want to trade a gentle horse for a bucking horse?"

I said, "Yes. I'll swap with you." I got down off of Blue Dog, pulled off my saddle and said, "Here's your gentle horse."

Sam's horse never did buck with me, but the next morning Blue Dog sure piled Sam, and he bucked him off every time he tried to ride him. I didn't show Blue Dog to Cody because he was a gentle horse. Well, I got ahead of my story about two years. This year of 1894, while we were breaking out these broncs, we kids, Tode and me, sometimes would gallop up Magpie Hollar or draw to the Jennings' ranch about three miles from our place. Cal Jennings had a whole flock of kids, both boys and girls. One day when I was up there, Cal said, "Kid, let's take off a couple of days and go up on the mountain fishing."

This suited me fine. Always liked to fish when there was anything to fish for. The next day we packed old Blondy, one of Cal's horses, with a bed and some grub and headed for the Big Horns. In going through the town of Big Horn we bought some fish line and hooks. We followed the old stage road up the mountain by way of Red Grade. When we got to the top of the mountain, we turned left, followed a cowpath down onto Little Goose Creek. Right about where William Henry Harrison now has his summer home, Cal and I pitched our camp. We caught a lot of grasshoppers, then we each cut down a long willow and trimmed off the branches. We peeled off the bark so the willows would look like real fishing poles. After putting our fishing outfits together, we went to the stream to get enough fish for sup-

64

per. After we had each made a couple of casts, we had plenty of fish for supper—four of them, all natives averaging about a pound each.

The next morning we were out fishing soon as the sun was up. We only fished until noon, as by that time we had all the fish that old Blondy could pack out of there. We only had about two hundred fish at a pound average. There were no game wardens, but lots of fish. We only took what our two families could use, with a few for our neighbors.

A few days after the fishing trip, Bill Cameron, our near neighbor and old-time cowboy and a good one, came to our place. He said that Doctor Newell of Sheridan wanted a mate for his brown driving horse. In a trade Doc would give Bill his bay race horse. Well, Doc didn't have any race horse, just a well-built, well-muscled horse that was gentle and had a little more speed than the average cowpony. Bill wanted this horse for a rope horse. Bill knew just about all of the horse outfits in the country, so we headed for old Jim Murray's Bar U U horse ranch over at the mouth of Box Elder Creek, where it empties into Piney Creek. The old Scotchman was at home. When Bill told Murray what he wanted, Jim said, "Yes, I think I can fix it up for you. Tomorrow morning we'll go up Box Elder and make a little horse roundup."

The next morning when we were all well mounted, we rode up Box Elder eight or ten miles, right up to Lake DeSmet. By now a lot of horses were in on the creek for water. Jim took the north side of the creek. Cameron took the south side, while I brought up the rear. Down the creek we went. The horses were wild. Murray and Cameron could only hold about half the horses on the creek. I came along in the rear at a high gallop. When we hit the wings of the big corral, we were in high gear. Those long wings extended out a quarter of a mile from the corral

65

gate. We corralled most of the horses, all except a few old wild renegade mares that broke back up Box Elder. This made no difference, we didn't want them any way. We had about a hundred head in the corral. While Murray was cooking up some dinner or lunch, Bill was looking at the horses. He decided on a young brown gelding. We cut the horse into a small pen, then ran him into the chute where Bill put a hackamore on the horse and looked at his mouth for age. The horse still had two colt or baby teeth, which meant that he was a four-year-old.

After dinner Bill paid Murray sixteen dollars for the horse. This was six dollars above average price for an unbroke gelding. Murray had out on the range about fifteen hundred head of horses. Two years after the deal with Cameron, Murray offered to sell to me unbroke geldings at ten dollars per head. As I remember, it was 1898 or 1899 that Murray closed out his horse business at five dollars per head with the slicks or unbranded stuff free of charge.

That afternoon after leaving the Bar U horse ranch, we spent the night with Tom and Winnie Kazee, who lived on Piney Creek just across the stream from the Flying E cow ranch. And here is where three old-time cowboys met and talked over old times. Tom Kazee, an old-time wagon boss for the Flying E, was elected first sheriff of Sheridan County in 1888. Bill Cameron and Jumbo McKenzie were cowboys for the same outfit. These three men all had been top cowhands. They could tell some interesting tales about when they first came to Wyoming Territory in the early 1880's.

Before leaving the Kazee place I swapped horses with Jumbo. Traded off a cream-colored horse for a half-broke dapple-gray bronc branded JUM on left thigh. When we got back to the Bard ranch we kids went to work on our broncs. Bill Cameron and his wife and his brother lived on the old Jack Burnside

66

place next to our place. This summer of 1894, Bill was punching cows for Doctor Newell and George L. Smith, who owned the Bar N outfit down on lower Prairie Dog Creek. Smith also owned a drug store, Bar N (— N), in Sheridan right on the corner where the dime store is now located.

How come Bill was home? He had about a month's vacation in between the spring roundup and the fall or beef roundup. After Bill got this Bar U bronc broke to drive in harness, he did trade for the race horse, which he called Doc.

That fall when the granger roundup wagon pulled out on the range and started gathering cattle, I went along as horse wrangler. Got a dollar a day and our cattle gathered, which were not many at this time. This granger roundup wagon was only out about two weeks. We usually camped in some nester's or granger's field or pasture. There were no night guards to stand, and the horse wrangling was easy. I had time to break out two broncs. One was for Frank Kirkpatrick, and one for a fellow by the name of Tompkins. I got ten dollars from each man. This was easy money, just like getting money from home and not having to write for it. Jim Simpson, the big colored man who had come up from Texas with a herd of long horns, was our cook. At one time Jim was about the best roper on the range. When he got a little too heavy for riding, he took to cooking. He knew how to wrastle Dutch ovens, pots and pans, and what kind of fire to have so that he would not be burning everything black like some fellows did that didn't know much about camp cooking. We all slept in a big tent when the weather was bad. When the weather was good, we rolled out our bed most any place where we could find a level spot.

One night we sure got fooled on the weather. Didn't put up the bed tent. Just rolled out our beds and crawled in. The fellow with his bed next to mine hadn't been long away from Arkansas when he pulled off his old granger boots and, instead of putting them under the bed, stood them both up out in the big open. He put his socks in the boots. Along sometime during the night it began to snow. About daylight the wind blew the tarp from off my head. When I looked to see how my neighbor was coming along, there he was, digging the snow out of his boots and shaking out his socks. There already were four inches of snow on our beds and it was yet snowing. It didn't take us long to get dressed and to start running foot races to warm up a bit. Simpson over under the fly of his wagon was having a lot of trouble trying to cook some breakfast. The wind was blowing out the fire just about as fast as he could build it. It was about ten o'clock before we had breakfast. We then shoveled the snow off a level spot and set up the big bed tent and set up a Sibley heating stove that has no bottom but sits right down on the ground. It warmed the tent up in a hurry. Here we spent the rest of the day and that night. For pastime we played freeze-out for turkeys. When some fellow would put up one of his wife's turkeys, usually about six of us would take out a stack of twenty-five chips (beans or matches). These beans or matches were valued at a penny each. After the six players had bought twenty-five beans each, the game started. It was draw poker. Once a player lost all his beans he couldn't buy back into the game. He was froze out until another turkey was put up. There is one thing for sure, these turkey men had to fix things up with their wives before they would give up the turkeys. These kind of poker games were referred to as flat-rock games.

Working along with this granger wagon were Frank Kirkpatrick, Charley Story, and C. W. Stroud,[1] the fellow that got his boots snow full. While most of us were busy playing freezeout, Story wrote up a song with a verse concerning every man of the granger wagon. One verse I remember quite well went something like this:

> *There's old Camel Stroud who is ded stuck on a flat*
> *rock game*
> *Humps his back like a humble bee and never over-*
> *looks an old HD*

HD was Stroud's brand.

These granger fellows were a mighty sprucy lot, believed in wearing clean shirts. Any time our wagon camped near their place, they would go home for a clean shirt, they said. One evening when everybody had gone home for a clean shirt, Simpson sorta shook his head and said, "Kid, what do you think of it?"

I said, "I don't know. What do you think,"

He said, "You know them fellers are not foolin' nobody. They's just goin' home to sleep in a warm bed and to cuddle up close to their wimmin folks."

Along with the outfit there was one old granger who would light a candle, stick one end in a whiskey bottle as a candle-stick. This outfit he would place near the head of his bed and read half the night. Well, we didn't like this very well, so one of the boys swiped a spud from the sack, took it to bed with him and when the old fellow got busy reading, he put the light out with the spud. The old fellow was sure on the prod about this. When he lighted the candle again, he dared anyone to put it out. No one said anything. When he went to reading again,

<hr>

[1] In later years, Stroud moved into Sheridan. For several years he was water commissioner of Sheridan County. Charley Story also moved into Sheridan where he was an early-day newspaper man. Later he served as mayor of Sheridan. Frank Kirkpatrick also served one term as mayor of Sheridan, with Bill Dunning as chief of police.—Author's note.

George Gardener took his six-shooter from under his pillow and shot the light out, blowed up the whole works, candle stick and all. This was enough for the old granger. He didn't try reading in bed any more.

With the roundup over, it was time for us young fellows to get back in school at the Willey school house, which was next to the old FE cow ranch. When Tode and I headed for school we were both riding broncs. From down Prairie Dog Creek there came George Gardener and his sister Ella. George was mounted on a bronc. Ella had a nice gentle pony and was riding a side saddle. She was sorta hazing the bronc for George. We had broncs hobbled in the school yard. We had broncs staked or picketed to green logs on the old FE cow ranch. There were quite a lot of big kids going to this school. During the noon hour or recess time, we would go back of the school house and dance quadrilles. George and I each had a mouth organ and could play some good lively dance tunes. Our teacher was a young fellow by the name of Cubious. He wasn't a Cuban, but he looked like one. He was always sleepy. About three nights a week he was out tomcattin' around, keepin' company with a young widow who lived down the creek. About half the time during school hours, he would cock his feet up on his desk and go sound to sleep. When it came time for classes one of the big girls would go and wake him up and say, "Mr. Cubious, it's time for classes."

With us big kids, we didn't care whether he went to sleep or not. We went ahead and did our school work, and we saw to it that the little kids behaved themselves.

We rode broncs to school until the sledding got good. Then we went to driving broncs on our jumper sled. At the Willey school there was a good barn with several stalls. We bronc bustin' kids had the two back stalls where the little kids were in less danger of getting kicked.

70

I remember one day when the snow was a foot or more deep. We were driving down across the meadow on the Burnsides' place when we heard that awful howl of the gray wolf nearby. About four hundred yards off to one side we spotted a big gray wolf upon a small knoll. He was just starting to bed down in the snow. We whipped up our broncs and drove down to Bill Cameron's place. He got his 30-30 carbine from the house, ran to the barn, put the bridle on Doc, his saddle horse, mounted him bareback and took off up across the meadow. At the backside of the knoll, Bill tied Doc to some brush. Then he began to crawl on his hands and knees through the snow up to where the wolf was bedded down. When the wolf either heard or scented Bill, it raised up out of the snow and was ready to take off. It got a 30.30 right back of the shoulder. After Bill had dragged the big gray down to where Doc was tied, he took one rein from off the bridle and tied one end of the rein around the wolf's neck. The other end he tried to Doc's tail. And here he came riding Doc and dragging the wolf through the deep snow. I've seen lots of wolves and killed a few myself. That was the largest wolf that I ever saw. How much bounty Bill collected, I don't know, probably twenty dollars.

MORE ROPIN' AN' RIDIN'

THE SPRING OF 1895 WAS A LATE SPRING. We were just about out of hay. We had only enough left for our work stock, a couple of saddle horses and three or four milk cows. Of a morning we would drive our little bunch of range cattle out onto a big flat where there was quite a lot of old grass. One evening there came to our place a couple of nester kids from down Prairie Dog Creek, Henry George and George Gardener. George was a good roper. These kids helped me drive the cattle up to the big flat.

"Any strays in this bunch?" George asked.

"Yes," I said, "that little blocky-built two-year-old over there, the only one with horns. He's a stray."

"What brand's he wearin'?" George asked.

"I don't know," I said. "It might be the map of Mexico. Never did look to see."

After George had roped the steer around the horns, Henry caught the steer by the hind feet and stretched him out on the ground. After putting George's loop on the front feet, I started partin' the hair and lookin' for the brand. George said, "What's on him?"

"Damned if I know," is how I answered him.

"Take this front foot rope and keep him stretched out tight, and I'll take a look," George said.

While George was partin' the hair and tryin' to trace the brand, I gave Henry the high sign, and we both stepped our horses up at the same time. When the steer felt the slack, he got on to his feet and took in after George. When he tried to get behind my horse, I took off across the flat and Henry did the same. By now the steer was crowdin' George so close that he took off across the flat on foot. He outran that steer for fifty yards. All the time the steer was gaining a little, until he got close enough for George to grab him by a horn. After a little tussle the steer went on across the flat. Now it was George who was on the fight.

He said, "I'm goin' to whip both of you —— —— ——."

"You're not going to whip me. I'm not gettin' off my horse," I told him.

"I'll get on old Beaver" (that was his buckskin rope horse), "and I'll rope you ———, and then I'll work you over," he shouted.

By the time George got to old Beaver, Henry and I were gone. We didn't see George for about a month, then he said, "Come go home with me and stay all night."

George was sleeping out in the yard in his roundup bed. I slept with him. Along some time during the night it felt like the whole earth had fallen in on top of me, and there was George standing off to one side laughing.

He said, "Now I'm even with you for turnin' that wild steer loose on me."

Here is what George had done. His stepdad, old Dandy Downs, had some green ash fence posts cut. George got the biggest one in the pile, stood it on end, and let it fall across me. It didn't break any bones, but I was pretty sore across the middle for a day or two. I couldn't complain because that was a dirty trick we played on George.

Back in those good old days there were no arenas to rope in. We nester kids just went out on the range and did our roping. We never were particular as to what we got our rope on. We liked to rope mavericks best of all. They were wilder and could run faster. Then it was sorta fun burning your brand on one of those slick's ribs. It wasn't just because we wanted the maverick. It was more for the devilment of the thing.

One time Bill Levitt and Elias Martin, two nester kids, came from Little Goose Creek over to our place. They wanted to do some roping. We went up into Magpie Hollar where the Surrena brothers had some cattle ranging. There we began roping calves. No mavericks, as there weren't any in the bunch. We had just roped a big calf when I saw the two Surrena brothers heading down our way. It sure didn't take me long to bust that calf and get my rope off. Already Bill and Elias were headin' down Magpie Hollar or draw with me not far behind. Here came the two brothers as fast as their horses could run. Well, that was quite a race. We went right down Magpie to Mead Creek. Crossed the creek, took up a side draw headin' off towards Little Goose. The two brothers were only about four hundred yards behind. We were gaining a little. At the head of the draw, instead of going on towards Little Goose, we ran around a knoll and headed down a draw towards Mead Creek. There the brothers lost us. From start to finish this was about a five-mile race, with our horses dripping wet with sweat. We rode into a box-elder grove, pulled off the saddles, and waited about an hour for our horses to cool off a bit, and for the brothers to start headin' back home.

About forty years later when I was spending the night with George Surrena, I asked him if he remembered this calf-roping deal. He said, "You bet I remember it. If we could have caught you kids we were going to give you a damn good lickin'."

In Sheridan out near the Coffeen school there lived a couple of Negro boys who had a collie dog that was a heeler. They thought it fun to see their dog heel the horses of us nester kids and to try to get us bucked off. One day when I was riding a gentle horse into town, these two Negro kids were out with their dog. When I saw the dog coming for my horse, I just dropped a loop over the Dog's head and started for up town with my horse in a fast gallop. The dog wasn't hitting the ground only once in about every twenty feet. Here came the Negro kids yelling, "Please, Mister, don't kill our dog. We won't do it again." And they never did. At the Powers brothers' livery barn (where Boyd's Super Market is now located) Boot Powers pulled the rope from the dog.

It was along about the first of May, 1895, that I rode over to the Moncreiffe brothers' ranch, just south of Big Horn, to see

74

about selling a polo pony to Malcolm Moncreiffe. This was the same hot-blood pony that had bucked me off in '94. When I got to the Moncreiffe ranch, the foreman's wife told me that the men were out at some corrals in what was called the mountain pasture, branding cattle. In these branding corrals there were four hundred head of yearling heifers waiting to be branded. While the branding irons were heating, William Moncreiffe,[1] the older of the two brothers, a tall, lanky Englishman, was out in the middle of the big corral looking at the heifers.

I noticed one heifer walk out away from the others, shake her head, and paw the ground. About that time someone yelled, "Look out, William." About that time William saw the heifer and made for the corral fence, with that wild heifer fanning his

[1] It was the year of 1916 or 1917, while I was foreman for William Moncreiffe, or Billie, as he was called, we were spending the night at the Jack Moore ranch on Box Elder Creek. That was the year that Frank Mondell was running for Congress. Jack Moore said that when Mondell and some of the white-collared birds went out into the country to spear some votes, Mondell came to his place.

Mondell said, "Now Jack, who is at the ranch next to you?"

Jack said, "I told him there was Billie Moncreiffe, a tall, lanky Englishman with a lot of freckles on his face. And that there was Floyd Bard, a little sawed-off guy with pop eyes."

The next day when Billie and I were out riding the range, he said, "You know I would hate to be a little sawed-off popeyed guy."

I said, "Well, I'd just as well be that as a long, lanky Englishman with freckles all over my face."

Moncreiffe and I were always betting on something such as how many cattle there might be in some certain bunch. We'd play pitch to see who would wrangle horses of a morning, or who would open all the gates while riding pastures looking for strays. One time when we went to Billings, Montana to buy a couple of hundred steers, we each made a bet as to what a cattleman might look like. On a piece of paper we each wrote a description of the man that we had never seen. We never knew who won this bet. The man never showed up. This was one of our big bets. It was fifty cents. All for a little fun. One time when we bet a nickel on something and Moncreiffe didn't have the money in his pocket, he wrote out a check for the full amount, which I never cashed. I yet have the check somewhere in the house, our home in Big Horn.—Author's note.

coat tail. That was a close race. When William landed well up on the top rail, the heifer hit the lower rails. From then on until the branding was over, William stayed out of the corral.

These heifers had been trailed in from the Gillette country from the TJ ranch, owned by an Englishman by the name of Hamilton, who came to Wyoming along in the 1880's. That is where the Moncreiffe brothers first landed after coming to the United States. These heifers were probably the starter of the Moncreiffe cow business. At one time the Moncreiffe brothers were running about three thousand cows on their Dutch Creek holdings. They worked them off and on for a good many years.

PUNCHIN' COWS
FOR THE BAR N OUTFIT
OF LOWER PRAIRIE DOG CREEK

EARLY IN THE SPRING OF 1895, I made a trip down Prairie Dog to the Bar N to see Sam Bell, the manager, about a job of punchin' cows for the outfit. Sam says, "O. K. Kid, they tell me that you are a pretty good roper and rider, and you know something about handlin' cattle. And that's the kind of man the Bar N needs. I'll give you a job at forty per month and that's five dollars above the average wage of the average cowboy. Come back about the twentieth of May, that's when the PK wagon starts the spring roundup. You and Perry Hulse will be the cowboys for the Bar N. You'll be repping along with the PK wagon. You two fellows will have two mighty good strings of horses to ride."

I told Sam that sure sounded good to me, that I'd be coming for the job on the eighteenth. I had thanked Sam and was starting to leave for home when Sam said, "Kid, put your horse in the barn and stay for dinner. Soon as Perry Hulse and Baldy Goodrich come in from feeding the cattle, we'll eat."

I knew both Perry and Ed Goodrich. They were both sorta baldheaded. Ed was called "Baldy." In the summer months Ed usually rode bucking horses in Cody's wild west show. During the winter months he would get himself a job feeding cattle and breaking a few horses on the side. After dinner when I was getting ready to leave, Ed says, "Kid, it was only last week that I finished breaking a horse for old McCarty, the old horse man over on Tongue River. The horse was pretty bad about buckin'. I took most of that out of the bronc. He has the makin's of a top saddle horse. Old Mac swapped this horse to a Missouri kid for a month's work grubbin' sagebrush. If your pony is gentle, I think that you can swap horses with the Missouri kid." There being nothin' that I liked better than a horse trade, I rode over to old Mac's place. Out on a flat near the house the kid was grubbin' sagebrush.

When I rode up to the kid I says, "Is Mac to home?"

He says, "No, he isn't. Is there anything I can do for you?"

"No," I says. "I guess not. Just came to see if I could trade a gentle horse for a bronc something that my mother and sister couldn't ride."

The kid says, "I've got just the horse for you."

Here's where two kids swapped horses.

We had built a branding fire and were getting ready to vent or cancel out the Y brand when old Mac rode up. He told the kid to go back to grubbing sage, that he would vent the brand. It was done by burning a little Y upside down on the left shoulder, just above the original brand.

While I was saddling up this good-looking sorrel bronc, Mac said, "Did you see any horses between the Bar N and here?"

77

"Yes," I said. "One little bunch up near your outside gate."

"Guess I'd better ride along with you and see what they are." Old Mac wasn't interested in the horses, he just wanted to see me get bucked off, and he come pretty near seeing it.

Out near where the kid was grubbin' sage that bronc blew up. Without any spurs I had a tough time riding that bronc. Old Mac just reared back in his saddle and laughed until the tears run down his cheeks. The sagebrushin' kid just stood there with his mouth open. He didn't know what to say.

Mac says, "I'll ride with you to the outside so that you won't have to get off of Bob Cat to open the gate."

While I was riding through the gate, Mac swung the gate shut, hitting Bob Cat in the rear end. Once again the old Irishman had a good laugh, while it was all I could do to ride that Bob Cat. At the gate Mac turned back towards home.

In making the four miles back to the Bar N, Bob Cat blew up and bucked seven times. Then he gave it up as a bad job, and I was mighty glad of it, 'cause I was about ready to give up. Come to find out this was one of the worst buckers that Mac ever raised, so he told me some two or three years later when I met him in Sheridan. This time Mac came up grinning and blinkin' his eyes. The first thing the old Irishman said was, "Hello, my lad, have you got any more of those horses that your mother, your sister, aunts, and cousins are always riding?"

I told him, "Not since I got that one from you."

Then Mac began to laugh. He said, "My lad, I'm going to tell you a little joke. About a week after you and that kid traded horses, the kid dressed up, got on that bay horse you traded him and started for the Squirrel Creek school house where they were having Sunday School. Don't know what happened, but right there in front of the school house that horse blew up and bucked the kid off."

I knew this horse would buck because one time when I thumbed him in the neck and shoulders, he bucked with me, but he wasn't hard to ride, not like Bob Cat. I broke him of bucking and sold him for a very good price.

It was on the eighteenth of May that I saddled up Blue Dick, a four-year-old blue roan gelding, and tied my bed and war sack or duffle sack on another one of my saddle horses. Then I said good-bye to Mother and the rest of my family. It was after midafternoon when I rode into the Bar N ranch.

After I had eaten lunch, Perry and I went out into the pasture and rounded up the cavvy, which as I remember had eighteen good-looking saddle stock. That afternoon Sam cut the cavvy in two, giving a part to me and a part to Perry who wasn't too hot as a cowboy, but was a hand when it came to riding circle, going on day herd, and standin' night guard. Perry got the best circle horses, while I got the good cow horses and rope horses. In my string was little Dick Warren, Frank Warren, and Big Duck Warren, the best all-round cow horse that I ever rode. These horses were raised and broken by Larry Warren, an old-time horse man who came from Colorado along in the early 1880's. He settled in the Prairie Dog Valley not far from the Bard ranch.

For circle horses I had three Bar U horses raised by old Jim Murray; one was named General, a long-backed brown. A chestnut sorrel was named Siroc, after Jesse James's notorious horse. The other horse, a roan-flanked sorrel, was called Tode. All were tough as whang leather and mighty good circle horses. For a night horse I had a small strawberry roan raised on the Bard ranch. The other two were good Mexican horses, good anywhere. One was named Fondy; the other was Rossceis or something like that. In Perry's string, he only had one cutting horse named Yellow Dick, a dun-colored buckskin. Some of his circle horses had been raised by Mr. Wallop. They were branded with the quarter-circle-bar-quarter-circle brand ⌣ on left thigh. Among those horses there was one named Roanie Wallop. He was a race horse, the fastest horse on the roundup. There was one that Perry called old Skunktail, a flea-bitten gray. A little sorrel he called Henry. On cold mornings Henry would hump up and crow-hop around until Perry thought him a real buckin' horse.

Over at Dow's dam on Dutch Creek we caught up with the PK wagon. The PK was owned by the Patrick Brothers, John and Al. Their range foreman was Harry Fullmer. The wagon boss was Walt Hampton, a wild one but a good cow man. I already knew most of the cowboys with the PK wagon. There was the late John Duncan of the Eaton ranch, Sam Culbertson of the Little Goose Valley, Gus Newell of lower Tongue River, who rode the rough string. There was Neri Wood, who was called the "pot hound pup" because he branded PUP brand. There was Charley Hill from Badger Creek who used the IT brand. Haywood Robinson and Mat Bedsaul were Virginia cowboys. Haywood was a cousin of Hampton and Mat was the PK horse wrangler. Jim Simpson was our cook. The night-hawk was a fellow that came down from the Milk River country of Montana. He was called "Hair-on-the-Neck" because he never shaved his neck. There was Black Perry, who wore a big black mustache and sorta talked through his nose. I never knew what country he came from. He was a queer one. And there was Eddie Donley, a young lawyer who had cattle on the PK range. He had no bed and he's the guy that slept with me. That summer I was the PK barber. Three or four of the cowboys, once or twice a week, would get me to shave them or cut their hair. For shaving, a cowboy would lay down on the ground with his head bent back over a rolled up bed. Down on my knees beside him I would lather his face and give him the shave of his life, which was about like pulling teeth.

The PK cattle ranged over an area of about fifty miles square, but their main range or home range was mostly of the Dutch Creek country. While we were rounding up the Dutch Creek country, we rounded up about thirty head of yearling heifers, all fresh branded. The brand had just begun to peel. Who the brand belonged to nobody knew. It was a maverick brand because it wasn't on record and had never been recorded. These heifers were without a doubt mostly from PK cows and they were rebranded with the PK iron. We found out afterwards that this maverickin' was done by a big town kid whose father was a lawyer and a judge. One day there came into the roundup a sleeper. That's a bull maverick that's been castrated, sometimes ear marked, but not branded. This sleeper wasn't ear marked. He was a red two-year-old steer, probably belonged to some granger. He was more gentle than the average range cattle.

Right away a young nester claimed this sleeper, said it belonged to his mother, that she neglected havin' it branded. Well, we all knew the nester was lying. The boss told him so. Our wagon boss told the young nester, who was workin' along with the PK wagon, that if he was claiming this sleeper, he just as well take the rest of his cattle from the herd, take his string of cowponies and head for home, that he was blackballed. That meant that he never could work with a regular roundup wagon any more.

Out on the range that summer of 1895, the PK had a wagon; the OW had one wagon and a part of the time there were two wagons. Bill Munsen was the boss of the regular wagon. Frank McKenney was the other wagon boss. The U Cross ⅄ had a

81

wagon with Jim Berrett as wagon boss. There was O Four Bar OЧ on Upper Tongue that had Simon Duncan reppin' with the PK outfit. During that summer there were quite often reps. out workin' with other wagons. Workin' with one of the OW wagons was Charley Thex from Otter Creek, who was workin' for Circle Bar ⊖. Charley rode a good string of horses and took good care of them. A part of them he could ride; a part of them he couldn't. When Neri asked me to ride three of these horses, I couldn't very well refuse because he had been good to me, in helping to get back some of the Bard cattle from the "71" outfit. Two of these broncs were mighty hard to set on when they turned loose to buckin'. One big rangy sorrel came near kickin' the spurs from off my boot heels while I had the spurs hung into him to keep from getting bucked off. Down on Buffalo Creek most of us cowboys got sick from drinkin' alkali water. We had what was called "the back door trots," only there wasn't any back door, and we trotted around in back of some sage-brush. For several days about all we drank was coffee and juice from canned tomatoes.

This spring of 1895, the U Cross shipped in and turned loose on the range several thousand head of two- and three-year-old churn-dasher steers. They were dairy stock of all breeds and colors, mostly from Kansas and Nebraska. They were so damn slow they were hard to handle. They never kept up with our range cattle.

One day when we were rounding up on Buffalo Creek and I wasn't feeling too good, Simpson says, "Kid, you had better roll a can of tomatoes in your slicker and tie it on the back of your saddle. When you get thirsty you can open the can, drink the juice, and eat the tomatoes."

I was trying to drive some of these churn-dashers down the creek towards the roundup group. It was a tough job, and I was nearly exhausted. I stopped long enough to open the can of tomatoes, and, when I finished eating them, I put a few small pebbles in the can. Just then down the creek came a bunch of cattle with a few big, wild, native or Texas steers among them. This was one point in my favor. Soon as this bunch of cattle hit the churn-dashers and got mixed with them, I was right there rattling the can and screamin' like a wild Indian. This did the trick. Down the creek the whole caboodle went, with the big steer leading. I just kept those cattle on high gear to within a half-mile of the roundup ground. There I threw away the can and slowed down to a walk. But those big steers didn't slow down at all. When they hit the roundup they went right on through and out on the other side. There weren't cowboys enough to hold them.

When I got to the roundup with the churn-dasher doggies, everyone was speculating as to what went wrong with those big steers. No one asked me anything, and I didn't tell them anything. A few days later while Sam Culbertson and I were on day herd together, four of these doggies were coming into our herd. Sam says, "Let's rope them and take a fall out of them."

I was riding big Buck Warren. Sam was on a PK bronc. I didn't have any trouble in roping my doggie, bustin' him and takin' off my throw rope. When I looked to see how Sam was comin' along, he had just roped his doggie when his bronc went one way and the doggie, the other. They all went down together.

I yelled at Sam to see if he was hurt. He said, "No, but for God's sake head off those two old outlaw steers."

In the herd there were two big steers that were probably eight or nine years old. One was white with some red on the side of his jaws. The other was a red brockle-face, big as a box-car, and ornery as they make 'em. There was a big wild bull that stayed with the steers. When they saw us with our ropes down, they made a break to get away. I soon had the white steer and bull back in the herd. The red steer I could do nothing with. Big Buck probably could have handled him on the end of my rope, but I wasn't sure my rig (saddle) would hold together. About all I could do was to keep in sight of the steer until he stopped with some range cattle about four miles from our herd. There I left him until he cooled down a bit. Then I took the whole outfit on high back to the herd where Sam was getting a little uneasy about me. He thought I had roped the steer and had got in some sort of a jackpot. For several years these steers had been dodgin' the shipping pens. But this was one year that they were penned or corralled and shipped off to market.

While we were camped down near the mouth of Clear Creek, there came a rain that lasted all forenoon. That afternoon we borrowed a fish net or seine from a rancher. The net was five or six feet wide and twenty or thirty feet long. On each end of the net we tied a throw rope. I took one end of the net while one of the other boys took the other end. We mounted our horses and swam them across the big hole in the creek, dragging the big net in between us. When we landed on the opposite bank we had about two gunny sacks of fish in our net. There were a few whitefish, some suckers, trout, and a lot of nice catfish. Some weighed five or six pounds. There was one fish about twenty inches long that looked like a bullsnake to me. But Gus Newell said it was a mountain eel and was good to eat. When these fish were dressed out, some of them had to be skinned, that is, the catfish and the bullsnake as the cowboys called it. In a Dutch oven Simpson fried a part of the fish nice and brown. In another one he fried the bullsnake or eel for Gus. He ate nearly all of it. And that was O.K. with us boys. We didn't want any of that snake anyway.

84

When we took the net back to the rancher, we took along a quarter of beef to pay for the use of the net. It was just the night before that we had butchered a yearling heifer for beef. For beef on the roundup it was most always the yearling heifer that was considered better beef.

Along that fall during the beef roundup when we were camped on Dutch Creek just above Dow's dam, a rancher, or dry farmer, drove into our camp with his wagon box half loaded with water melons. There probably were fifty of them. He wanted to swap them for a quarter of beef. Well, a cowboy never passes up that kind of trade. Soon the dry farmer was headin' for home with a quarter of beef and us cowboys had melons for a week or two.

While camping here at the dam we made a roundup that took in the Dow Prong and Granger Prong of Dutch Creek. We caught in this roundup one big, old, outlaw steer. To keep him from slipping off from the herd during night guard, two cowboys roped him and tied him to a big box-elder tree. Some time during the night the steer broke his neck, or it might have broken his heart to be treated this way. The next morning he was as dead as a door nail.

Once when we were camped down along the Powder River, just below the mouth of Wild Horse Creek, the wagon boss said to us cowboys, "Tomorrow morning you boys catch your best circle horse. It's going to be a long circle that we'll make, and it will be in the wee hours of morning that we'll leave camp."

It was usually about four in the morning when we ate breakfast. About two o'clock this morning, the night-hawk had the cavvy in the rope corral, and we were eating breakfast. We didn't know much about what we were eating as it was too dark to see. When it came to catching our circle horses, it was so dark we could hardly tell one from the other. I had just got my throw rope off my saddle, when along comes the Pot Hound Pup with his bridle. He says: "Kid, catch Big Brownie for me. It's too dark for me to see."

I just finished roping Brownie when Perry Hulse showed up with his bridle. He says, "Kid, catch Roanie Wallop for me. I know he can stand this long ride."

Then along comes Gus Newell. He says, "Kid, would you mind tossin' your loop over onto Keghead for me? Maybe this long circle will take a little of the buck out of him."

By the time I had caught General, the long-back Bar U brown, and had saddled up, most of the outfit were already headin' up Wild Horse Creek. Bill Munsen, the OW wagon boss, was leadin' the circle. Out on this circle there were U Cross cowboys, OW cowboys, and PK cowboys; countin' reps. and all there were probably seventy-five cowboys headin' up Wild Horse with Munsen in the lead ridin' an ornery, wall-eyed pinto. One thing about Bill Munsen, he never let the grass grow under his circle horse's feet. He just kept driftin' right along until we came to the head of Wild Horse. There we met up with Sleepy Jim Vaughn, workin' for SA outfit over on SA Creek. Jim took a part of the cowboys and drove all the country to the south of Wild Horse, right down to the Powder River. Munsen took the rest of the cowboys and drove the country to the north and east of Wild Horse. Before we left the head of Wild Horse, Bill told two cowboys to head back down the creek and to drive all cattle down the creek to the roundup ground at the mouth of the creek.

Bill says, "Don't drive too fast. There will be other cowhands comin' in from side creeks and off the ridges with more cattle."

Bill took me all the way round right up to the last cowboy where he sent me down a side creek that led into Wild Horse. Then he took the ridge to the north. I went down this side creek, whoopin' an' hollerin', drivin' all cattle ahead of me on a trot. Then Bill came off the ridge with another bunch, but he didn't go far until Bill's pinto threw up his tail all in and couldn't go any farther.

Bill says, "Kid, you take the cattle on down the creek to the roundup ground. And tell Henry Pelz, one of the OW cowboys, to get a fresh horse and come after me."

And that is what was done. By the time the last of the cattle were in the roundup, it was about three in the afternoon. We were all tired and hungry. Cowboys and horses alike were pretty well played out. By the time we had finished eating and had caught our cutting horses, it was too late in the day to try and work that big roundup. It was the largest that I ever saw. The roundup was bedded down, night guarded and worked the next day.

With each outfit cutting out their own cattle, the whole forenoon was spent in working the roundup. What cattle were not wanted were turned back on the range. The afternoon was spent in branding calves, with each outfit doing its own branding. The U Cross outfit after branding turned their cows and calves back on the range. The OW and PK took all their cattle back to their home range. For the PK it was the Dutch Creek country. The OW went to Hangin' Woman country. The U Cross had just finished working the roundup. Jim Brett, of the outfit, was sitting on his good cuttin' horse with a leg up around the saddle horn, talkin' with a couple of cowboys. A cow broke out of the herd nearby, and when Jim's horse started to bend the cow back into the roundup, he went out of there so fast that Jim was left lying in the sagebrush on his back. When we found out that the boss of the U Cross wasn't hurt, we all had a big laugh.

One fellow says: "Jim, that's a good cuttin' horse of yours, if he had someone to ride him."

87

When we got to doing some backtrackin', it was figured out that the most of us had ridden about sixty miles during that long circle. That fall while we were out on the beef roundup, the PK wagon was camped on Clear Creek, in what was called the Yorkie water gap. Sam Culbertson and I had the beef herd in on water. Most of the herd had drank and were bedded down. We were lying in the shade of our horses about half asleep when two coyotes came over a little ridge chasin' a jackrabbit right into the beef herd. Some of those big, wild steers went out of there about ninety to nothin' with the rest of the herd right on their heels. Out into the hills the herd went with Sam and me tryin' our best to hold them up. The best we could do was to bend the lead steers back into the rear end of the herd and get them to millin' around. Around and around we went like a merry-go-round until the herd got pretty well run down. We just held the herd there until it settled down and went to grazin'. Well, that run didn't do that beef herd any good. It took several pounds of taller off their ribs. Not long after this the PK headed for Dutch Creek and the Arno shippin' pens along the railroad track, about eight miles out from Sheridan.

After the herd had been worked into three or four different bunches ready for the pens, three hundred yards was as close as we could get to those pens. No matter how we tried, we couldn't get that first cut of two hundred steers any closer. The boss came to where I was sittin' on Big Buck Warren. He says, "Kid, you go to our horse cavvy. Get the horse wrangler to help you cut out about a dozen horses. When you get back here you throw those horses into the lead of those steers and head for that corral gate like Hell beatin' tan bark." Well, I didn't know how fast that was, but when I put that dozen cowponies through that corral gate we were sure makin' time. The steers were right there on our heels. When I ran the horses up in the corner of the alley, the steers went right on down the alley and into a big pen, and that's the way the rest of the herd was penned. We had those stock yards full of beef cattle—a trainload of them, which were loaded in stock cars and shipped to an eastern market. By the time the last steer was crowded into a stock car with about twenty-four or twenty-five others, the car was packed just about like a can of sardines. When one steer got down, the others were prodded over a bit so the down one could get up. Sometimes one of those long horns would get caught or wedged in between the slats of the side of the stock car, and the horn would have to be sawed off to free the steer. All kinds of things could happen. Sometimes a steer would take a kick at something and get a foot wedged. Then a slat would have to be sawed out to free the animal. The shipper, the fellow who went to market with the cattle, met up with all kinds of grief while ridin' in that caboose or way car on the tail end of the stock train.

Why worry about that? Soon as supper was over and no night guard to stand, we'd be catchin' our top horses and tailin' it for Sheridan, where the town was wide open to all kinds of entertainment for a cowboy. After we did some shopping, we'd hunt up some of this entertainment. There were no less than eight saloons along Main Street, where there were all kinds of gambling games. Some of these saloons had some kind of music. Another might have some fellow all dolled up and singin' some of the late songs.

Down on Grinnell Avenue where the most of the cowboys headed for were two sporting houses—each had a dance hall with some high-steppin' gals. At the end of the dance hall there was a bar and a bar maid. At the end of each dance, a fellow took his partner and went to the bar. After a fellow dug up a four-bit piece (fifty cents) out of his jeans and handed over to the bar maid, in exchange she would hand you back two whiskey glasses filled to the brim. This looked simple enough, so I went and asked one of the gals for a dance. Me being only sixteen, she gave me a queer sort of look, but didn't say anything 'till we started to waltzing. Then she says, "Kid, you're startin' kinda young in sowin' your wild oats."

"Well," I said, "I just as well start young and get it over with."

When the dance ended, and we marched up to the bar for our drinks, the bar maid poured our drinks from two different bottles. When I sorta hesitated about drinkin', my partner says, "Kid, that's pretty fiery stuff. If you don't want it, just throw it into the spittoon when you think nobody's lookin'."

After I had paid the maid fifty cents for the two drinks, the bar maid handed to my gal a little red check and stamp on this check in black—"10¢."

"What's that for?" I asked.

"That's my commission on our dance," the girl answered. Then, to top the thing off, she pulled her dress up above her knees, rolled down her stockin', took out a small pocket book that was half filled with checks and some green backs.

I wasn't at this joint long 'til I headed back up town to get my horse from the livery stable and head for camp. There at the stable I ran into our wagon boss. He says, "Kid, let's go to camp."

"O.k.," I said, "that suits me."

On our way out of town we were riding by one of those sporting places, when the boss says, "Kid, let's go in and dance once more."

It being a warm night, the dance-hall door and windows were open. We rode right up to the door. Before I knew what was up, the boss had grabbed Red Bird with the spurs. That big PK gelding jumped through the door and landed out on the dance floor where four couples were dancing a quadrille. The faster the boss rowled Red Bird, the faster he bucked and kicked. There were cowboys and gals goin' out of the windows and doors, anywhere they could get out. One gal could only make it to a settee at the end of the hall. There she began to scream and cry and run from one end of the settee to the other end. I sure felt sorry for this little gal. She was really frightened. The show didn't last long. Some of the cowboys took the boss and Red Bird outside, but he insisted on going back in to dance a quadrille. When the dance was about half over, he ran into the madame's bedroom and came out with a chemise or night gown on over his clothing. He got on Red Bird and back up town he went singing.

I headed for camp and a little sleep before Simpson yelled, "Come and get her."

The boss was a good cowman and business man. But when he hit town and got lit up, he was a wild one. When we went back on the range for our final or last beef roundup of the season, the weather was bad. It was rainy. Mat, the horse wrangler, quit his job. It was then that the boss put Haywood Robinson to wranglin' horses. Haywood thought this job was beneath him. It was a kid's job. When he says, "Kid, I'll trade jobs with you until the roundup is over," I said, "O.K. But I'll draw my wages from the Bar N and you can keep your PK wages."

I was gettin' five dollars more a month than he was.

With plenty of grass and water and cavvy well broke into camp life, and no dry herdin' or any night guard to stand, the job was easy. I just finished draggin' up some wood for Simpson when Billie Moncreiffe rode into our camp at Hay Spring, at the head of one prong of Dutch Creek. Billie was ridin' a white pony. He had a tin cup in his hand and was comin' for a drink of water. He said that he and his hired man, Louie Colson, had a camp down the creek a half a mile or so, and that they were close herdin' four hundred yearling heifers. He was in a hurry to get back and relieve the Swede so that he could come for a drink of water. The Swede was ridin' a strawberry roan, an old cowpony that was gettin' sorta bench-kneed. Louie couldn't talk much English. When he started jabbering away, we couldn't make head or tails of what he was sayin'.

(I didn't see any more of these two men for about two years, and that was when William Moncreiffe had leased a part of the Dutch Creek country and was puttin' up some fences.)

A TRIP TO CHICAGO

WHEN THE PK OUTFIT GOT BACK to Arno, I didn't help pen those wild steers. I was horse wrangler. But when the beef was loaded in the stock cars and ready to go, the outfit was short one shipper to go along with the cattle. When someone suggested that "the kid" take the job, I said, "That's O.K. with me. I'd like to take a train ride and see what a big city looks like." After signing up a shipper's contract, we were on our way to Omaha. But I never got there. When we were sidetracked at Aurora, Nebraska for feed and water for the cattle, we shippers, three of us, had an all-night stop over. We spent the night with an old couple who had a roomin' house and eatin' joint not far from the stock yards. The next morning, when the cattle were loaded back in the cars and were ready to go, I found out that my contract was for four carloads of fat cows that were consigned to the Chicago market. These were OW cows.

When Bill Munsen had handed a ten-dollar bill to me saying, "Kid, here's some money to help pay your expenses," I just sorta wondered what was up. Now I knew. The other shippers had jobbed me. They didn't want to take this long trip to Chicago. Well, it didn't make any difference to me. I was young and tough as an old bull hide. I could stand almost anything.

We were travelin' on a mixed train. The cows were up next to the engine where they wouldn't get much of a jolt if something went wrong. The train was about thirty cars long with the caboose at the rear. That's where I rode a part of the time. When the train would stop to refuel or change crews, I would grab the prod pole and make a run for the front end of the train to see if any of the cows were down. I'd not much more than get there when the engineer would toot four long whistles and one short one. That meant all aboard, and we're leaving here. Well, I had my choice. I could either ride in the cab of the engine or I'd climb up the ladder on the end of a car and walk the full length of the train back to the caboose. It wasn't too bad up on top of the cars for there was a pretty good board walk, something like a narrow sidewalk. The only thing wrong was that a fellow had to make quite a step from one car to the other. We had to be careful, as we might fall down in between the cars and get run over. I hardly ever had much time to sleep or eat, as I was always on the jump. When there was any sleepin', a fellow had to take it on the run. Just folded up your coat as a pillow, stretched yourself out in one of those long, leather-covered seats tied hard to the wall of the way car. I'd just get to sleep when the brakeman or conductor would say, "This is the end of our division. Here's where you change way cars or cabooses. You'll find another down there on the side track. You can tell it. It's got a green light on the tail end. Just open the door and walk in. And if you want anything to eat there's a beanery just across the street. You'll have plenty of time. It will be thirty minutes before your train leaves town."

At the eatin' joint I was about half through with the lunch when the engineer tooted all aboard, we're leavin' town. About all a fellow could do was to take one more big drink of coffee, much too hot, grab up a chunk of meat and bread and make a run for the tail end of the way car. By then the train was leavin' town. You just grabbed hold of the guard rail of the back step and swung aboard. Well, that was worse than mountin' a buckin' bronc. If a fellow missed mountin' the bronc, that didn't matter so much. If you missed mountin' that way car, you stood a good chance of gettin' run over. That could happen. I knew one cowboy who got both legs cut off just below the knees. He didn't give up ridin'. Was off the job about a year. Got himself some cork legs—a whole new outfit, and went back to makin' a hand on the range.

When those trainmen would say, "Kid, you'll have plenty of time to get a lunch before leavin' here," I didn't believe them. They were about like the weather prophet, just didn't know when they were tellin' the truth. It's been said that there are two kinds of liars in the world: one a natural liar, and the other is a weather prophet.

When the trainmen would say, "Kid, we'll be here thirty or forty minutes," I'd make a run for some eatin' joint, throw down a fifty-cent piece on the counter, ask for a sandwich and a doughnut, please. I didn't wait for any change, just hightailed it for the way car and got there the same time the whistle blew. It was seven o'clock in the morning when I arrived at the Chicago stock yards. There was only one fellow ahead of me. This fellow was lookin' for suckers. Right off the bat he says, "I am one of the Fish brothers of the dry-goods store. How about some new clothes?"

When I told him I'd just as well spend some money that way as some other way, we started out together. We walked a short way then boarded a street car. There were two other fellows aboard the car. One was sellin' tickets; the other was drivin' old Dobbin hitched to the end of the car. In between the rails there was a well-beaten horse trail.

I was no more than seated when we were headin' for uptown. Every little way we had to stop to let some one else climb aboard. Soon the seats were all taken, when in walks a lady. It was then I thought of what my mother told me one time, "Always be polite to the ladies and treat them with respect, but keep your distance." The first part of this I remembered all right. I gave up my seat to the lady. With Fish it was different. He didn't seem to care how many women folks stood up. He just sat there holdin' down his seat like a cowboy holdin' down a doggie. By now that streetcar was a load for old Dobbin to pull. When the driver hit the old horse with the whip, the old fellow did all he could, and that was a little too good. It just sorta upset some of the folks that was standin' up. One big, good-lookin' gal landed right on Fish's lap. She didn't make any move to get up. She just sat there and began to laugh. The more she laughed, the madder Fish got. When he got about as mad as an old wet hen, the gal got off his lap, thanked him for the seat, and left the car. Then we all did laugh. Later on, when I asked Fish why he got so mad, he said, "Them damn gals make me tired. Always landing on a feller's lap." The way I looked at it, there was nothing to get sore about.

At the Fish Brothers store I found out that they were not out after suckers—but western trade. They had a good line of clothing. Here I dressed up like a millionaire—new suit of clothes, everything new even to a derby hat. (Mother later said she was going to set a hen in it. But she never did.) I hadn't any more than landed there in Chicago 'till I was ready to do some backtrackin' for Wyoming. I didn't know anyone, and no one knew me. One evening Fish took me to see a show. I got quite a kick out of standin' on a street corner and talkin' to a policeman and watchin' the people rushin' up and down the street as if they were tryin' to catch a train. There must have been a shortage of hats in Chicago. A part of the men were goin' bareheaded. I had never seen anything like that before, only once, and he was a crazy sheep-herder. When someone told Perry Hulse that he could grow hair if he'd cut the crown out of his hat and let the sunshine in on his bald head, Perry was one of those fellows that would try anything once. So he cut the crown out of his big black Stetson and went that way all summer, rain or shine. Well, all Perry grew was a lot of blisters that became scabs. These he would rub with beef taller 'till they got loosened up. Then he would pull off the scabs as big as two-bit pieces. All that monkey work didn't do any good. When the roundup was over, he didn't have any more hair than what he started with.

I never went to Chicago again. Too far from home. I used to go to Omaha with cattle every fall right up 'till about the time I got married. My wife said she thought it best not to go there any more. From what she had heard, about all the stockmen went down there for was to chase around with the women and have a good time. About this there was no argument.

CATCHIN' WILD HORSES

THIS FALL OF 1895, when I got back to the Bar N, there was nothing much to do. The roundup was over for the season. I stayed at the Bar N three or four days helping to wean some calves, when along comes Charley Hill who had been workin' for the PK. Charley had been paid off and was headin' for his ranch on Badger Creek. Charley says, "Kid, just as well go home with me, and I'll help you to get those two young geldings that you missed gathering last year at Willow Springs. Charley Hill was about as wild as they come. He had a homestead at the forks of Badger Creek. One prong of the creek was named Hill Prong. Hill wasn't so much of a rider as he was a bronc man. He only had a few horses of his own but broke a lot of horses for others. He had a good set of corrals for handlin' horses.

In with a bunch of the McCarthy horses we found the two four-year-old geldings that I wanted. They were all as wild as rabbits. That didn't make any difference to us. We were each mounted on a good horse, and we could run the legs off that bunch. We nearly did that before we had them corralled. When I asked Charley the best way to handle those two broncs, he says, "Neck them together. You can't loco one without locin' the other."

I didn't want to use my throw rope. Hill says, "Kid, I'll give you a piece of my bronc rope. It's more soft and won't burn the bronco's neck so much."

After wrastlin' those broncs around for a while, we got them close enough together that we necked them. Not like a boy neckin' a girl—we necked those two broncs about four feet apart. When the corral gate was open, the broncs left that corral on high running close together. When they tried to separate, they couldn't do it. By the time I got those broncs to the Bard ranch, they had halter broke each other. Their necks were quite sore for a few days.

One bronc belonged to Tode, who named him Good Eye because it had a little white spot in one eye. Mine I named Bob, after the man that I got him from.

97

Hill helped me head the broncs up Badger Creek a little way. Then he said, "Good-bye, Kid. See you again some time." But he never did. When he left the Badger Creek and went into Montana to live, he joined a posse that was out looking for a murderer who had escaped jail. Charley knew this fellow. So did I and most everyone around Sheridan. He was the fellow who had shot the thumb off Swede Charley Olson, night marshal of Sheridan, in 1893 or 1894. He went up into Montana where he killed an old man in cold blood and was to be hanged, but broke jail. When the posse corralled the killer in a brush thicket, he fired a shot into the posse. The bullet struck Charley in the head, killin' him instantly. The posse opened up fire and killed the murderer almost instantly. I was sorry to hear of Hill's death. Charley was a rawboned man about five feet eight or nine. He wore a dark mustache. He was a little wild at times, but a nice fellow at that.

IN TOWN AND OUT

IT WAS LATE IN THE FALL OF 1895 when I went to Sheridan to join my family who were already at the Windsor Hotel, which Dad had leased for eighteen months. The man who had been running the hotel had lost most of his trade. When he offered Dad eighteen months' free rent if he would come and build up some trade, Dad took him up. Mother and us kids didn't like the idea of leaving the ranch. All this kind of stuff was Dad's idea. When the Bards moved into Sheridan, Bill Cameron, his wife, Laura, and Bill's brother, Henry, had moved on the Bard ranch for the winter. I was yet on the granger roundup. I remember well the last roundup of the season. It was at the forks of Cat Creek. There wasn't so many cattle in this roundup, but plenty of grangers. They were so plentiful around the herd of cattle that it was almost impossible to get an animal cut out of the roundup. Al Willey, the boss of the roundup, says, "A part of you damn grangers go out there about two or three hundred yards and build a fire and stay there until it comes your turn to work the roundup." And that's what we did.

It being a cold day, we didn't object to sitting there by the fire. In riding from the roundup to the fire, I dropped one bridle rein. When I reached for it, my horse blew up and bucked me off. After the roundup was all worked, the grangers took their cattle and headed for home. There were several grangers going my way. Among them there was a kid about three years older than me. We got to talking about swappin' horses. Charley wanted to try out my horse. Charley hadn't much more than got in the saddle 'till my horse blew up with him. The horse started to bucking and running towards a wire fence near the Willey school house. The horse didn't hit the fence, but made a quick turn to the left. That left Charley hangin' on the top wire of the fence. Charley didn't get hurt, but he left a few pieces of clothing hanging to the wire fence. It was no horse trade. Charley didn't want my horse.

The following day I went to Sheridan and the Windsor Hotel for some more book learning. The teacher of the seventh and eighth grades was Miss Lena Stover. She was the same one who was attending the Banner school in the summer of 1889. Lena was a wonderful teacher, and if we kids didn't learn anything, it wasn't Lena's fault. We did learn a lot that winter while attending school. And at the hotel we learned a lot of things that we never knew before. Dad was the day clerk, George Rexford was night clerk. Big Gus was head cook. Nigger Bob was second

99

cook. They were both tall, husky men. Mammie Freel and her sister, Laura, were the waitresses, and Mrs. Jack Bell was the chamber maid.

Out in the back yard of the hotel there was a big wood pile for the hoboes to try out their muscles before Gus would give them a handout (something to eat). These hoboes had to cut and split wood for an hour before Gus would feed them. I got quite a kick out of watching the hoboes when they headed for the wood pile. They would take off their coat if they had one, fold it up and lay it down on a block of wood. They then would look the wood pile all over to choose something easy to saw and split. The next thing was the ax. After looking it over a few times, they would run their thumb over the edge of the blade to see if it was sharp. They would start to work on the wood pile, or put on their coat and walk away to some residence where they'd get a handout without blistering their hands.

Mrs. Jack Bell, the chamber maid, was certainly a nice woman. Her husband, Jack Bell, I knew in the summer of 1890 while wrangling horses for the nester or rustler wagon, as the big cowmen called the wagon. One night, while the HAT wagon was camped on Powder River, three cowboys rode into our camp. One was Jack Bell, who slept with me. The others were Ranger Jones and Ed Tway, "Eat-'em-up Jake," as he was called by the cowboys. This was the same Ranger Jones who was shot to death at the Muddy Bridge. I only saw Jack Bell a few times that summer. He lived somewhere up on Crazy Woman Creek. Whether he was married at this time I don't know. After the Johnson County cattle war, Jack came up into the Tongue River country up around Dayton. There he got in with three men who had a contract to furnish the McShane tie camp with beef. The camp was located upon the Big Horn Mountains in the Tongue River district. There were several hundred men working for the McShane Company, located in four or five camps. They cut down pine timber and hewed it on two sides with a broad ax to make railroad ties. These men were called tie hacks. The ties were hauled by team and bobsled from timber to the Tongue River, where the ties were unloaded during the high water of spring time. The ties were shoved into the river and were floated down to a big flume near Dayton. From the flume the ties were hauled by wagon to the tie yard in Sheridan.

As I remember, Jack Bell was only working for the three men who had the beef contract. When these men were arrested for butchering of estray beef, Jack was caught in the net. Being unable to furnish bond, he had to lay it out in jail until the trial came up. During this time Jack gave Dad a bill of sale of everything he owned except his wife. Jack didn't want the lawyers to get everything that he owned. When the trial came up, Jack was cleared of the beef steal. The other men got some kind of sentence. Soon after the trial Jack and his wife took their saddle stock, some other property, and left the country. We were sorry to see the Bells leave, as they were two nice people.

When it came Christmas time, the sleighing in Sheridan was good. The weather was cold, well below zero. To celebrate Christmas Day, Bob Brown, an old-time cowboy now a saloonman, who was liked by most everyone but a few old cranks, went to Ed Campbell's livery stable. There he hired Ed and four lively livery horses and a light bob sleigh. Down the street they came. Ed was in the driver's seat with the two teams on a fast trot. The sleigh bells were sure ringing "Merry Christmas." Ed and Bob each had on buffalo overcoats. Bob was riding in the back part of the sled. He had a quart bottle of whiskey from which he took a nip now and then. They weren't doing anyone any harm, just driving up one street and down another singing Christmas carols. A few of the town cranks didn't like them any too well, and they told the town marshal so. As I remember, it was C. H. Grinnell who came to arrest Bob for disturbing the peace. Bob told old C. H. if he'd just put that off until tomorrow, they could double the fine and he would pay. Bob and C. H. being good friends, this was agreed to.

On week ends I would go out to the ranch usually on Friday afternoon. On Saturday night there was most always a dance somewhere in the neighborhood. These were called "kitchen dances." At this time there were only a few dance halls in the country. The only place to hold a dance was in the kitchen of some ranch home, which was none too large. Four couples would be called on to the floor for a dance. Whether it was a square dance or a round one, it didn't make any difference. Only four couples were allowed on the floor. Most always there were four times as many men as there were women. The men didn't get enough dancing even with daylight just around the corner. With the women folks it was different. They were ready to drop in their tracks, but they wouldn't own up to it. Jim Simpson, the roundup cook, was usually the fiddler and a good one. When the last roundup of the season was over, Jim would take his fiddle under his arm, mount a saddle horse, and head for our neighborhood. Jim was most welcome where he went in among his friends. He had lots of friends among the grangers. He usually made his home at the George Harper ranch. Mrs. Harper had lost a hand from blood poisoning. She had four small children to look after. While Mrs. Harper took care of her family and did a part of the house work, Jim Simpson did the rest. He did most of the cooking. Jim was neat and clean about everything he did. He spent several winters at the Harper ranch, helping with all kinds of work.

Most always on week ends while at the hotel in Sheridan, I

had to tend office as the clerk. I remember one time while I was behind the desk, a big, rawboned carpenter with a black beard came into the office. His name was Kaufman. He was behind on his board bill about two months. When Dad asked Kaufman for a part of the bill, the carpenter blew up and invited Dad to come outside. Nothing pleased Dad more than to do a little boxing with the gloves. Dad was quick as a cat and hit as hard as a mule kicking. He only weighed about 140 to 150 pounds but had plenty of dynamite in either fist. On his right hand he wore one of those KP rings with a big set. Every time he hit the carpenter, Kaufman would lose a few black whiskers. Dad was just playing with the fellow, not trying to knock him down. Sam Kaufman saw that he had overmatched himself. He took out up Court House Hill right in Main Street, with Dad after him. At a hundred yards Dad was winded. The next time the carpenter came to the hotel, he paid the board bill. He boarded at the old Windsor during the rest of the winter.

That winter at the hotel I did almost everything there was to do, except the chamber-maid work. Here I balked. But I did catch the new chamber maid in the family wash tub takin' a sponge off. It was just after school, and I was in a hurry to go skating. I went up the stairs with two pails of coal, pushed open the door of the girls' living room, so intent on the skating party that I didn't see the maid until I was in the middle of the room. She gave a scream, and I dropped both coal pails. Down the stairs I went two at a time. I don't know who was the most frightened. I guess it was me. It wasn't the maid's fault, she just forgot to lock the door. You never know what kind of a jackpot a feller can get into.

There were two girls in Sheridan, sisters, whom my brother and I used to take on skating parties. Along about ten o'clock, when the party was over, the four of us would head for the kitchen of the hotel. One of us boys would stay with the girls, while the other, Tode or me, would go and unfasten the hook that held the kitchen window. Once inside the kitchen, we would go to the pie rack and get the kind of pie we liked best. This we would cut into four quarters, with each of us taking a quarter. When Gus began to miss his pies, he put up a holler. Then we switched to beefsteak. We would go to the ice box, get two large tea-bone steaks, grease up the top of the range like Gus did, and fry the steaks. When Gus made a holler about this, we were at the end of our string and didn't bring the girls home with us again.

As I remember it was along in March, and spring wasn't far away, when Jumbo McKenzie came to the hotel. Jum was all dolled up in a nice new suit. He didn't even have on his cowboy boots, looked more like a banker (only a lot better looking). We were very much surprised in seeing Jum again. The last time we had seen Jum was in the fall of 1892, when he and Bill Wallace were on their way to Alberta, Canada. They had stayed over night at the Bard ranch, got the White Cap horse, and put him in with some other saddle horses that they were driving ahead of them. Now here was Jum at the hotel. He said that he was on his way to Buffalo to get married. When Mother asked him who was the lucky girl, he said, "Lois Newell." I was sorta surprised at this. Lois was only a year older than I was. She was in school over in Buffalo at the same time I was. Lois was a beautiful girl with dark eyes and dark hair. Jum was more on the blondy side. They would make a fine-looking couple.

After a day or two at the hotel Jum went on to Buffalo, got married, and then took his young bride up to Fort McCloud, Alberta, Canada.[1]

[1] Two years later, just after their son was born, Jum was drowned while trying to swim his horse across a stream that was running bank full just

By spring, 1896, the Windsor Hotel had the best trade of any hotel in Sheridan. Our regular boarders were Mr. E. A. Whitney, two school ma'ams, and a lot of others. The Windsor was doing a better business than the Sheridan Inn, which was more of a railroad hotel, and for some of the big bugs, when they hit town, such as the big cowmen, Buffalo Bill Cody, and his son-in-law named Boal, who married Cody's oldest daughter.

At one time Boal was manager of the Inn. The Inn never did cater much to the common run of people. It wasn't doing too good either. But in later years, when the white collars flocked there for some of their high-falutin' parties, the Inn did much better.

When the grass started greenin' up in the hills, us kids were like a bunch of penned-up yearlings that had been kept in a feed lot all winter. We wanted to get out into those green hills and kick up our heels. That's about the way Mother felt, too. There was no holdin' us Bards in town once the grass was green. Only Dad, he liked town the best.

About the first of May, Mother gave Dad notice that she was movin' back to the ranch and takin' us kids with her. There were four of us. Tode, my sister, Florence (Dot), my kid brother, Dick, and myself. Dad didn't like this movin' idea none too well.

The Camerons had only agreed to stay at the Bard ranch until the first of May, so when Dad couldn't go with us to the ranch, he had George Rexford, the night clerk, go to the ranch with us. George knew the ranch from one end to the other. He had worked on the ranch before.

We were a little late getting back to the ranch, and the spring work was already piling up. There were fifty or sixty yearlin' calves to dehorn and some calves to brand. Some of the neighbors came and helped with this work.

after a big rain storm. Lois came back to Sheridan and became a nurse, and a good one.—Author's note.

There were horses to round up, colts to brand, a few young studs to castrate, and some three- and four-year-old geldings to be kept in our horse pasture. These we would break out later on. While Tode and I were busy at this work, Rexford was busy with the ranch work, cleanin' ditches ready for irrigation, plowing up some of the old meadow, and plantin' it to grain.

There were fences to be mended where the snow had mashed them down on the brow of a hill. There were all kinds of things to be done.

WE SEND FOR
RATTLESNAKE JACK, THE WOLFER

ONE MORNING WHEN WE WENT OUT into our horse pasture to wrangle in our broncs, there was a mare runnin' around whinneying for her colt. Soon we found the colt or what was left of it, which was a few pieces of hide and some bones. The wolves had visited the pasture some time during the night. They had killed the colt, bitten a yearlin' colt in the hind leg just above the ham string, tore a three-cornered chunk of flesh from the thigh of one of the broncs we were breakin' to ride.

Rattlesnake Jack being the official wolf-trapper of our neighborhood, he came and set some wolf traps. This Rattlesnake Jack was a queer old duffer. One time while he and his two kids were camped near our place, Jack told me of his life. Jack had a good education. At one time he lived in Chicago and was a druggist, owning his own drugstore. Due to his health and some woman trouble he sold his drugstore and with the two kids, Albert and Lillie, came to northern Wyoming and learned to be a wolfer. In the summer time the three of them lived in a tent, just moved from place to place as the work required. In the winter time the kids were put in school, sometimes in town. Other times they were boarded with some ranch family and attended some rural school. During the winter months Jack would camp in some old cabin. Most always he had a rattlesnake or two in his camp as pets. He claimed that he pulled the poison fangs from the snakes and that the snakes were harmless. While Albert and Lillie were out in camp, Jack would keep shaved and respectable lookin'. When the kids were in school, he didn't care how he looked. He let his hair and beard grow all winter right up to when the kids were comin' back to camp. I had heard it said that Jack kept so full of dope that a snakebite was harmless to him. When Jack died along about 1900, it was from a rattlesnake bite. What became of Albert and Lillie I never knew. They were two nice kids.

BRONC RIDIN' FOR BUFFALO BILL

ONE DAY GEORGE BIRCH AND CY COMPTON, two Wrench hands, bronc riders, came to our place lookin' for Wrench horses. I remember they took the saddles off their broncs so they could cool off a bit. They had dinner or lunch with us. George was a Buffalo Bill man. Had been a rider in the show and was going again this season, and so was Cy, who was just a kid of about eighteen.

George got to talkin' about the wild west show, as to how they rode pony express and how the handkerchief was picked off the ground by a rider on a pony on a fast gallop. Well, this talk was all interesting to Tode and me. Some day we wanted to go with Cody's wild west show. Most all that summer we two kids practiced these two stunts: ridin' pony express, and pickin' up the handkerchief, with our gentle pony on the run. We didn't need any practice in ridin' buckin' broncs, we were gettin' plenty of that in breakin' broncs to ride. I guess we must have gotten pretty good at this kind of work. It was in 1904 that Tode went with Cody's wild west show to Europe, where he did all the stunts that we used to practice.

In the early spring of 1900, George Birch wrote me a letter stating there was a job for me ridin' buckin' horses in Cody's show. The wages were sixty dollars per month, everything furnished except a saddle and a forty-five six-shooter for shootin' blank shells. Well, I had both the saddle and the six-shooter. But I couldn't very well take this offer, as my plans were already made. In a few days I would be leavin' for Alberta, Canada.

BREAKIN' MORE BRONCS

ALL THE SUMMER AND FALL OF 1896, we were busy breakin' horses to ride and some to drive. When we weren't breakin' in our own broncs, we were breakin' some for our neighbors. Got five dollars per head. We swapped horses with most everyone who wanted a horse trade. When no one showed up for a horse trade, we swapped horses with each other. About two miles out from Sheridan on Prairie Dog Creek there lived Stephen George, an Englishman, a retired beaver-trapper. Uncle Steve, as we all called him, came to Prairie Dog Creek along about 1880. He got to choose his homestead, the best in the little valley. Now, sixteen years later, Uncle Steve owned his homestead, about four head of Durham cattle, and a few horses. No one knew how much money he had. This he kept cached out around an old straw shed. Uncle Steve had two young geldings for me to break to ride. When I got the first one broke and took him home to Steve, he says, "Just a minute, Kid, you stay here at the house while I go out and get the five bucks you have comin'."

When I took the second horse back to Uncle Steve, he says, "Kid, here's the five bucks for breakin' the bronc. I've no use for him. You take him home with you and ride him 'till I call for him."

I named the horse Judge, and had him five years. He bucked me off five times, and I got five dollars for ridin' him. Never did break him of buckin'. Judge was the best horse I ever rode when it came to running wild horses over the Dutch Creek hills. He could run all day. Didn't seem to tire him. He was the most sure-footed horse I ever rode. No breedin' at all, only Clydesdale and mustang. He was a freak, a long-backed bay, about eleven hundred pounds, sorta dish-faced, snaky eyes, stout on the end of a rope when he didn't buck a fellow off. He didn't like a rope at all. One day when I roped a cow just for the fun of it, Judge blew up and bucked me off, jerked the cow down, and dragged the cow into a little brush thicket. There Judge got astraddle of the rope, which was tied hard and fast to the saddle horn. In that little brush thicket the horse and cow were both down and couldn't get up without some help. Well, I wasn't givin' that horse any help 'till I got good and ready. I was plenty sore at him for the way he had bucked me off. After about thirty minutes, I got the mess untangled. I took the rope off the cow, which seemed all right. Judge was sorta skinned up a bit, with a rope burn on one hind leg. That rough deal sorta broke him from buckin' every time I took down my throw rope.

I was always on the lookout for some nice-lookin' young gelding that might make a top saddle horse when broke to ride. One day I found one, out on the range not far from Sheridan. It was a brown four-year-old gelding about eleven hundred pounds, wearin' the P7 brand on the left thigh. Right off I knew who owned this brand. It was Sid Skinner, the ice man of Sheridan. Sid used to work two mares on his ice wagon, and they each had a colt. These two colts were sired by a Thoroughbred stud of Billie Wagoner, a horse man livin' on the Tongue River. This brown geldin' was well halter broke and gentle as a kitten. Knew all the streets and alleys in Sheridan, since he followed the ice wagon from house to house, taggin' along beside his mammy when he was a suckin' colt.

When I asked Sid what he wanted for the young geldin' he said, "Kid, that colt will cost you plenty. Nothin' less than forty dollars will take him just as he stands."

This price was about twice the price of an average bronc. But I paid it and took Brownie home with me and turned him loose in with some more young geldings that we kids were breakin' to ride. When it came Brownie's turn to be rode, he just went along fine and dandy for a quarter-mile or so. All of a sudden, he downed his head and bucked me off. I went right over his head and lit on my feet. The second jump he swapped ends, and his rear was in my face. He just kept on swappin' ends, tryin' to get rid of the saddle. He didn't buck any more for about a year, when he bucked me off again.

Us kids were not ridin' broncs all the time, only part of the time. We did lots of other work durin' hayin' time, threshin' time, and on Sunday. That's when the broncs got a rest, and that's when we rode our girlin' horses—something real gentle that warn't spooked at nothin', not even a pair of divided skirts and a white shirt waist like the gals used to wear. Just a gentle pony that would crowd up close to the gal's pony so that we could hold hands. We didn't have convertibles or anything like that to do our courtin' in, just rode along and held hands. Sometimes we would get a kiss or two if our ponies were willing to crowd up close. There have sure been a lot of changes durin' these past sixty years!

It was this summer of 1896 that Sheridan had its first real wild west show put on by Dick Reed, Sr., and Shorty Jennings. The race track and fair grounds were on land owned by Rube Cornwell, just across the highway west of the sugar factory. As I recall, it was the third of July that Tode and I drove ten head of yearling heifers to the fair grounds. These heifers were for the kids under fifteen to ride. Some of these heifers were trained buckers. One light-red line-backed heifer we named Diamond would swap ends and buck like a real bronc. This wasn't only a wild west show. It was the annual picnic where the neighbors all got together on the Fourth of July. They had been doing that for years. I remember one time when several families of us, back in the 1880's, went in the mouth of Little Goose Canyon and had a Fourth of July picnic camp for a couple of days. While the men were fishin', the women folks did the cookin' and took care of us kids.

This Fourth of July of 1896, there were to be two birds killed with one stone: the picnic and the show. Most all of us knew what the picnic would be like with lots of good things to eat, yellow-legged chickens all fried up nice and brown, strawberries and cream, lots of good ice cream and lots of other things. We didn't know anything about a wild west show, only what we had seen out on the big, open range. On the third of July, we kids took the heifers to the fair grounds and put them in the corral. There were a few country folks makin' camp down along Little Goose Creek. The Crow Indians were then settin'

111

up their tepees along near the north end of the fair grounds. After the heifers were corralled and fed some hay, Tode and I went up among the Indian tepees lookin' for a horse trade. At the Horn tepee we were sittin' on our horses admirin' the new tepee when Mr. Horn says, "You sell 'em pony?" He pointed to Tode's saddle horse, the one he called Muggins.

Tode says, "Yes, I sell him for twenty-five dollars."

At that Horn says, "Wait. Papoose she talk." Then he yelled something in Crow.

The papoose was a beautiful Indian maid who looked to be about sixteen. Her eyes were big and brown. Her hair wasn't black and coarse, but brown and freshly brushed. It was braided in two braids. She wore a bright-colored blanket over her dress. To me she looked like a Thoroughbred. Mary Horn came and stood beside her Dad, who talked in Crow to her. Then she says, "He wants to buy your horse. He's got the money, twenty-five dollars."

Tode sold Muggins to the Horns, but we couldn't deliver the horse until the following day, as Tode had no way to get back to the ranch. The morning of the Fourth when we went to deliver Muggins, Tode was ridin' the horse he called Goodeye. Goodeye looked very much like Muggins. When Horn saw Goodeye, he wanted to buy the horse, so he would have a matched team. Once again Mary came and did the talkin' for her dad. She says, "How much you want for this horse?"

Tode says, "Twenty-five dollars. Same as the other one."

After Mary had talked with her dad, she says, "No. He only got twenty dollars. All the money he got."

Tode says, "No. I have to have twenty-five."

Once again Mary talked with her dad, then she says, "He wants your pony. We all want your pony. He says twenty dol-

lars is all that we have. For the other five dollars I'll be your
squaw for a little while."

Well, we kids had done lots of horse tradin' and got all kinds
of things to boot in a trade. One time I traded horses with Charley Tompkins and got an old Sharps rifle. But never before or
since have we ever been offered boot in a horse trade like this.
Now Tode was stumped. He didn't know what to say. We must
have sat there on our horses for five minutes or more. All the
while I was wishin' that Goodeye belonged to me. Finally Tode
says, "Guess I'll keep my horse," and headed for the picnic
grounds.

After the community lunch was served, we all headed for
the show grounds and the grandstand. Lots of folks were there
ahead of us. Things were now shapin' up pretty fast. Over on
the north side of the show grounds the Crows were mounted
on their ponies bareback. Both the Indians and their ponies
were nearly naked. The ponies were ridden only with a war
bridle. All the bucks had on were breechclouts. Some of the
Crows had forty-five six-shooters and blank cartridges. We cowboys were grouped over on the south side. Up at the north side
of the race track there was the old Deadwood stagecoach, with
two matched teams of bays hitched to it. Up in the driver's seat
was Mr. Chilcot, a big man who wore a black beard. Ridin' on
top of the coach as a messenger or body guard was O. P. Hanna.
On the seat beside him was a dummy man all fixed up until it
looked like the real thing.

At one o'clock there was a pistol shot, and here came old man
Chilcot down the race track with the four bays in a high gallop.
Then here came the Crows yellin' something in Crow and firing
their six-shooters. From the south side came the cowboys as
fast as their ponies could run. Right there in front of the grand-

stand a sham battle was fought. O. P. Hanna was busy with his sawed-off shotgun, then he threw the dummy off the coach. An old woman in the grandstand yelled, "My God, they have killed a man." She collapsed, fainted dead away, and that was more excitement.

The battle didn't last long 'till we had the Indians on the run down across the show ground. We were smokin' up the Crows and they smokin' up the cowboys with forty-fives. We were all mixed together like a stampeded beef herd. When the battle was over, some of the Crows were powder burned some. During the battle an old buck came at me ridin' full speed, yellin' something in Crow. He didn't have a six-shooter, but I did. When he saw my gun, he tried for a getaway, but his pony wasn't fast enough. This old buck got pretty well powder burned on his bare rump.

After the smoke had cleared away and the dummy was removed, the buckin' bronc ridin' was next on the program. There was plenty of good buckin' horses on hand, with only two riders to ride them. One was a kid of my age, seventeen years old. Jim was an average rider who lived just three miles from the Bard ranch up in Magpie Hollar or Magpie Draw, sometimes called Jennings' Draw. The other rider was Claude Gadcliffe, a young fellow that had come up from Texas the year before and was now workin' for Doc Brundage as a ranch hand. Claude was a slender-built blonde, the prettiest rider that I have ever seen. Jim was a heavy-built kid with not too much action. He rode a buckin' horse anywhere from its ears to its tail. When Claude rode a bucker, he rode straight up as if he was a part of the horse and saddle. After bronc ridin' was over at the end of the second day, the new fifty-dollar saddle was given to Jim. Claude got nothin'. The crowd wasn't satisfied with this decision of the judges. Two of the cowboys went all around through the crowd with their Stetsons in their hands, passin' the hat to everybody who cared to donate something towards buyin' a new saddle for Claude. It wasn't long 'till they were back with sixty dollars in those two hats, ten dollars too much for a new saddle. Well, they just gave the whole caboodle to Claude. He might want a new bridle or something in the cowboy line.

There were yet three good buckin' horses tied to the hitch rail that hadn't been ridden or even saddled. The crowd wanted to see them ridden. Claude says, "Bring them onto the track and I'll ride them."

There were no chutes, not even a decent corral. I don't remember how it came about, but I was the kid who led the buckers in on the race track. Maybe it was because I was ridin' an extra good snub horse. Well, I knew Blue Dick, my top rope horse, could handle most anything on the end of a rope. The first in on the track was a big bay called Dynamite, a little spooky about saddlin'. I had him snubbed so close up to the saddle horn the bronc couldn't do much until Claude was up in the saddle and rarin' to go. It was a good show we saw. The next horse I led in was a keen-built bay with a sorta brockle face, called Rain-in-the-Face. He was built like a quarter horse. That was the best buckin' horse of the whole show. Claude rode Rain-in-the-Face straight up with his right hand in the air. The Hardin' Gray was another good show horse. When someone led a little black mare mule in on the track to be ridden, Jim says, "I'll ride that one."

The mule was no trouble to saddle or mount. When Jim hooked the mule with his spur and pulled off his big black hat and hit the mule over the front end and over the rear end, that was the best show yet. The mule snapped ends so fast that Jim didn't know whether he was goin' or comin'. He was grabbin' for everything on his saddle. When the mule quit buckin', Jim was chokin' the saddle horn with both hands.

Back in the pioneer days, sixty years ago, there were lots of horses on the range. In among this amount of horses, there were a lot of mean, ornery ones, just bucked natural like, snapped ends, sunfished, and did just about everything a bronc could think of. It was all natural the way they would buck. A rider just rode them to a finish. There was no pistol shot to tell him the ride was finished at the end of a half-dozen bucks. With those old natural buckers doin' their best there weren't many bronc riders bucked off: like they are today. It's the flank cinch or surcingle that makes the buckers of today so damn tough to ride. A half or more of the buckin' horses of today wouldn't buck a jump if that flank cinch wasn't ticklin' their belly. They just buck and kick to get rid of that flank cinch. This kind of buckin' is both dangerous to the rider and the horse. Never know when they will lose their balance and fall on the rider. Take those broncs that are ridden bareback. When they buck off a rider, they just keep on buckin' and kickin', tryin' to get rid of that flank cinch. There was no saddle to get off, so why was that bronc buckin' and kickin' high up in the air, 'till it lost its balance and fell and broke a hind leg? I saw this very thing happen at one of the rodeos. Well, that is the difference between sixty years ago and today.

Now back to our wild west show. The next thing on the program was yearling calf ridin' for kids fifteen and under. This was good, with most of the kids being bucked off. Among the kids there was a Crow Indian about forty years old. He had plenty of wrinkles on his face. When he wanted to ride one of the yearlings, the judges said, "No. It wouldn't be fair to the kids." But after some argument the Crow was allowed to ride. It was then that Diamond, the line-backed heifer, was roped and surcingled with a wide strap. The Crow rode the heifer about like Jim rode the mule; about the only difference was that the Indian got bucked off the fourth buck. Then Diamond landed on him with all four feet. The Crow was skinned up some. He went limping back to his tepee, sayin' heap something, I didn't quite hear what it was.

The Gypsy kid who came with some of the race horses rode Diamond to a standstill.

There were all kinds of races, trotting horse races, running races, and foot races. There was a polo game between the Moncreiffe team and some Englishmen who lived up around Beckton. There was a steeple chase, mostly for the Englishmen. They rode pancake saddles and jumped their mounts over everything they came to.

After two days of the wild west show, we all went home satisfied, figuring that we got our money's worth. Our next wild west show would probably be staged out on the range somewhere, and there might be some ropin' done, too, with us grangers or nesters.

The ranchmen, who yet were wearin' the name of granger, were bothered quite a lot with some of the old long-horned cows gettin' into our hay meadow or grain field. When the wire fence was too high to jump, the cows would crawl between the wires. About the only way to stop this was to rope the critters and put a "cowpoke" on their neck. Tode and I used to do teamwork on this job. We always had a few cowpokes on hand and some rope to tie them on with. One of us kids would rope a cow by the horns. The other would rope the heels and stretch the cow out on the ground. Then one of us would put the poke on her neck. These cowpokes were made of green saplings about the size of a baseball bat, about four feet long. They had two prongs, shaped like a big turkey wishbone. We would put the poke astradle of the cow's neck. On the topside of the neck we would tie the two prongs together with a short piece of rope, pretty well up against the old heifer's neck. Now the most of those cows couldn't crawl between the wires. They seldom jumped over the wire. Nothing would stop one cow from comin' through the fence. We were gettin' pretty sore at this cow, when she busted down the fence and came into the grain field. Most always there would be half a dozen others following her. One day when I saw the old cow and her tribe makin' for the fence, I grabbed Old Betsy, the sawed-off shotgun. I didn't take time to saddle the wranglin' pony, just mounted him bareback and up through the meadow I went in high gear. When the pony jumped a small irrigation ditch, he just kept on jumpin' 'till he bucked me off. I skinned my face up a little when I took a header into the alfalfa. By the time I had located Betsy and was back on the pony, the cow was in the grain. We all headed for the hole in the fence. It was quite a race to see who would get there first. The cow was a little handicapped with that cowpoke on her neck. Well, I won the race. I opened up with Old Betsy on the cow with both barrels right back of the shoulder. At first I thought I had killed the old brute, but I didn't. One thing for sure, she never came through the fence again.

The grangers usually started puttin' up their first crop of hay just after the Fourth of July. That's what the Bards were doing. We had been in the hayfield a couple of weeks when we got word from the Wrench ranch that they had gathered two of our saddle horses while makin' a horse roundup, and they would hold the horses 'till further notice. Not to lose any time in the hayfield, I saddled a horse after supper and headed for the Wrench ranch three miles north of Sheridan. In going through town I noticed that the broncs in front of Bob Brown's saloon all were wearin' the Wrench brand. I tied my horse to the hitch rail or rack and went into the saloon to see who the riders were. There was Jim, the Red-Nosed Kid, Claude Gadcliff, and Gus

Newell. They were bellied up to the bar and havin' a drink. Gus says, "Pistol, will you have a drink?"

I says, "No, thanks. Just had supper."

Gus says, "You're probably after the two horses that we gathered. If you'll wait 'till we get something to eat, we can ride out together."

I told them to go ahead and get their supper, that I would visit awhile with Bob. When they came back, they were pretty well lit up, and so were the coal-oil street lamps. We were just starting out of town when Gus and Jim started shootin' at the street lamps. Jim was yellin' "Powder River, let 'er buck."

Claude says, "Come on, Kid, we're leavin' here."

Well we left there on a gallop. Gus and Jim were yet shootin' at the lamps. When Claude and I got to the Wrench ranch, we took the saddles off of our horses and turned them loose in the horse pasture. Upstairs over the cook house we went to bed in Claude's bed. Claude was soon asleep. Not me. I just figured there would be some trouble later on. When the two drunken devils entered the cook house later, one said to the other, "I wonder where those ⸺ ⸺ ⸺ are."

When they came up the stairs, I raised up on one elbow. The Red-Nosed Kid says, "There's one of the bastards. I'll part his hair for him." At that the Kid put a bullet through the head of the bedstead, only a few inches over my head. At that I jumped out of bed and says to the Kid, "You damn fool, you're liable to kill some one." I didn't mind so much about my hair bein' parted, I didn't like the names they called me. When I was a kid of eight or nine, my dad said: "Son, never call anyone a bastard or a son of a bitch. He probably has a nice mother the same as you. Never call anyone those names, not even in a joke."

I never did care much for this Red-Nosed Kid, as some of us had named him. The situation wasn't improving any. I don't know what might have happened if the town marshals hadn't shown up and arrested Gus, the Red-Nosed Kid, and the Bard kid. They didn't see Claude. He was in bed and did not get up. The marshals were overstepping their boundary. They were going to take the three of us and put us in jail. The Wrench ranch boss said, "No. I'll see that my men come in town tomorrow afternoon and pay their fines."

The marshal said to me, "Kid, see that you are there, too." When I tried to tell him that I had nothin' to do with the shootin', he said, "Save that to tell the judge."

I had known Judge Hook since the spring or fall of 1887, and when I walked into his office, he said, "What have you got to say for yourself."

"Nothin'," I said.

"Well, what's the story," he wanted to know.

After tellin' him all about what happened, he says, "Young man, I shall fine you one dollar for bein' in bad company. The costs will be two and a half. Three-fifty all told."

That was getting off light, although I had done nothing, not even yelled "Powder River."

For his yellin' the Kid was fined eighteen dollars, and Gus was fined twenty-four dollars. Claude was the fellow with all the luck. While we were ridin' from town back to the Wrench ranch, Claude told me that he had grown up down in Texas near the Mexican border. One night while he and one of his brothers and a neighbor boy were at a Mexican dance, they got into a fight. He cut a Mexican all to hell, then headed north. He didn't locate anywhere 'till he went to work as a ranch hand for Doc Brundage, just had to lie low for awhile.

"If I had gone to ridin' broncs," he said, "they might have found me, as good a rider as I am."

Over this damn monkey work, I had lost a half-day in the

hayfield. With sixty acres of alfalfa and timothy hay to put up, a half-day out of the hayfield meant quite a lot. I was the hay stacker. We had a good hay crew, even if they were all kids like Tode and me. George Rexford had left the ranch as a hired man and had gone back to the Windsor Hotel with Dad. A much better ranch hand, Hardy Wells, had taken his place.

Here is about the way our haying crew lined up. These were kids from Sheridan who were spending their vacation on ranches. There was Monie, or Bones Arnott, a lawyer's son; Gould Reed, son of Dick (Cob) Reed, one of the first auctioneers of Sheridan, who had helped put on Sheridan's recent wild west show. There was Jay Newell, the son of Wallace Newell, a newspaperman of Sheridan. Percy Metz, the son of Judge Metz, used to give us a helpin' hand now and then. We had two mowing machines, one with a five-foot sickle, for one was a McCormick. The other was one of the old Planters with a chain drive, not much good, always breakin' links. It was not much good in heavy hay, so we just used it as an extra now and then when Tode got a little behind on the mowing. Tode did most of the mowing. For a team he had one gentle horse that was called the bronc horse. Alongside this horse there was a bronc, a half-broke horse. The mowin' machine was the ideal place to finish breakin' the work stock. A half-day of pullin' the mower through heavy grass or hay was about all one of the broncs could stand. Then Tode would take another bronc.

After the hay was mowed down and left to cure a day, it was raked into wind rows. There us kids, town kids and granger kids, would get busy on the end of a pitchfork handle and start pilin' the wind rows up in little doodles or cocks as they were called, about a bale to the doodle. A hayfield sure looked nice with all these little haycocks. After the Columbian haystacker was pulled out into the hayfield and staked down, we were ready for action. Gould and Bones each had a gentle team hitched to a buck rake and were buckin' in hay, about eight or ten doodles to the buck-rake load. After drivin' the buck rake up on the stacker head, they would back up the team, leavin' the hay on the stacker head. Then Jay would drive the old stacker horse out to the end of a fifty-foot cable, dumpin' the hay over onto the stack. There Hardy or I did the stackin' of the hay. There were times when it took the both of us to do the hay-stackin'.

As soon as a field was cleared of hay, the irrigation water was turned on. Hardy was the irrigator, but he always found time to help with the stackin.' On hay stackin' days us kids would get hungry along about ten in the mornin', and a little tired. That's when Mother or my sister, Dot, would bring to the hay-field a sandwich for each of us. Sometimes we would have ice water or homemade root beer to drink. This handout and about thirty minutes of rest were mighty welcome to us kids. Now we all felt freshened up, both the stackin' crew and the teams.

During the next hour and a half we all worked like beavers right up 'till noon. Mother always had a big dinner cooked up for the haying crew. Hardy, the only man on the crew, didn't eat so much. With us kids it was different. We were about like half-grown wolves. We were always hungry. It took a lot to feed us, and what we liked best was beef, same as the wolf who butchered every day or two and didn't care whose beef they butchered. With us grangers it was different. We never butchered a beef wearing a brand, unless it was our own brand. When we butchered a slick, no matter whether it was one of our own or a maverick off the range, we didn't hang the hide on the corral fence, unless it was wearin' our brand. It was against the law to have an unbranded hide hanging on the corral fence. If a fellow got caught at this, he was accused of maverick-ing. No one at our place was ever convicted of this, because there was no unbranded hide on the corral fence. This was another one of the laws invented by the White Caps. This law never did them any good. We grangers could outsmart them on this. We had to beat them at their own game. In later years I know for sure that a cow outfit, while moving their cattle from one range to another, took three head of my cattle, a two-year-old heifer and two two-year-old steers. While cuttin' strays from their herd, they sure overlooked mine. Took them right along. I never did hear of the steers. Two years later the heifer came into a roundup about a hundred miles from our place. I never did get her and don't know what became of her. She probably raised some mavericks for someone. The steers were probably butchered for beef or died during some blizzard. That could be anyone's guess.

During the summer months the grangers took their turns at butchering a yearling for beef. This beef would be divided up among a few neighbors. Most all grangers had an ice house. They put up their own ice, helping each other put it up. They usually cut or sawed the ice from some beaver dam. Back in those good old days, the granger had to do most everything to make a livin' except take branded stock that wasn't his. Most of them paid no attention to the maverick law that some of the big cowmen or cattle barons hatched up for their own good.

When my dad came to Wyoming Territory during the summer of 1876, he cooked on roundups and cow ranches. He knew a lot about the cowman's game. When he sold his homestead on Little Bear Creek in the spring of 1882 and came overland to Buffalo, he didn't stop except to make camp for the night. He already knew that the cowmen were claiming the range from Buffalo south into the Powder River country and farther south than that. He took no chances on steppin' on the cowman's toes.

123

They already had hired gunmen lookin' after their interests. It wasn't considered healthy for a nester or granger to file a claim, a homestead or squatter's right on some choice land that the cowmen were claiming. A nester or granger wouldn't any more than locate on some of this land 'till a gunman would show up and tell the settler that he would find the climate much healthier if he moved on farther north. Maybe it would be best to head back east or wherever he came from, that he might be found frozen to death during one of these Wyoming blizzards. Some of the immigrants took the hint and went back home or farther to the north. Some of these settlers didn't take the hint or warning, just stayed on until the second warning, when his cabin was half built. If he didn't heed this second warning, the cabin was never finished. Dad knew quite a lot about the cowman's game. When he headed north with his two covered wagons and his family, he didn't look for a location until he was north of Buffalo. Here the cowman hadn't yet claimed the big open range country as his, and never would. The cattle war of 1892 was the starting of the finish of the cowman and his White Cap scheme. He was licked, and he knew it. What the so-called rustlers and the Lobo wolves didn't take, he, the White Cap, sold off and quit business, leavin' a few cows on the range to raise mavericks for us grangers. These cows were not left intentionally, but they were so wild and ornery that they always dodged a roundup.

AT HOME ON THE RANGE

WE KIDS WHO SPENT HALF OF OUR TIME out on the range knew the rough country where these cows were ranging. We knew where most of the wild horses of the Dutch Creek Hills were watering. We sure used to give those wild horses a run for their money. Sometimes we corralled them, and more often they outsmarted us. There were times when we would rope them out on the range. This was done mostly in the winter time when there was a lot of snow on the ground, with the wild ones in a weakened condition and us kids on a good grain-fed horse. By doing some relaying we roped many a wild horse that had no owner and no brand. It just belonged to the lucky one who dropped his loop over the stud's head first. We never bothered much about the wild fillies, unless it was an extra good one.

In the summer of 1896, we finished haying along about the middle of September. Our hay crew, the town kids, had gone to Sheridan and to school. Tode and I weren't goin' back to school, for a while at least. There was yet a lot of work to be done. There would be a second crop of hay to put up, some grain to be threshed. There were the broncs to finish breakin' to ride before winter set in. It was only a couple of days after the first crop of hay was up that, early one morning, I saddled up a four-year-old bronc that had only been ridden three times. We named this bronc Jim. When he got to liking sugar, we named him Sugar Jim. Jim was a dark-steel gray, sired by our trotting stud and a mustang mare. Jim was a gentle, barnyard-raised colt. He never did buck, but he wasn't yet bridle wise. When I headed for the Dutch Creek Hills to see about some of our stock, I took some lunch on back of the saddle. By noon I was up on the divide between Dow Prong and Straight Prong of Dutch Creek, not far from a big spring. I was sitting there beside Sugar Jim eatin' my lunch, when I noticed about forty head of wild horses go down into a draw for water at the spring. I knew this wild bunch, as I had run them several times. There was a draft-built gray three-year-old filly in this bunch that we had passed up before. But now we wanted this filly. The Merrills, who were living on the Perkins homestead, three miles up Mead Creek from the Bard ranch, had a gray filly. They wanted a mate for her.

With the wild ones down in the draw, I mounted Jim, tied my throw rope hard and fast to the saddle horn, and headed down the draw. Some of the horses had already drank and were headin' out away from the spring. Before the herd knew what was up, I had a loop made and was headin' towards the gray filly which was now climbing the bank of the draw. I let out a couple of war whoops and gave Jim his head. He took right in after the filly, and out across the little sagebrush flat we went. The filly was too frightened to run her best. Jim was frightened enough that he was running his best, which was O.K. When I dropped the loop over the filly's head, we all landed in a heap. I landed on my feet and grabbed hold of the bridle reins. During the next ten or fifteen minutes there was sure a tug-of-war being fought on each end of the rope. Finally Jim won out. He had that filly choked to a frazzle. It was then that I made the rope into a hackamore and headed for home. I had quite a battle with those two broncs for a mile or two until the filly was halter broke and Jim was better bridle wise. It was near supper time when I got back to the ranch. The two broncs were just about all in, and so was I.

I said to Tode, "Here's the filly. The rest is up to you."

The next morning he headed for the Merrill place with the filly. When he came home, he had the burro and two bridle bits. We already had the burro traded off to Ed Sutton for a nice black saddle horse. Ed had a coal mine not far from our house, and he wanted a burro to pull the coal car from out of the mine to the tipple where wagons were loaded. When Tode asked the Merrills five dollars to boot, they didn't have the money, so they gave him the two bridle bits. They had been made by one of the Merrill boys, who was a blacksmith.

We didn't have the black saddle horse long before we sold him for a little better than forty dollars. That was a top price for a saddle horse. Tode and I had done a lot of horse trading, but this was the most complicated trade of them all.

Down on the old FE cow ranch there lived a family with a boy just my age. He was a red-headed kid called Lew. On down Prairie Dog Creek another couple of miles, there lived another kid called Al. He was a year older than Lew and me. We used to ride a lot together out in the hills. One time the three of us went over on Dutch Creek for some of our horses. Just above the Dow dam we located a gentle bunch that we wanted. The line camp of Lew Burgess and Jack Cato was nearby. While I was waiting for my two chums to go farther up the creek for more horses, I cooked up a nice dinner at the line camp, even made a pan of hot biscuits.

Well, we never got to eat any of this lunch. Down the creek came Lew and Al with a wild bunch. We didn't have any time for lunch, just headed for Prairie Dog with the whole outfit. Lew was ridin' up near the lead when an old mare started to break with some others following her. Lew shot the mare through the middle and stopped her right in her tracks. The young horses headed back into the bunch and stayed there. We had no more trouble. I often wondered about the lunch that was left for the line riders.

This kid, Al, was quite a fellow for talking. He was rawhidin' someone, makin' fun of someone, most of the time. Al had an uncle here from Iowa, and one Sunday when us kids didn't have much to do, Al wanted to show the uncle around a bit. He wanted us to go with him out in the hills. Al was makin' a big talk as usual. When it came my turn to get rawhided a bit, he says to me, "What you pack that six-shooter around for? You couldn't hit the broad side of a barn."

I says, "Throw up your hat." He sailed a new hat up in the air and I put a hole through it. Then he stepped off his horse and I did the same thing again when he reached for his hat. All together I shot five holes through that big hat. Al's mother was pretty mad about the hat deal. Al never did forget it.

It was the next year after he got married that he was butchering beef for market in Sheridan and wasn't fixed much for butchering. The cattle were wild and a little difficult to corral. One day when Al went out into his pasture to shoot down a beef, I happened to be ridin' by. He called, "Come in here and shoot this beef for me."

When he told me which cow to shoot, I rode around in front of the beef and shot it in the forehead, killing it instantly. Al says, "I see you haven't forgot how to shoot."

"No," I answered, "and I probably won't as long as there are forty-five cartridges bein' made."

That old forty-five kept me broke half the time in buyin' ammunition. But it was useful in more ways that one. In killing a rattlesnake it came in handy. Instead of having to hunt a stone, I'd slip down off my horse and shoot the snake's head off. Too, those little yappin' prairie dogs made good targets.

Over on what was called the Granger Prong of Dutch Creek, Al Willey had a school section of land leased. It was a 640-acre pasture up and down the creek, all fenced with four wires and pitch posts. On the east side of the pasture he had built a good horse corral, with a wing extending out from the gate about two hundred yards. This corral was on the outside of the pasture fence. It was a good place for corralling some of the wild ones. Over in the Dutch Creek Hills I knew where there were some mustangs rangin'. They were mostly buckskins, about twenty head of them. Running with this bunch there was an extra good buckskin filly, about four years old, that I wanted. She was a slick, no brand. One day when I was mounted on a bay gelding that I called Snip, I headed off towards the hills to give those buckskins a little run, and to try and corral them at the Willey corral.

Up along the Dow Prong of Dutch Creek, I jumped the buckskins. They took off down the creek with me after them on a fast gallop. When they got to the forks of the creek, the mustangs doubled back up the straight prong. The only way to head them off was in makin' a run up over the little divide between the two creeks. Near the top of the divide Snip threw up his tail, was winded, wouldn't go any farther. It was only about fifty yards to the top of the divide, so I took it on foot as fast as I could run.

Up Straight Prong there came the wild ones on a fast trot. When I started shootin' into some sandrock just in front of the leader of the mustangs, they went back down the creek just as fast. By now Snip had his wind and was O.K. Right at the forks of the creek I met the mustangs. I headed them back up Granger Prong. When they hit that school-section fence, I knew that I had them in my sucker sack. When those mustangs went through the corral gate they were kickin' up the dust. I was right there to slam the corral gate shut. There were two nice buckskin fillies in the bunch, a light one and a dark one. After lookin' them over a time or two, I decided on the dark buckskin, which was the larger of the two and probably a year older. She looked to be a four-year-old. After roping the filly and anchoring her to the snubbin' post out in the center of the corral, I turned the rest of the horses back on the range. After puttin' the hackamore on the buckskin, I halterbroke her right there in the corral before headin' for home, but I never did break the buckskin of bucking. When a horse buyer came along, I sold the filly for twenty dollars, enough money to buy a lot of ammunition. The forty-five was my friend. There was something about that old forty-five that I liked. I most always took her with me out into the hills. Never knew when she might come in handy. She put me on an equal footing with all kinds of problems. Most of the rangemen had a six-shooter of some kind.

MEETING A DUDE RANCHER

As I REMEMBER, IT WAS THE YEAR OF 1896 that I met up with the first dude rancher of the country. I don't remember his last name. He was called Harry. One day he and a friend came to the Bard ranch with a team and buggy and wanted to buy fifty head of cattle, mostly young stuff. As I remember they were there a couple of days while we were gathering the cattle which they bought. Harry had along his cowboy, a Charley Long, who at one time was horse wrangler for the PK outfit. They had not yet bought any cow horses. Charley was ridin' a black livery horse, hired from a stable in Sheridan.

It was up to Charley and me to take these cattle to Harry's place over near the Beckton mill. I don't know who Harry bought the place from, probably George T. Beck. It was a good-sized ranch, with quite a lot of buildings. One big building, located up on a small knoll, was called "the big house." Harry and his wife lived there.

The morning Charley and I left the Bard ranch with the cattle, I was ridin' a bronc. We were all day in drivin' these fifty head of cattle over to Harry's ranch. We got there too late to eat supper with the ranch help. Charley and I went up to the big house where Harry and his wife and friend, Sherman, were havin' dinner. We were not asked to eat with them. We had our supper out in the kitchen with the cook. Well, this was O.K. After supper was over, Charley was asked into the living room. I went down to the blacksmith shop and was talkin' to Bill Burgess, the irrigator, until bed time, when along came Harry with a pillow. He threw it over to me sayin', "I guess that you can get in somewhere." Then he headed off to the big house where there were several spare bedrooms.

Bill says, "Kid, you can sleep with me."

The next morning Charley asked, "How did you make out?"

"O.K." I said. "How about you?"

"Fine and dandy. Had one of those spare bedrooms with a double bed all to myself."

At this I sorta blew up. While they were at the Bard ranch, Mother gave them the best bed in the house and we all ate at the same table. Now where the difference was could be anyone's guess. The fifty head of cattle had to be rebranded and our brand vented or cancelled.

Harry says, "Kid, you take Charley's horse and help George Leach with the ropin'."

"You just do that ropin' job yourself. I didn't come here today to do any ropin'. I came to see that these cattle were properly branded," I told him.

"Well," Harry says, "if you won't help with the ropin,' we'll have to put off the brandin' 'till I can find someone to help George."

After we argued for awhile, I got on the livery horse and we went to work. One of us would rope the animal by the head, the other would rope the hind feet. When the animal was stretched out on the ground, it was then branded. The last steer to be roped was a husky two-year-old. When it ran by me, I roped both hind feet, jerkin' the livery horse down. I didn't get hurt but the horse was skinned up a bit. The next time the steer was roped, it was the steer that got jerked down.

After the branding was done, I saddled up my bronc and was leavin' when Harry said, "Kid, we're havin' some beer. Will you have a bottle?"

"No," says I. "You just keep the beer for some of your friends." I shouldn't have said that. I should have kept my mouth shut and have done like the Nigger that got kicked on the head by a mule—just consider the source.

When I got home and told the folks about this dirty deal, Mother felt hurt. Dad was madder than a wet hen. He said something about he never wanted to see another damn dude. And that's the way we all felt about dudes for several years. Then we met up with the real dudes, some of the nicest people to be found anywhere.

The fall of 1896, the grangers were to meet in the George Master place down Ash Creek for their fall roundup. The mess wagon was camped near where some oil wells are now located. I was the PK wrangler, Walt was the boss, and Jim Simpson, the cook. When I left the Bard ranch, there were seven horses in my string. One was packin' my bed. Everything was fine and dandy until along the Wrench horse pasture. Here the county road was fenced with four strands of barbed wire, right up near the railroad track. Up the track came a switch engine. Near my horses the engineer popped off a lot of excess steam. Goodeye and Buck got so frightened they ran through the four-wire fence. Buck cut an artery in his neck and soon bled to death. Goodeye was cut up so badly that he had to be shot. I was sure mad at the engineer, but there was nothing to be done about it, only to go on to the roundup.

A tough bronc to sit.
"We wasn't riding for no rodeo
or making any grandstand plays—
just used any kind of saddle with a good saddle horn."

Branding Bee.
"It was sorta devilish fun
burning your brand on one of those slick's ribs."
Courtesy the Library, State Historical Society of Colorado

At the wagon there were about fifteen grangers rarin' to go. Most of them were men thirty-five or better. Most of them were out for a good time. I was the only one not old enough to vote! Several of us rode one afternoon about twenty miles over the Five Mile Flats. Here we scattered out and spent the night with some granger. That night I spent with the Wallace family, not far from Parkman. The house was near the railroad tracks. All night long there were trains or switch engines racing up and down the track. I wasn't used to so much noise, and I didn't get much sleep. We had breakfast about five o'clock, then all the grangers started to rounding up the Five Mile Flats and the Hidden Water country, which was plenty rough.

It was a little after noon before the roundup was worked, and we were headin' for camp. Fred ——— and I were ridin' together up a draw through the Hidden Water when we heard a cowboy yell, "Hold on a minute. I've got one of your yearlings, and here it is."

The cowboy was George Blake, workin' for the Spear outfit. In each saddle pocket he had a quart bottle of whiskey. In a gunny sack there were three more quarts. George said the grangers gave him the money, about seven dollars, and had him go to Ranchester after the whiskey. George opened a quart and gave us a drink. My drink was a small one. I didn't want to get sick. Fred took a big drink.

Up near the divide we ran into our herd that was gathered that day. Most of our grangers were with the herd. Right at the Masters gate most everyone stopped for a drink or two. While they were havin' the drink, I rode on to camp about a half-mile away. Simpson had dinner waiting. I was nearly through eating when Fred came into camp and said something about he and Walt whippin' any two men in the outfit. Fred was a small man with a heavy mustache. After turnin' his horse loose, he went and heaped his tin plate up with food. Then he sat on the ground with his back up against a rolled-up bed. That's when the whiskey hit him smack between the eyes. All we could do was to drag him over in the shade of a tree and leave him there till he sobered up. Several of those grangers were lit up until they thought they were kids. While we were roundin' up the herd to get a yearling heifer for beef, one granger bet me fifty cents that he could rope a calf before I could. I had my calf roped before he had a loop made. After cutting the heifer out of the herd, we headed her down Ash Creek to the mess wagon. Walt didn't bother about cinchin' his saddle up some more, but I did cinch mine up good and tight. When opposite the wagon we were in a gallop. Walt roped the heifer. The saddle with a loose cinch sorta kicked up, and Walt went right over Pete's head, hittin' the ground on the back of his neck. When I saw some of the grangers run out to where Walt was lying, I went ahead and roped the beef and dragged it into camp. While some of the grangers were carrying Walt to our bed tent, a couple of grangers helped me to butcher the beef. By now Walt had come to, but thought that he was going to die and wanted to make out his will. Along with the wagon there was an old cowman, Bill Garrard. Bill came with pencil and paper. He said, "Walter, I understand that you want to make out your will."

"That's right, Mr. Garrard."

"Well, Walter, who do you want to will your property to?"

"Her name is Hanna. She's a school teacher. We were plannin' to get married."

"What have you got in the way of property that you want to will to this young lady," Bill asked.

"My saddle and bridle and roundup bed. I guess that's all, unless it's my chaps, spurs, and six-shooter," Walter said.

Well, Walter didn't die. The following year he married the

school teacher, and became one of the most prosperous ranchmen of Sheridan county.

Fred didn't know what was going on. He was dead to the
world. Some of the men were in for burying him, but the ground
was so hard that it was impossible to dig a grave. Then someone
suggested dumpin' him over the bank into Ash Creek. After
carryin' Fred out onto the bank of the creek, Neri Wood, the
Pot Hound Pup, preached the funeral sermon. Then someone
says, "I think he's still alive. I can see him breathing. We'd better give him one more chance."

Fred was then carried over to the bed tent and put to bed.
The next morning he was O.K. These late fall roundups were
the grangers' vacation. They enjoyed it all just like a bunch of
kids during Christmas vacation.

When it came time to go back to school, Tode and I didn't
go along with Mother and the two younger ones, our sister and
kid brother, who were moving back to the Windsor Hotel to be
with Dad. Tode being now 16 and I, 17, we thought that we
were too big for school, that we were now grown up. We decided to stay on the ranch and run the outfit and save the expense
of a hired man. Without much to do we made O.K. of a morning.
While Tode was doing the chores at the barn such as harnessing
the team, feeding the team and our two saddle horses, and
milking the cow, I got breakfast. By the time he came back to
the house with the milk, breakfast was ready. We didn't have
much breakfast—only a couple of tea bone steaks apiece and a
stack of buckwheat hot cakes and coffee. Some mornings we
had oatmeal. And that's all we had. During that winter we ate
so many buckwheat cakes that we began to scratch and dig like
a parlor dog with a batch of fleas. We didn't know what was
wrong. We took off our underwear and looked for graybacks.
We looked up and down the seams for lice, but didn't find even

a nit. We didn't know what was causing all this scratching until an old bachelor came by and said it was too much buckwheat!

After breakfast each day Tode would water the stock, clean out the barn stalls, and hitch the team to the feed wagon or sled, owing to weather conditions. During the winter months we usually used the bobsled and hayrack. By the time Tode had the feed outfit ready, I had the dishes washed and put away and the kitchen swept. There were three hundred head of cattle to feed. Part of these cattle were two- and three-year-old steers belonging to a cattle-dealer by the name of Waters. There were three big loads of hay to be hauled for the three hundred head of cattle. In each load there was a ton or more of hay. We used to figure a ton to one hundred head of cattle, big and little. During real cold weather the cattle required more hay, especially the steers. Some days we hauled out four loads and scattered the hay out over the meadow where the manure would be left as fertilizer. On raw, windy, cold days the cattle were fed in some sheltered place down along the creek where there was quite a lot of brush. There were times when a blizzard would come raging up the valley at about ninety miles an hour. At such times we didn't try any hay hauling. No use. The wind would blow the hay off the rack faster than we could pitch it on. The cattle just had to sorta hump up in some sheltered place and wait until the blizzard quieted down a bit.

On ordinary days we finished with the feedin' usually about one o'clock. By the time we cooked dinner—it wasn't lunch, 'cause we were as hungry as a she wolf with a litter of pups— and had eaten it and washed the dishes, the day was pretty well shot. It was then time to start doin' chores. We didn't fool around with any broncs. We kept in the barn just one gentle saddle horse each.

For amusement we would ride off to some of our neighbors

to a party or dance. If it was a party, we kids played all kinds of games. Some of them were kissin' games like tin, tin, come in. The older folks played cards. It was usually a four-handed game of high five or pedro. At midnight we had a nice lunch, then everybody went home. On dance night we usually went early and stayed late. When there was no fiddler handy, I would put my fiddle in a flour sack, mount my horse with the fiddle under my arm, and head for some kitchen dance. The music wasn't much, but it was all we had. Sometimes there were two fiddles. Other times it would be a fiddle and an Oregon or banjo. Sometimes those old fiddles sounded sorta scratchy or a little squeaky, but they kept good time.

It was along towards spring when I was returning from a dance with my fiddle under my arm that my saddle horse stepped in a hole and rolled over. Not on me, but on the fiddle. I didn't get hurt, but the fiddle did. It was smashed to pieces. I never had another fiddle for about twenty years. Then I bought from a pawn shop for fifteen dollars a fiddle, case and all. I still have this fiddle stored away in my clothes closet. That's the way Tode and I spent the winter of 1896 and 1897.

PUNCHIN' COWS
ON THE MUSSELSHELL

IN THE SPRING OF 1897 WHEN THE LEASE on the Windsor Hotel in Sheridan expired, Dad and Mother came back to the ranch and went into the dairy business. There were already a few broke milk cows on the ranch of Durham stock and some heifers that could be broken to milk. They were a little wild and had to be handled like a bronc. We had to tie up one hind foot for awhile. There was a creamery already established at Big Horn, the first creamery in Sheridan County. It was making both butter and cheese. This creamery had been built by the ranchers, who sold stock at fifty dollars per share. Mother had bought and paid for two shares. Who the manager of the creamery was I don't remember. It was probably J. F. or "Cheese" Brown, who was a professional cheese-maker. He came to Johnson County in the 1880's and settled first on Crazy Woman Creek out south of Buffalo. In the early 1890's, he moved to Sheridan county, locating on the Henry Coffeen ranch in the Banner district. There he began milking cows and making cheese. It was good cheese which he sold to the ranchers. The cheese was made into five-pound cakes about as big around as a water pail. The ten- and fifteen-pound cakes were much bigger, about the size of a large dish pan.

When the creamery was put into operation, Mr. Brown moved into Big Horn with his family. He built a nice little four-room cottage and became the cheese-maker of Big Horn. The whole milk was hauled to the creamery by lumber wagon and team. Mr. George Moose, our neighbor, had the milk route for our neighborhood. As I remember, he made the trip every other day. When the milk cans were brought back to us, they contained buttermilk and whay left over from the cheese-making. This was very good for the pigs and laying hens.

In the spring of 1897, I only stayed at the ranch long enough to help break some of those "bronco" heifers to milk. Then I headed out onto the range to try and find a job of breakin' horses or punchin' cows. About the time I was makin' arrangements for the trip, a young Iowa cowboy showed up and wanted to go along. He had an old blue roan saddle horse raised by Yellow Weasle and Grouard, branded CF quarter circle CF on the right thigh. Mitchell called his horse Blue Dog. Blue Dog was gettin' old, couldn't stand a day's hard ride, about the same as Mitchell, who didn't own a bed or a horse to pack it on. His aunt and his cousin, Lew, rigged him out with a roundup bed. For a pack horse Lew and I went over in the hills and roped a wild stud, a three-year-old brown that had a wire scar on one front foot. No one wanted this slick. We had all passed this slick by at one time or another. He was no good as saddle stock, but would probably pack Mitchell's bed. That is, if he could get it tied on.

For me, I was fixed up O.K. Big Brownie was my saddle horse. For a bed horse I had a white-faced sorrel gelding, a good one, that would follow Brownie from mornin' 'till night. The morning that we were ready for our trip, we tied up a hind leg on the wild stud and tied the bed on hard and fast so it couldn't be bucked off. Before we let that hind foot down, we tied the stud to the saddle horn of Mitchell's saddle. The stud did a fair job of buckin'. But old Blue Dog could handle him. The Iowa cowboy, however, didn't know anything about handling a bronc at the end of a hackamore rope.

We went out by way of Sheridan. Stayed our first night at the Bar N ranch. The next night we spent at the OW. By now the stud and Mitchell were pretty well broke in. We yet had to tie up the stud's hind foot to tie on the bed. The third night was spent at the Circle Bar cow ranch on the head of Otter Creek. Here we got to see a block house or fort built of flat rock upon a knoll not far from the ranch buildings. The block house was about fourteen feet square with one door and no windows. There were several port holes where a cowpuncher could stick his rifle barrel out in case of an Indian attack. This block house was built when Sitting Bull went on the warpath down at Pine Ridge or Sioux Reservation.

139

We were at Grant Dunning's ranch for four days. There Mr. Oliver Wallop, an Englishman, had established a horse camp along in the early 1880's. In the early 1890's, he sold his horses and camp to Grant Dunning. Mr. Wallop then moved to another ranch about three miles south of Big Horn. It must have been Sunday when we pulled into the old horse camp, 'cause the next day was wash day. There was a Cheyenne squaw who came and helped Mrs. Dunning with the washing. Mrs. Dunning gave the squaw fifty cents, then Grant played the squaw a game of freeze out to see whether it would be a dollar or nothing. They each took fifty chips or matches and started playing draw poker. It took the squaw about thirty minutes to clean Grant of his chips. Then she says, "Heap good." And she headed for her tepee not far away, on Otter Creek. As I recall it, Grant had some of the bucks grubbing sagebrush off his hay meadow.

We stayed over a day at the Dunning's and helped Grant with some four-year-old broncs that he was breakin' to ride. Among these broncs was a good-looking bald or white-faced strawberry roan that he called The Irishman. Grant wanted to swap The Irishman to me for Brownie. There was no object in swappin', as The Irishman probably would never be as good as Brownie. When I told Grant so, he says, "Pistol, you're probably right about that."

Our next stop was at the Hugh Hunter horse ranch near Ashland, Montana on the Tongue River. When I asked Hunter for a job breakin' horses to ride, he says, "My horses are mostly all draught stock, and there is not much ridin' to do until the spring horse roundup. It's a month early for that, but I'll hire you to stay here and look after the ranch while we all go to Miles City to the stock convention. I'll give you thirty-five per month and your friend can stop here with you. We'll probably be gone a week, then I might give you a job ridin'. Got about seven hundred head to round up and brand the colts." Then he asked me if I had ever done any sod bustin'.

"Yes," I told him, "a little down in Wyoming on my dad's ranch when I was bronc bustin'."

"O.K. then," he said. "I'll show you the breakin' plow and the two teams that you will be using. That big gray team is as slow as molasses in January. The roan and bay are like a whirl wind. Don't work them together; put a fast one with a slow one. Work them strung out, same as on a wagon."

Well, there wasn't a man in the world that could do this, that is, to hold the plow handles and four lines and follow one of those old foot-burner walkin' plows, but I said, "O.K. I'll get the job done."

That night about supper time George Brewster and his young wife and baby son from the V Quarter Circle U ranch up Tongue River near Birney drove in with a team and buggy to the Hunter ranch, and spent the night there. The following morning the Hunters and their baby daughter; the Brewsters; Jimmie Greisenger, the horse foreman, and Mac, the ranch foreman, all left for Miles City. I hitched the gray team onto the walking plow and busted sod 'till noon. During the afternoon I busted sod with the fast ones. Had no trouble at all. The only trouble we had was with the Scotchman Hunter's coyote hounds. Among them there was a big Russian wolf hound that jumped the dog fence and left the ranch. When they all came back to the ranch, Hunter felt badly about the hound jumpin' the fence.

"It might be best that you go down to that big Indian camp, probably they have him," he said. "Stay around all day and see if you can find the hound."

It was only five or six miles to the Indian camp at the edge of the Cheyenne Reservation. That night Mitchell and I came back to the ranch without the hound.

The next morning I asked Hunter, "How about that job of ridin'."

"Ah, out of the by God, I guess I won't be needin' you any longer," he said. After paying me off, he got in a wagon with his two hired men and drove away, probably to see what kind of job I had done with sod bustin'.

Mitchell and I were nearly ready to leave the 7OL horse ranch when the Scotchman came around the corner of the barn.

"Ah, out of the by God, I am going to hire you over," he exclaimed.

"No," says I. "You're not hiring me over. We're all packed up and leavin' here."

"Well, if you hear of my hound, let me know."

That day we rode close onto forty miles to the old Diamond ranch on Rosebud Creek, and there was Hunter's hound. He had been there for three or four days. The man at the Diamond said that he would be going over past the 7OL in a day or two and that he would take the hound with him. The following day we made it to what is called Pea's Bottom over on the Yellowstone River. Here is where the Greisenger family lived. The ranch buildings were on the opposite side of the river from us. Henry Greisenger, a brother of Jimmy, came across the river in a boat.

I put my bed in the boat and got in with Henry and led Brownie behind the boat. We swam my two horses across the Yellowstone.

The next trip Henry brought across Mitchell and his outfit. We spent the night with the Greisenger family, Mr. and Mrs. Greisenger and two good-looking girls and a kid brother.

The next morning when we got ready to leave, Henry says, "The kid will ride out away with you and direct you to the RL horse camp, where they are now gathering horses for the spring

142

roundup. You can probably land a job there as a cowboy or bronc rider. I'd advise you though not to hire out as a bronc rider as they have some tough ones to ride."

The kid brother, who was probably twelve years old, rode with us about ten miles, then he said, "See those little buttes over there. That's about eight or ten miles from here. The RL is about four miles to the right of the buttes. Well, the kid must have been left-handed or cock-eyed. The camp was three or four miles to the left of the butte. When we got to the buttes about four o'clock in the afternoon, it was snowing hard. We had been following an old wagon road that led up to a small cabin on a creek.

Inside the cabin there was an old cook stove, a table, a couple of benches, and a cupboard. We unloaded our outfit and hobbled our horses up in the bend of the creek. It was, I think, about the twenty-fifth of April. The snow was blowing. In the cabin there was some stove wood with which we built a fire in the cook stove. We rolled our beds out on the dirt floor. About dark the storm was over, but the weather was quite chilly. We didn't have any food with us. Here we spent the night. The following morning the snow was four inches deep. We didn't bother about cookin' breakfast. There was nothin' to cook. All that day we rode in a half-circle to the right of the buttes with nothing to eat but four sagehen eggs. We scared a hen off her nest and found five eggs. After breaking one to see if they were good, I put the other four in my coat pocket. At an old campground we found a large-sized baking powder can. We built a fire of dry sagebrush, filled the can about half-full of alkali water, and put it to boil. When the eggs were hard boiled we ate two each. That was our meal the second day. Our last meal had been a good breakfast before we left the Yellowstone.

After we had finished with the sagehen eggs, we started again ridin' in a half-circle. About five o'clock we hit an old wagon road. Mitchell's horses were played out. While he unsaddled his horse and took the beds off the bed horses and hobbled the horses, I rode on up the road toward the buttes to see what was ahead of us. All I could see was the old cabin that we had left that morning. That night we scraped away some snow and rolled out our beds and crawled in for the night.

The next morning we didn't roll out any too early. The sky was clear, but it was cold. We thought it best to go to the old cabin and start ridin' the country over to the left of the buttes. Before we came to the cabin, however, there were fresh wagon tracks in the old road. At the cabin we got the surprise of our lives. A camp tender for a sheep outfit had been there and left some supplies. There was a case of eggs, one of corn, one of tomatoes (large-sized cans), and a sack of flour. This sure looked mighty good to us, as hungry as we were. The first thing we tackled was the tomatoes. We each had a can and divided another one. We built a fire in the cook stove and hard boiled a dozen eggs. After eating these we made up something out of flour, canned corn, and water, stirred it all together and baked it on top of the stove. The Iowa cowboy said it was corn fritters. Whatever it was, it tasted good.

The weather was yet windy and cold when I left the cabin. I was walkin' and leadin' Brownie. The bed horse was following. The slowpoke was yet at the cabin. Out a hundred yards or so from the cabin I heard a rumbling noise that sounded something like thunder. Here came a wild bunch of horses, forty or fifty of them, on the run with a lone rider after them. Away went my bed horse with them. After steppin' up on Brownie, I galloped over to the rider.

"Can you tell me where the RL horse camp is," I asked.

"Yes," he answered. "I'm headed for there. If you can follow me, I'll take you there. I didn't have any trouble following him (I was mounted as well as he was), and he (Charley Green) took the wild bunch to the camp corral. Billie Neal, the boss of the RL had just ridden over from the ranch on the Mussel-shell River. When I hit him for a job, he started looking me over from my granger boots to the top of my hat. Finally he says, "Are you a bronc rider?"

"No, Sir, I am no bronc rider," I told him.

"You could ride one if he didn't buck too hard, couldn't you?"

"Well, I might."

"I'll give you a job at thirty-five dollars per month punchin' cows."

"O.K.," I said, "But I have a partner back along the trail somewhere."

"If he's a cowboy, we can use him, too."

About an hour later the Slowpoke, as he was called by the RL cowboys, came ridin' in. He got a job with no questions asked. Mitchell had on cowboy boots, a big Stetson hat, and buckskin gloves. He was about twenty-five and wore a heavy mustache.

As I remember it was the twenty-eighth of April that we rode over to the RL ranch, where there were about forty cowboys, mostly bronc riders. Here we spent two days waiting for the first of May. That's when the two roundup wagons would be leavin' for the range country. The RL was a good outfit. It had the best cavvy of saddle horses to be found anywhere, half- and three-quarter Thoroughbreds. This was a real old cow ranch. The buildings were made of cottonwood logs. The cook's cabin was big and roomy. The ranch cook was a Negro called George. He was a good cook, neat and clean, and sure was busy feedin' this bunch of cowboys. He had to set up two tables and

145

a half before they were all fed. He only had one table that would seat twenty cowboys.

During my two days at the ranch, I waited table for George and helped with the dishes. This paid off. George used to give me extra pie and cake. When he'd see me anywhere near the cookhouse he'd say "Boss, don't you want a piece of pie or cake?"

On the first of May, the two wagons left the ranch. With Billie Neal's wagon there were most of the top hands, all with eight or nine top cow horses in their string. All together with Neal's regular roundup wagon there were about thirty-five cowboys. The "79" outfit and N Bar N outfit were workin' the range along with Neal's wagon. This was the year the Ryan brothers, owners of the RL, sold their entire herd of cattle to the 7–7, the Paul McCormack outfit of the Crow Reservation.

With what was called the holding wagon of the RL, George Storms was our boss. He was a small, heavy-set man, very dark complexioned, with a large black mustache. He possibly had some Spanish blood. Lew Ship, a big, good-looking man, rode the rough string, mostly broncs. Johnnie Backus, an Arizona cowboy and a top hand anywhere, was with us. There was a small, wild Dutchman called taps. Also there was Al Holmes, who was raised in Kansas, I think. There were two kids about my age who had never worked on a roundup before, plus the Slowpoke and myself, the night-hawk, and the day horse wrangler. Our cook, Dutchie, was a German who was married and had a homestead in the Musselshell Valley. That's about the way our crew stacked up. We didn't ride circle or make any roundups, just held what RL cattle the other outfits rounded up. Our wagon did move along on the range with the regular roundup. We usually camped several miles off to one side where there was plenty of grass and water for the herd that we were holding.

146

The day that we left the RL ranch, we moved out some ten or twenty miles on the big, open range and made camp. The next day, the second of May, it snowed most of the day. The snow melted fast, and we stayed in camp, sat around in the bed tent and whittled on cottonwood bark, and got acquainted with each other.

This summer of 1897 was rainy and wet most of the time. It was hard wheeling for the mess wagon and the four work horses. We didn't have a bed wagon. Everything was piled on the mess wagon. Storms played me for the tenderfoot of our crew when he gave each of us our string of saddle stock. I had six head in my string, culls of the cavvy, except one little sorrel gelding that hadn't wintered too well. He had not yet shed all of his winter coat of hair. When George roped this horse out of the cavvy, he says, "Kid, here's another one for you."

After puttin' the bridle on Clipper, as I named him, I took a piece of bark and scraped all the old, dead hair from his back, then put on the saddle. When I mounted Clipper and turned him around a few times, I knew that I had a real cowpony. I would not have got him, but George, our boss, didn't know the pony. He just thought that he was another counterfeit. When George saw that I knew something of roundup work, he teamed me up with Johnnie Backus doing top work, going to the other wagons for cattle that had been gathered. When there was ropin' to be done, it was Johnnie and I who did it. We stood night guard together, went on day herd when it came our turn, that is, if we were not elsewhere after more cattle.

One morning George says, "Kid, you ride over to the ranch and bring back a bed wagon. Clark, the man who is lookin' after the Thoroughbred mares and colts will help you find a team and harness. The only spare rig on the ranch is that old stagecoach. You'll probably have to work it over some."

147

At the ranch the only work horse to be found was a brown gelding, about 1,100 pounds, a four-year-old that had only been worked a few times. For a mate we found a little old cowpony that was gettin' gray up around the head. The harness was O.K., except the collar was about three sizes too large for the cowpony. The old coach looked more like a big old buckboard. The running gears were O.K. The bed or box of the rig needed some repairs. There was no seat. Clark and I spent about four hours puttin' the outfit together and gettin' the team hitched on. Another hour was wasted before the team would pull the bed rig out of the barnyard. Once I got that team traveling, we made good time to the roundup wagon. That was the most willing team that I ever saw. The old cowpony was willing to do his part, and the work gelding was willing to let the old pony do it all.

We cowboys each took our turn with this outfit hauling in camp wood. We camped three or four days in a place, so it took quite a lot of fire wood. When it came my turn, Storms went on horseback to pilot me around. He took me up on a steep knoll where there was plenty of pine wood. It was so steep up there that, with no brake on the rig, the team ran down the knoll. They hit a stump, which stopped the runaway. The temporary seat had collapsed, and I was flat on my back in the bed of that old stagecoach. Neither the team nor I got hurt. We didn't go for wood anymore up on knolls or steep places.

This was Johnnie Backus' second year with the RL. He had a good string of horses. Here is what Storms dished out to me: Clipper; old, gray Lizzie; Custer, a small bay switch tail, no good at all; old stiff-knee, that was always falling down when he hit a gallop; two geldings, owned by old man Baldwin, who had the Musselshell post office and store, and whose cattle the RL was looking after. These two horses were no good. The gray

148

Last day on the trail.
"It was the shipping pens for those steers,
but for us cowboys, a shave, some new clothes,
and a little fun on the town."

Floyd Bard (on horse at right), foreman of the E4 Ranch, rides roundup.
"I came along in the rear at a high gallop . . . ."

Hot men, stubborn cattle.
"When we hit the wings of the big corral, we were in high gear."

was mean and ornery to saddle. The brown was high strung and nervous. He would stampede and take you for a swift ride every once in awhile. The only two decent horses in my string were Clipper and Brownie, my own horse.

The two kids my age and Slowpoke had some good horses but couldn't ride them. They were always gettin' bucked off. Then we'd have to run the horse down to catch him. Storms made these Monkey Ward cowboys ride with a twenty-foot hackamore rope in their hand, so, if they got bucked off; they could hold their bronc.

All that spring, with too much rain, the Musselshell River was on the rampage, running bankfull, with plenty of drift wood afloat. Several times that spring we had to swim cattle across the river. I was riding the Baldwin gray when we hit swimming water. That pony kept going down 'till just his nose and eyes were above water. I was sure enough scared, there was no guessing about that. Another time when we were swimming cattle across the river, there were several calves that wouldn't take to the water. They always broke back and headed for the range. When we got them rounded up, we stampeded them for the river. When a calf jumped into the river, we would jump our pony into the river, grab the calf by the ear, and head for the opposite bank. What calves broke back again, we would round up and do the same thing over. After that when there was any swimming to be done, I took Brownie, who swam high with half his body above water.

One night when Johnnie and I went on first guard at eight o'clock, there were close to two thousand cattle in the herd. It was raining. There was plenty of thunder and lightning. The cattle were restless and hard to hold on the bed ground. Storms was out with us. At ten o'clock he says, "Kid, you go and call second guard, and you come back with them. These cattle are goin' to be tough to hold."

149

When we got back to the herd it was milling and milling around like a merry-go-round. The thunder was poppin' like a pistol. The lightning was something awful. There were little balls of fire jumpin' from horn to horn on the cattle. There was a little flicker of light on the tip end of the ears of our night horses. A part of the herd was already in a gallop, running and bawling. Those cattle were sure scared. Looked like their eyes were poppin' out of their heads.

We cowboys were ridin' in a gallop tryin' to hold them. To me it looked like the end of the world. When I met Storms he yelled, "Kid, go to camp and call third guard, then you can go to bed."

I had just got into bed when there was a rumblin' noise and the clatter of hooves and horns. Right after this the cowboys rode into camp. They said the herd had stampeded and got away.

Well, it wasn't the end of the world the next morning. The sun was shining. Storms says, "Kid, you and Johnnie catch your top horses and try to head off those lead cattle."

With mud ankle deep we didn't have any trouble headin' off the cattle. About four miles from camp we headed off the lead steers and were bendin' them back into the herd when Storms and the other boys came to help. That was the worst night that I ever put in, and I don't want anything more like that. We now had two thousand head in the herd. That was plenty for the kind of crew we had. The herd was headed towards Custer Junction and the Crow Reservation. It was strung out for more than a half mile, probably nearer a mile. Johnnie and I were ridin' point. Some of the other boys were ridin' on either side of the herd. Slowpoke, with the two kids and Taps, were drivin' drags, the rear of the herd.

One of those kids named Ed was tryin' to rope calves when

his saddle turned under his pony's belly. Up through the herd came the pony, buckin' and kickin' that new saddle, and stampeded the lead steers. Once again Johnnie and I had to bend those lead steers back into the herd.

On the north side of the Yellowstone River, just a little way above Custer Junction, we met Billy Neal's wagon. It had some five hundred head of RL cattle. The two herds were put together and night herded that night with four cowboys standin' or ridin' two-hour shifts. We weren't takin' any chances on losing the herd at the last minute.

The next morning we started to swim the herd across the Yellowstone over onto the reservation side. Jimmy Holmes, top cowboy of Neal's wagon, pulled his saddle off his big buckskin horse, put on a lifesaver's belt, mounted the buckskin, and swam the horse on the lower side of the lead cattle. This was a beautiful sight to see, these twenty-five hundred head of cattle swimming the Yellowstone River. There were a few small calves that wouldn't take to water. Also, there was one old, fat, dry cow that refused to swim the river. Jim Webb, an RL cowboy, roped the cow and took her out to swimming water. Jim went a little too far. When the undercurrent hit the horse, it turned Jim's horse over onto its side, losin' Jim. The horse swam ashore. Jim was havin' a tough time of it, until Charley Green threw the end of his throw to him. Jim was towed ashore. (This was the same Jim Well who in later years was sheriff of Billings, Montana. He was killed by a sheep herder.)

When the old cow was about to land on the Crow side of the river, some Indians rode up. The cow swam back across the river. This time she landed under a bluff. She was left there until the calves were roped, hog-tied, and loaded onto a wagon and ferried across the river. Paul McCormack was there taking pictures.

When we were now on the Crow side of the river and headed for camp, George Storms says, "Kid, you and Al Holmes bring that old cow up to the top of the bluff and take off the rope."

There was a rough trail leading down to the little flat where the cow was standing. She was sure on the fight, pawin' the dirt and bawlin'. I was mounted on the stampeding brown. I told Al that I wasn't going down there on this crazy damn horse. Al says, "I wouldn't go there on this old gentle horse."

At that Al got off his horse and started throwing rocks at the cow. I remember pickin' up three rocks about the size of a goose egg. With the first two I hit the cow in the ribs. The third rock was a little heavier. I took aim at the forehead and let drive. I hit the cow smack between the eyes. She went down as if shot. Al says, "Won't have any trouble takin' the rope off now."

When I came back with the rope, Al asked, "Is she dead?"

"Dead as a door nail."

Al says, "What we goin' to do now? We'll get canned or have to pay for the cow."

I told Al not to say anything. Just leave it to me. When we rode into camp, I threw Jim's rope over to him. Storms says, "You got it off all right?"

"We sure did," I answered. And there was nothing more said.

Just in the edge of the small town called Custer Junction, there was a ferry boat that took our wagons across the river. Above the ferry cable, there was a wide riffle where we crossed the cavvy. Here the water was little better than belly-deep to a horse. That night most of the cowboys went into town for a little fun. Lidge Green, Charley's brother, had a saloon and dance hall. When we entered the saloon, some of the 7—7 (seven bar seven) cowboys were already there. Lidge was tendin' bar and had on a bartender's cap. Charley grabbed his brother's cap and threw it onto the barroom floor. Then he shot a bullet through the cap. Some of the other cowboys did likewise. On a chair sat a 7-7 cowboy by the name of Con. Con was so drunk that he couldn't see the cap, so he emptied his shooter into the floor beside the chair. Lidge didn't say anything. He had been a wild cowboy himself. It seemed that Con and some other puncher were gunning for each other over some sort of a grudge. It was said that if ever they met face to face, one was apt to get shot.

The next day was a busy one for the RL cowboys. Quite a few cattle had to be roped to see what brand they had. In this RL herd there was about four hundred cows with the RL brand worked over into what was called the Window Sash brand. Here is the way it was done. This is the RL R̩ . This is the window sash ⊞ after RL had been worked over. Where the cow thief made the blunder, he failed to burn out the rounded part of the RL. These cows were rebranded with 7-7 same as the RL cattle were rebranded. Some time during the day eight dance-hall girls came by train from Billings to Lidge's dance hall. That night there was a real party put on. That night several of us boys were at the bar, and Con was there, too. In walked another cowboy. Who he was I never did know. He was at one end of the room, and Con was yet at the bar. All the cowboys at once made a quick get away. When I saw those two men standing there with their hands near their six-shooter handles, I left there in a hurry. It came to me that the man must be Con's enemy. No shootin' took place. The two men just stood there, each waitin' for the other to go for his gun. Con didn't move. The other fellow started backin' towards the door. He backed through the door and disappeared. It was then we all took a long breath.

The morning we were leavin' the Junction for the RL range

to gather more cattle, Storms says, "We'll ride two together. Scatter out on the range and gather all the saddle horses that we can find. Our cavvy needs more saddle horses. You boys all ride your top horses." At this I put my saddle on Clipper.

When Storms saw how I was mounted, he says, "Kid, we'll ride together." Out about ten miles we jumped a wild mare and colt. With them was a bay saddle gelding that Storms wanted. He said, "I don't like the idea of running that outfit fifteen miles to a corral."

Well, he didn't have to do that. He was mounted on what he called a three-quarter bred. This young sorrel gelding was three-quarters Thoroughbred and a quarter mustang. Was plenty fast, but a little spooky of a rope. When Storms made no effort to take his rope from the rope strap, I tied my rope hard and fast to the saddle horn. I roped the gelding that was trying to keep up with the wild mare and colt. The whole outfit was in high gear. Clipper was running so fast that I didn't have time to take up the slack of the rope. Got one front foot in the loop with the neck. Jerked the gelding down, and dragged him about twenty feet down the slope before we came to a standstill. While I was getting the outfit straightened out, Storms sat there on his horse looking the outfit over. He wasn't sayin' anything; neither was I. We just headed off across the range to where the wagon would be camped.

We started to building up another herd when Storms says, "Kid, it's about time that you rode that stiff horse on herd again."

At this I blew up, saying, "To Hell with you and that damn horse. If you want him rode, you do it. I'm leavin' this outfit. Figure up my time while I pack my outfit."

When I rode into the RL ranch for my wages, there was a Texas cowboy there. He was called the N Bar freak. His name was Bob Roberts. He was a queer sort of young man, had been punchin' cows for the N Bar outfit until he got canned for takin' a shot at a cowboy by the name of Martin, who was in the habit of tellin' someone what to do. When Martin started ordering the freak around while they were out on day herd together, Martin came into camp fast as his horse could run. He said that the damn crazy cowpuncher had taken a shot at him.

Roberts was now at the RL looking for another job. He had a saddle horse, a pack horse, a bed, and a camp outfit. When I told Bob that I was headin' north lookin' for another job, he asked to go with me. George, the Negro cook, hadn't forgottten me. He gave me enough provisions to last several days. Wherever night overtook us, that's where we camped.

After leaving the RL we headed to the northwest, traveling up the Musselshell River. At the Musselshell post office, where the RL got its mail, I asked Mr. Baldwin if there was any mail for me. He found a letter that had been there for more than a month. It was from my folks. It was the first letter I had received since leaving home.

After leaving the Musselshell we went by the way of Flatwillow grass range. At a place called Fergus, we spent the night and a part of a day. There were two Fergus brothers. They had a good outfit, both cattle and horses. The horses were mostly of the mustang breed, quite a lot of buckskins. Their horse brand was F on the right shoulder. I had quite a visit with one of the Fergus brothers. He told me that the Fergus family came to Montana in an early day. Fergus county was named for them. I would have liked to have had a job with the outfit, but they were full-handed.

From here we traveled across a lot of open range country to the head of Dog Creek, then on down Dog Creek to the Morris store and post office on the Missouri River. Here we crossed over on a ferry. From here we kept our course to the north and west until we came to Big Sandy, Montana. I couldn't have stood much more of that freak. I had to keep an eye on him at all times. I never knew what he might do. One time in camp he says, "Let's have a shootin' match."

When I asked him what he meant, he says, "Set up a tin can and shoot at it to see who is the best shot."

Well, I just had to beat him in shootin'. No tellin' what he'd be shooting at next time. I didn't trust him farther than the end of my six-shooter barrel. When we got to Big Sandy we parted company right off. He went to work for the VT cow outfit. I didn't want to work with him, so I went to the TL.

I asked Sam Miller for a job at the McNamire General Store, but Sam said they only needed one man, a bronc rider. He asked me if I was a bronc rider.

"Not as a professional rider, just an ordinary bronc rider I can make out O.K.," I told him.

When Sam saw that I had a good outfit he says, "O.K., Kid, you're hired at forty per month. This evening after supper Red Bob, our foreman of the cow and calf wagon, will be in town. You can ride out to camp with him."

Bob was about forty-five years of age, a rawboned man with red hair and mustache. He was a fine man and a good wagon boss. On the way out to camp, Bob told me about the broncs I would have in my string. There would be four eight-year-old geldings raised by the Fergus outfit. "They had only been ridden a few times, when they got away from our cavvy. During the last four years they have been running up in the Bear Paw Mountains until a couple of days ago," he said. "When we got them back, we necked the four of them to some old gentle cow-ponies in our cavvy."

Bob's wagon was camped two miles north of Big Sandy near some big branding corrals on Big Sandy Creek. At camp we turned our saddle horses and my pack horse in with the cavvy. Then I rolled my bed out in the tent where several cowboys were already in bed. Bob went to his tepee. Everything was dark in the bed tent, but I could hear the cowboys talking about the Fergus broncs. One cowboy says, "I wonder who is going to have to ride that bald-faced buckskin. They say he's a tough one to sit."

Another cowboy says, "He's probably no worse than that light-colored buckskin."

They didn't have to worry over who would have to ride those four broncs. I already knew who took on that job. The next morning at the yell, "Come and get it," we all rolled out of bed. Every cowboy in the outfit was a stranger to me. They were givin' me the once over as if to say, "I wonder where in Hell Bob got that Kid."

After everyone had helped himself to some breakfast, I went to the mess box, got a tin plate, tin cup, knife, and fork. At the Dutch ovens there was plenty of good beef steak and hot baking-powder biscuits, some good coffee—and that was it. When I had my plate filled up, I went and sat on the ground beside a young fellow who had all the ear marks of a cowboy. This cowboy was about twenty-five, a small man, who told me he was from the Powder River in Wyoming and that his name was Smithie. From there on he and I were good friends. With breakfast over, we all took our throw ropes and headed for the cavvy that was inside the rope corral.

Bob says, "Kid, just take any one of those broncs that are necked. If you'll wait till I get this mess wagon team harnessed, I'll help you with that bald-faced buckskin."

That's when the cowboys really did size me up from my granger boots on up. When I pulled the cinch up against that bronc's ribs, he went right over backwards. We had quite a bit of trouble in saddling the bronc. When I was mounted, he didn't care which way he bucked. He went in every direction at the same time, and I didn't care which end I whipped him on with that old rawhide quirt. All at once he made an extra high buck and came down on his side. It didn't hurt me, 'cause I lit off to one side.

Bob says, "Kid, if you don't whip him so much, he probably won't throw himself. Do more spurring."

And that's what I did. That was the orneriest horse that I ever had anything to do with. One time when we came to a puddle of water about knee-deep, he laid down and I had to wade out. Usually when he quit buckin', he would start runnin' backwards. One time he stuck both hind feet in an old badger hole and went over backwards. This time I held him down and whipped him with the quirt until he had enough. The other buckskin was more gentle but was hard to mount. Two different times I came near going over the top of him. The third time I was going to mount this bronc, Bob says, " 'Kit Carson', you help the Kid with that bronc."

Kit says, "Kid, what do you want me to do?"

"Put your rope on his front feet and we'll take a fall out of him. And while he's down, I'll mount him."

When that bronc got up on his feet, he was buckin' and I was going after him with my right spur. This Bob couldn't see. Bob yells, "Rake him, Kid."

When the bronc swapped ends and bucked back by Bob, he yells, "Kid, you sure have been raking him."

I didn't have any more trouble with that horse. The other two broncs, the pinto and sorrel, never did buck. Working for the TL there were three breed Indians, all top hands. "Kit Carson" weighed about two hundred pounds and had a black mustache, long hair usually done up underneath his hat. Baldy

Buck, another breed, was short and stout, and a good roper. Big Nels Value, a breed, was six feet. The best calf roper that I ever knew, "Kit Carson," was the only breed that worked with Bob's wagon.

After leaving the branding corral at Big Sandy, we went over into the Morias River country. There we met Dutch Herman's roundup wagon of the TL outfit. Dutch had gathered eight or nine hundred cows with calves. They were being trailed to the branding corral where the calves were to be branded. After the branding, the cows and calves were to be turned loose up in the Bear Paw Mountains. That was work for Red Bob's outfit. It was ten days before we got back to the branding corral.

The morning we had a part of the cows and calves corralled and ready for branding, the two ropers who were riding line on cows and calves in the Bear Paws hadn't shown up. The branding irons were hot. Bob says, "Kid, did you ever do any calf roping by the heels?"

"Yes," I nodded.

"Take my horse and start to roping," he said.

It was nearly noon when Jeff Warren and Creep showed up. By then we had branded about two hundred calves. After dinner Warren and Creep took over the ropin' job, while I helped with the branding irons. By three o'clock these two top hands had roped three hundred calves. That was enough for the first day's branding. These cows and calves were to be moved up into the Bear Paw Mountains, where Warren and Creep were ridin' line. We helped these two line riders head the cows and calves for the Bear Paws. There were yet better than three hundred calves to be branded the following day.

The second morning was the same thing over again. When noon came, the line rider hadn't shown up yet. That afternoon, with a fresh rope horse, I finished the ropin' job about the time

Warren and Creep came riding up. That's one time I got enough ropin' to last awhile. While we were moving the cows and calves to the Bear Paws, Bob rode into town to have a talk with Miller. That evening when he came back to camp, he says, "Tomorrow morning you boys all catch your private horses and pack your beds. The cow and calf wagon is through for awhile."

The next morning Bob's outfit headed for Big Sandy. Bob had already said that some of us would be layed off, that we could go to work in the hayfield. Near the stock yards at Big Sandy there was Miller waiting for us. When I galloped Brownie up to the lead of the cavvy to bend the horses into the corral gate, Miller called, "Come over, Kid." With me being the last cowboy hired, I was expecting to be the first one fired.

Miller says, "You and that Smithie that went to work just before you did, take this cavvy. Go to Dutch Herman's wagon and go to work. And that big pinto in the cavvy is a top cow horse. You ride him plenty."

It was noon when we throwed our cavvy in with Herman's. There were several dry farmers or Honyocks at the wagon along with the TL cowboys. Some of the Honyockers were riding work horses. Couldn't turn them around in a forty-acre field. After dinner, Herman, instead of mounting these dry farmers on some of the horses of our cavvy, mounted them on two top cowponies of my string. Then he went and set himself on the pinto that Miller told me to ride. All of this was against the rules of a cow outfit. He says, "Kid, you go and relieve one of the day herders."

This was spreadin' it on pretty thick. He probably thought that I had never worked on a roundup before. On herd that afternoon there were Smithie, Little Benny, and myself. The rest of the outfit were working the roundup and branding calves. Some of the calves belonged to Honyocker cows, and they were there to brand their own calves. That afternoon we three day herders talked things over among ourselves. I said that I was quitting that night. Smithie and Benny said they would stay on another day or two, and if it didn't get any better, they would quit.

The next morning I took my two horses and bed and headed back towards town. Out about three miles from Big Sandy the TL had a big haying camp. It was about like a roundup wagon. There was one bronc buster with a two-wheel cart breakin' broncs to work, a couple or three mowing machines cuttin' down prairie hay, and an old man grindin' or sharpening sickles. Also there was one kid raking hay; three buck rakes bucking hay to the stack yard; two men on the stack, stackin' hay while a kid drove the stacker team; and the cook with a helper. It was a real haying crew, the best that I have ever seen. This TL outfit was considered the largest and best outfit in the state of Montana. Here at the camp I stayed a day or two. When I asked the foreman for a job, he said that I had better ride into town and talk with Miller, that Sam did the hiring.

When I told Miller that I wouldn't work for Herman, but that I would take a job drivin' one of the mowers, he says, "Wait a minute. I've a better job than that. The Miltz family up in the Bear Paws have a nice little place. Mr. Miltz wants someone who can handle a half-broke span of mares. The wages will be forty dollars per month and board."

"That sounds good to me."

Miller gave me a letter and I headed up into the Bear Paws, some twenty miles out from town. The Miltz ranch was located in a nice little valley. Everything about the ranch looked neat and clean. The Miltzes were Germans. There were six in the family: Mr. and Mrs. Miltz, one son, Oscar, twelve years old, and three daughters, all good-looking girls. Annie was fifteen;

161

Lulu was seventeen or eighteen, and Agnes, about twenty-two or three. Here I was treated as one of the family. Mr. Miltz did the mowing of the prairie hay. With the bronco span of mares, I did the raking. Helping with hauling and stacking of the hay was Hobo Johnnie. This fellow was just driftin' and had stopped just long enough to earn a little grubstake, then he would move on. He was not asked into the home after supper, as I was. Just stayed out at the little bunkhouse. Oscar was a good mouth-organ-player. Lots of times of evenings, while Oscar was playing some good old-fashioned waltzes, I would dance with Anna or Lulu. One Saturday night a German couple, friends of Miltzes, got married. There was a dance in honor of the couple. Mrs. Miltz had supper an hour early so that us young folks could go to the dance, which was about twenty miles away. Sam Miller came with a team and buggy and took Anna and Lulu in the buggy while I went on horseback. We were only at the dance a couple or three hours 'till it was time to start headin' for home, if we didn't want a late breakfast. That forty-mile trip was worth it. We had a lot of fun.

When the hay was all in the stack, I sold my bed and bed horse to a young German for thirty dollars. After saying goodbye to this nice German family, I mounted Brownie and headed back for home. Every night along about supper time I would stop at some ranch for the night. One night I hit it pretty lucky. Stopped with a Swede family where there was a little dance. There were two darn good-lookin' Swede gals here who liked to dance. Nearly all night I danced with these girls. They were dancers, like most Swedes.

When I got to the Norris ferry on the Missouri River, it was about three o'clock in the afternoon, too early to stop for the night. When I asked if there was some place farther on where I could spend the night, he informed me there was a hay camp

out about forty miles. He also said there were two men riding
a tandem wheel just ahead of me. He said they were gamblers
from St. Paul. From what Norris said, I thought maybe these
two men might be some sort of road agents. When I saw some
big sand rocks along the road, I felt a little spooky, and while
passing by these rocks I had Brownie in a gallop and my six-
shooter handy. There was no need of this, as half a mile farther
on I overtook the two men. They were mending a flat tire on
their wheel. They were quite friendly. I doubt very much if
they were gamblers. That probably was a story that Norris
made up.

It was just getting dark when I rode into the hay camp and
asked to spend the night there. The foreman of the crew said,
"Just unsaddle your horse and turn him loose. We'll be wrangling our work stock in the morning. Go over to the cookhouse.
The cook will give you some supper. We just finished eatin'."

After my supper was set on the table, the cook, a heavy-set
man about forty years of age who walked with a limp, sat down
and was talking with me. In walked two young men, in their
early twenties. The taller one says to the cook, "What did you
do with our deck of cards that we left in here?"

The cook says, "I told you fellows if you didn't quit leavin'
those cards on my table, I'd burn them up."

The shorter of the two men started to cuss the cook, then
invited him outside. They got into a fist fight. The cook knocked
the young fellow down, then waited until he was back up on
his feet. Then the young fellow knocked down the cook. He
went right in on top of the cook and started to beat him up.
The cook says, "That isn't fair. I didn't beat you up when I
knocked you down."

It was then that the boss broke up the fight. The cook went
into the cookhouse to wash up, and I went with him. He was

skinned up some. The next morning at breakfast, I noticed the young smart aleck had a black eye.

On my homeward journey, I didn't go back the way I had come. Instead, I went by the way of Lewistown. One night I stayed at a stage ranch twenty miles north of Billings. At this ranch the stage changed teams. There was a good set of log buildings here, a stable that was large enough for twelve head of horses. The building where the family lived and meals were served was large and roomy. Off to one side there was a smaller building that had a bar and was used as a saloon. The family of father and mother had three teen-aged girls. I was offered a job tending bar and taking care of the stage horses for a month, while the man of the house went on a business trip. Taking care of the stage horses would have been O.K., but I didn't want any bar tending. I didn't know anything about it, so I thanked the man and kept on towards home.

When I came to the Big Horn River late one evening, the ferry man had gone home for the night. Now I could either swim Brownie across the Big Horn River or take off the saddle, put on the hobbles, and spend the night sleepin' on the saddle blanket. I didn't want to get wet, so I slept on the blanket 'till I froze out. Then I built a small fire and waited for daylight to come. I fired two quick shots from my pistol that brought the ferry man to life. Soon I was across the river. I was eatin' breakfast by the time the sun came up.

Two days later I was back home with my folks. I had been away about seven months. I had seen a lot of country, and I had got a lot of good experience. From Big Sandy, Montana to the Bard ranch on Mead Creek was probably four hundred miles. Brownie made this distance in ten days. Once again I went to work on the ranch to help to get everything done up before winter set in.

On the old Jack Burnside ranch there was living a family
that had come from Nebraska. In this family was a young lady
just my age, eighteen years. It is quite amusing to see how
much difference there is in a boy and girl of eighteen. Here I
was yet just a kid. This young lady of eighteen was a grown
woman, engaged to be married to a soldier boy stationed over
in the Philippine Islands. When I asked this young lady for
a date to go to the big dance at the Banner Hall, she says, "Sure,
I'll go with you. But don't get any foolish notions in your head.
I am engaged to a young man in the army. Soon as he comes
home from the Philippines, we are going to be married."

Well, I told the lady that I wasn't getting any foolish notions
in my head until I was old enough to vote. This gal was a good
partner in dancing. For looks she was just an average, built
like a quarter horse, weighed 140 pounds just the same as me.
We made a pretty good team. We dated each other for a year
or a little more. One day she told me that her boy friend was
sailing for the good old U.S.A., and that with good luck he
would probably be home by Christmas, when they would be
married. She said it would be best that we dated no more. So
we just kissed and said good-bye in a friendly kind of way.

About the most interesting date we had was the time we all
went into Sheridan for the Fourth of July and went to see the
Custer Battle Field. At nine o'clock nearly everybody was at
the depot with lunches waiting for the excursion train. As I remember, it was nine o'clock when the conductor yelled, "All
aboard!"

We all made a rush for the two passenger coaches waiting
on a side track. By ten o'clock we were on a side track near the
Custer Battle Field. From here we headed for the old battle
field, which was about a quarter of a mile. Upon a small knoll
we could see the larger cross or monument that marked the

165

spot where Custer had died. Out all around there were a lot of crosses, all freshly painted white. Over in a little draw two or three hundred yards to the east, there were several crosses in a group. Out from there were more crosses, just here or there. It was near noon when we turned back to the coaches and our lunches. Some of us younger folks went down to the Little Big Horn River to eat our lunches, while the older folks ate in the coaches where there was plenty of ice water to drink. At three o'clock we were on our way back to Sheridan.

After the gal had told me about her soldier boy being on his way home, I rode over to the 04 Bar cow outfit near Ranchester to see about a job breaking some horses to ride. Jim Davis, the foreman, whom I had known since 1890 or 1891 over in Buffalo, said that he had some young geldings to break, but that they were at the old OD ranch over on Rosebud Creek, some eight miles below the Kirby post office. The morning that Jim and I left the 04 Bar, we met a bunch of Indians. Among them was Howard Yellow Weasel, a young buck my age. Howard was riding a nice-lookin' young buckskin, a four-year-old that showed some good breedin'. This young half-broke gelding Howard offered to sell to me for ten dollars, which was only about half the actual value of the pony. I would have bought this pony but I didn't have that much cash in my pocket.

At the OD there were several log buildings in good condition, a good set of corrals. The ranch was yet owned by some of the Tompsons, early-day cowmen. It was now leased to the 04 Bar outfit. There were only two cowboys at this ranch, Simon Duncan and Frank (Smoky) Young. They were keepin' batch and haulin' hay to about six hundred cattle that were wintering on the ranch. Simon usually did the cooking. He sure did make good sourdough biscuits and flapjacks. The horses that I was breakin' were some Crow Indian ponies that would later be used as cowponies.

After breakin' out these ponies, I was only home a few days when I got a letter from the young lady who was already married to her soldier boy. She had been married for a month or more. One day there came just a note through the mail. It read something like this:

Dear Floyd:
Tomorrow night my husband goes to the Woodman's Lodge. Please meet me down at the Park Street bridge at eight o'clock. There is something very important that I want to talk to you about.

I should not have paid any attention to this note, but curiosity got the better of me. At eight when I rode up to the Park Street bridge, the new bride was waiting. I could see that she had been crying. I tied my horse in among some trees and went over to her.

"I am very unhappy," she began. "I don't love my husband half as much as I love you. Can't we go away somewhere and start life together someplace, some other state, where we are not known?"

When I told her that she was the one with foolish notions in her head, she began to cry as if her heart was breaking. She just stood there with her head on my shoulder, cryin' and beggin' me to go away with her. When I started loving her, she pushed me away and said, "Now that I am married to him, I am going to be true to him. But I don't love him like I do you. Won't you please listen to me."

I felt sorry for her, as she had been a dear friend to me, but being only eighteen, I wasn't wanting a woman to be tied down to for a few years. After explaining the whole thing to her and telling her in due time she would forget all about me, she said, "No, never. If you won't take me now, someday I'll be coming to you." But she never did.

I didn't have much to do with women for about two years, and that was down in Omaha. In makin' this trip to Omaha with beef cattle, along the way I met up with a couple of cowmen goin' to market with beef cattle, same as me. They were both married men, but one of them was a wild one. At one time he had been a rider in Cody's wild west show, so he told me. I didn't know these two men, just met up with them on that trip.

At Omaha stock yards our beef cattle were turned over to the commission house to sell. We three went to one of the big hotels to get rooms. We were at the desk registering for the rooms when a good-lookin' red-headed gal about twenty-five came walkin' through the office. We couldn't help take notice of such an attractive young woman. Even some of those old gray-headed men, with one foot in the grave, laid to one side their newspapers to have a look at this gal's well-shaped ankles.

Up at the third floor, when we stepped off the elevator and the bell hop was showing us to our rooms, which adjoined, I said to the bell hop more as a joke than the way he took it, "When will you be makin' the roundup?"

He says, "What do you mean?"

"Well, when some of us cowmen come down here, don't you round up some good-looking gals and let us cut out what we want."

"Sure, we'll do that. What kind do you want? Did you notice that red head down in the office," the bell hop asked. "Will she be O.K.?"

One of my partners says, "That gal sure looked good to me."

"What kind do you other gentlemen prefer?"

The other cowman said he liked blondes the best. The hop says, "I can fix you up O.K."

When it came my turn, and he asked me what kind of girl I wanted, just as a joke I says, "Do you have any married women on your list?"

He says, "I'll see." After takin' a little notebook from his pocket and going down the list, he says, "Only one and she's a big one, a Jew girl, and her husband is a traveling salesman."

When I asked him if the gal was big and fat, he says, "No. Just a big, well-built girl." I told him that would be O.K. for me.

The bell hop then says, "Some of these girls don't get through work 'till ten o'clock. Probably won't be here 'till eleven. You will have time to go around the corner to the Gaiety Theater and see a good show."

At eleven we were back in the parlor of our rooms when there came a knock on the door. One of the cowmen says, "Kid, you go and let them in."

There was the red head. With her was a gal probably twenty-two or three, a blonde, very small, a half-pint as they are sometimes called.

Right off she took it for granted that I was her boy friend. I told her there was a mistake somewhere, that the gal I had ordered was the biggest gal in Omaha, that she was probably the smallest one. She said that the other girl's husband was home and she couldn't come. That she was substituting for the married one. It was then there came another knock on the door. This time there was a good-lookin' blonde who apologized for being late, but said she had to work overtime.

I could see right off that I had been gypped on the deal. The red head and the blonde seemed like nice gals that were out for some fun and a little cash. This half-pint of mine was a gold digger. She wanted me to dig deeper for more money. All the money she got from me was the five bucks that was agreed to by the bell hop. She sure got plenty mad when I told her that she wasn't worth more than two bits.

That was the last time I went to Omaha, until the fall of 1916 when I went for an appendicitis operation.

MIXING COLLEGE AND WILD HORSES

In the fall of 1898 a man canvassed our county selling tuition at a hundred dollars each for the college at Big Horn. After Mother had bought and paid for a tuition, she said it was up to me to attend this college and to try to get a little more education, which I was badly in need of.

Over at the Big Horn Hotel, I found a place where I could batch along with three other men, Bob Wilkerson, Nye Barnett, and Bill Skinner, whose wife owned the hotel.

This winter of 1898, Mrs. Skinner had rented the main part of the hotel to a man and his wife, their two kids, and a brother-in-law. We four men kept batch in the annex of the hotel where there was one large-sized room, which was our living room and kitchen. There were two bedrooms. One of these Nye and I occupied. The two older men slept in the other room. Mrs. Skinner had taken their two kids and gone east for an all-winter's visit with some of her relatives. We four men divided the batchin' expenses, with each one furnishing part of the provisions. My part of the provisions mostly consisted of beef and spuds and wild-plum preserves, which Mother had canned for winter use. Most of the provisions that I furnished were from the ranch. I wasn't out much cash.

The college was named the Wyoming Collegiate Institute and was located on the side of the present Big Horn School. The college was built of brick. Preacher Austin was the professor. He lived on the Jackson ranch. Ralph Anderson was his assistant.

There were pupils of all ages from different parts of Wyoming attending this college. From the Big Horn Basin, some lived near Hyattville. There was Gus Allen and his sister, Grace; a young man, Jim Whaley; and Fred, a small man about twenty-two who wore a heavy mustache. This is the same Fred who was working along with the granger roundup wagon the fall of 1896, the same as I.

When it came Christmas vacation, Bob Hopkins, a kid that I had known over at Buffalo during 1890 and 1891, went with me to the Bard ranch. It was nice weather with no snow on the ground. For a little sport, we decided to try and corral a band of wild horses that was ranging over in the Dutch Creek Hills. There were five of us big kids or young men. We were all about nineteen. There were Bob, Lew, Tode and myself, and another kid whose name I don't remember. Lew lived on the old FE cow ranch.

The morning we were going to try for the wild ones, we all met down at the Willey school house. We were mounted on some of the best horses in the country. Some of us had our six-shooters buckled on just in case that some old wild mare gave us too much trouble. Over on the divide between Dow Prong and Straight Prong of Dutch Creek we jumped forty odd head of wild horses. Some were branded and some weren't. The branded stock were mostly old stray mares that had drifted into the hills several years previous. Now more than half the band were slicks that no one claimed. They just belonged to whoever got their rope on first.

When we jumped these wild ones, they took off, circling a big hill. I went around the hill from the opposite direction, headin' off the band, running them back around the hill right into the other boys, who headed them down Dow Prong. It was then I made a run for the lead of the band, headin' them off just as they were takin' off up a side draw. Here came the other boys as fast as their horses could run, bringin' up the drags. After bunchin' the band, I headed for Prairie Dog Creek with the wild ones following. Tode was riding on one side of the band and Lew was on the opposite side. Bob and the other kid was bringing up the rear. We held the band so tight together that they didn't have a chance to make a break to get away.

In making this run from Dutch Creek to a big horse corral on Mead Creek, about ten miles, we made it all in high gear, except for two or three hills where we slowed down to a trot.

It was probably ten or eleven o'clock when we corralled this band. Two of the boys stood guard over the corral while three of us rode home for our rope horses and a bunch of our gentle range horses. Upon our return with the gentle stock we turned them down on to Mead Creek and left Bob to guard them while the four of us did the corral work. These horses were so wild and snaky that we didn't take any chances in the corral on foot. It fell to Lew and I to do the ropin'. Tode and Al were tendin' gate. These slicks were anywhere from sucklings up to three-year-olds, except one buckskin stud that looked a year or two older. This stud was the leader of the band. Before we even went out to corral this wild bunch, I told the boys if they would let me have the buckskin stud, they could have the others. Either Lew or I would ride into the corral, rope one of the slicks around the neck, and head for the gate where we dragged it to the outside. There it was roped by the hind feet and stretched out. Then the ropes were removed, just like we were doing team work on cattle. After the ropes were removed, the slick was headed into the gentle bunch that Bob was holdin.' We left the buckskin stud until nearly the last. We didn't take anything under two-year-olds. When we roped the buckskin, it took both Lew and I to drag him to the outside. When the ropes were off and he was headed into our gentle bunch, he didn't stop there. Went right on through and headed for the hills. There wasn't a horse in our outfit that could head him off, so I lost my prize stud.

After we had twelve of the slicks in with our gentle bunch, four of us headed for the Bard ranch with the slicks and the gentle ones all mixed together. We took the whole works on high gear to the horse corrals at the Bard ranch. About the time that we had the outfit corralled, here come the kid who was left be-hind to open the gate and head the remainder of the wild bunch back towards the hills. We were very lucky in this venture that no one got hurt. Lew got his rope horse jerked down once.

When we divided the slicks, Bob didn't want any of them. He had no place to keep them. The rest of us got three slicks each. For my share I took two two-year-old studs and a roan coming three-year-old. This roan filly showed quite a bit of draft stock. This filly I traded to Dad for a black suit of clothes that he had bought while running the Windsor Hotel. It was yet nearly new. The only thing wrong with the suit was it had a swallow-tailed coat that was now going out of style. That didn't make any difference to me. If I didn't like the swallow tail, I could cut it off. The pants and vest were worth more than the filly.

By the first of the year, 1899, we were back in college. Every Saturday night there was a dance at the Skinner Hall up over the Skinner store. There we college kids had a good time danc-ing. Preacher Austin had a good, half-broke driving team, which Gus Allen, Jim Whaley, and I would borrow some night during

173

the week. With the team and a buckboard we would pick up Grace Allen and two more girls. Then we headed off to some ranch where there was a room big enough for dancing. By April first my college days were over. So were Nye's. He and Bob Wilkerson left Big Horn for Ashland, Montana and Hunter's 7OL ranch. Hunter had sold his herd to an Englishman by the name of Eckford who lived on a ranch near High River, Alberta, Canada. During most of the summer of 1899, Bob Wilkerson, Nye Barnett, Jim Hackley, Bert Pierson, a fellow by the name of Holmes, and one or two others trailed the 7OL herd of horses from Ashland, Montana to High River.

On April 4, there came a big snow. The snow was a foot deep on the level. Al, the kid who lived on Prairie Dog Creek, and I decided this would be a good time to try to capture another wild buckskin stud that was ranging over in the Dutch Creek Hills. This time I was mounted on the horse that I named Judge, a long-distance horse. Al had a good horse, too. A little farther up the divide from where we had jumped the wild ones during Christmas vacation there was another bunch of wild ones, with an extra good buckskin three-year-old stud in the bunch. When we jumped this bunch, Al says, "You give them the first run while I wait here for them to double back up the Dow Prong of Dutch Creek."

Down the divide between the two creeks the wild bunch went, through that snow that was about a foot deep. There was no trouble in following their trail. Sometimes I was in sight of them, sometimes I wasn't. When they left the divide and headed down the Straight Prong, I began to gain on them. By the time the bunch came to the forks of the creek and were headed back up Dow Prong, I overtook the drags. There I passed by. Now every little way some of the bunch would throw up their tails. They were all in, couldn't go any farther. Finally there were only two left to follow, a buckskin mare and the stud. When these two started headin' for where we had first jumped them, the mare throwed up her tail and was all in. Now I was fast gainin' on the stud. Al came galloping out from where he was waiting and soon overtook the stud and roped him. The stud was so near all in that he didn't put up much of a fight.

There near Prairie Dog Creek in what was called Lew Zanc Draw, Al suggested that we build a fire, heat his bridle bit, and brand the stud. He took all the leather from the bit and put it in the fire. While the bit was gettin' hot, he suggested that we throw a silver dollar—head or tails—to see who would get the buckskin stud. When he flipped up the dollar, I says, "Tails." When the dollar came down, it was "heads," so he won. Once again I lost the buckskin that I wanted to own. Again that summer I gave the first buckskin stud a run for his life, but failed in ropin' him. I never ran any more wild studs, only a few ridge-running geldings.

In the spring or summer of 1899, Dad got a job selling groceries for the Loverin and Brown grocery house of Chicago. His territory was the Big Horn Basin country, over the mountains from us. With a team and buckboard, a sample case, a bed, and a few extra clothes, he headed for the Basin country to take order for groceries.

Somewhere he bought a Spanish jackass and had it delivered to the Bard ranch. This jack we crossed with some of our smaller mares and started to raisin' what was called "cotton mules." In the South there in the cotton fields there was a ready market for this kind of mule. There was not much of a market for any kind of horse. The bottom had dropped out of the horse business. Most everyone was going out of the business. Horses were so cheap that the railroad wouldn't accept them as freight unless the freight was prepaid. Some horse men just quit branding up their increase. There was a horse man named Yorkie that had two herd of good horses ranging on Buffalo Creek. Yorkie offered to sell these horses at four dollars per head with slicks thrown in. Al wanted me to go with him and buy these horses. It looked as if there was no future for the horse business, so I said, "No."

That was a sad mistake on my part. Jess Britain bought this herd of horses. Only had them a year when he was selling horses to the Moncreiffe outfit at forty dollars per head as Boer War horses. Most all of the horse men sold out their horses just before the horse boom.

One day while in Sheridan I met my old friend, Bill Cameron, who said, "Kid, I am broke. Let's go over to Piney Creek an' break some horses. At this time Bill was forty and I was twenty. The first place we went to was the Sam Dickey ranch. Sam had a good ranch. When I asked Sam about a job breakin' horses, he says, "No, I haven't any horses to break. But I'll tell you what I got—a wild bay four-year-old stud out in my leased school section, ranging with about forty head of my horses. Don't know where that wild stud came from. Don't know who owns him. He is unbranded. Can't corral him. Don't want to shoot him. He's the makin's of a top saddle horse when broke. If you boys can corral the stud, you're welcome to him."

Bill always rode a good horse. This time he was mounted on a big sorrel Thoroughbred, raised by Mr. Allen over near Hyattville. My mount was a Crow Indian pony that was a good rope horse—that was the thing in halter breaking broncs. Out at the back side of the pasture we found the horses. The stud waved his tail in the air, let out a few horse snorts, and took off on a run, with the others following. They were near the east fence line. Bill says, "Kid, you just whip them broom tails over the rump and keep them acomin'. When the stud started to leave the herd, I tried to bend him back into the herd. I had my rope down, a whoopin' and hollarin' and whippin' every horse that I got close to.

Bill was layin' right to the stud, headin' him back into the herd. When we came to the pasture gate, Bill headed the herd across the road and into Sam's horse corral. Old Injun I headed right in with them. My rope was tied hard and fast to the saddle horn. When I dropped the loop over that stud's head, he come near jerkin' Injun down. We had quite a tussle with the stud before we got the hackamore on. Tied him to a corral post while we went in and had dinner with the Dickey family. That afternoon we headed up Piney Creek with the stud, which was tied to the horn of my saddle. When we came to the old Flying E ⫝⫝ cow ranch, where there was a good high corral where no horse could jump over the top, I said to Bill, "Here's where I am going to try and ride the stud."

Bill roped the stud's front feet. After he was down, I put my saddle on him when he got up. He bucked and ran around the inside of the corral, then he would buck some more. He came near piling me a couple of times. He had me pullin' leather with both hands. After riding the stud around the inside of the corral for an hour or more to sorta bridle wise him, I put my saddle back on Injun, and we headed up Piney Creek to the Jake Grubbs ranch.

When we arrived there, Jake and his son, Ernie, had just come in from the Powder River with some young geldings. I didn't know the Grubbs none too well. Cameron knew Jake quite well. They had both punched cows for the Flying E outfit along in the 1880's. At one time Jake was wagon boss. Here Bill Cameron and I got a job breaking broncs at five dollars per head. Jake had seven head to break. Frank Eldred, the harness-maker of Sheridan, had a nine-year-old bronc here at Jake's that we got

177

ten dollars for breakin'. Altogether, counting the wild stud, we had nine head to break. The morning we started in on these broncs, Jake and his son Ernie, who was thirteen, went back down in the Powder River on some business. About two hundred yards from the barn there were two good bronc corrals, round corrals with a gate in between the corrals.

After corralling this bunch of broncs, we started in on the wildest ones first. Bill being twenty years older than me, I rode all the first time or two. We would cut one of these broncs in a corral by himself. Then one of us would rope the bronc by the front feet, bust him, and after he was hog-tied, we would sorta pet him a little. We would thin out the tail some with our jackknife or just pull out some of the hair where it was a little too thick. Then we would take some of the kinks out of the mane where the old witches had been ridin' him, as the kinks were referred to.

Now with all this bein' done, we would put on my saddle. When that bronc got back on his feet with me in the saddle, he sure went some for awhile, tryin' to buck me out of the saddle. Then around inside of that corral they would run. Sometimes they would kick at my feet. Just about one ride like this and the most of them quit bucking.

Jake had a hot-blood, five-year-old gelding that he called Tony, that was a barnyard-raised geldin', that done more bucking than all the wild ones put together. Most of these broncs we rode a time or two, then we halter broke them. The nine-year-old was the easiest broke. Tony was the toughest one. There was one six-year-old gray that was corral balky. He had probably been fooled with by some other rider. When this bronc tried to rub me off on the corral fence, I would spur him so hard that he soon quit that.

I had him pretty well scratched up from his ears to his tail,

178

enough so that young Billie Grubb told his mother that one of the broncs had run into the wire fence and got scratched up a bit.

We were at Jake's place ten days. Rode all the broncs out twice each day. When Jake came home from the Powder River, Bill told him that the broncs were now broke. But I didn't think so. Anyway we had done a fair job, even broke them to a rope corral. This was done by tying a two-inch rope from one gate post to another gate post in between the two corrals. Here we run those broncs back and forth 'till they had some respect for a rope corral. Now they were cavvy broke. We had roped these broncs by the front feet until they were afraid to run by us. The morning we turned these broncs back to Jake as broke, after corralling them, we left our ropes and saddles at the barn. With our bridles we walked to the corral, put the bridle on one of the ponies, mounted him bareback, and rode it to the barn. Jake said that was good enough.

Here is the way we made out. Jake paid us thirty-five dollars for the breaking of the seven head. Frank Eldred, the harness-maker, give us ten dollars for breaking the nine-year-old. Bill Cameron sold the wild stud to a granger for forty dollars. When this was added up, we each got a little better than forty dollars for the ten or twelve days work. Nowadays the bronc breakers get fifty dollars a month for ridin' broncs. The owner of the bronc furnishes the feed and pays for the shoeing of the broncs. We never used to shoe any broncs. Just rode them barefooted. We rode them broncs in any kind of saddle, just so it had a good saddle horn to hang onto. We wasn't riding for no rodeo or making any grandstand plays. If us old-time bronc riders could of got the price that is paid nowadays, we probably would of been millionaires.

After breakin' of these broncs, I went home, and Bill Cameron went back to Sheridan to his wife and daughter. Not long after this Bill and his wife separated. Bill drifted up into the northern part of Montana. There at the Missouri River he got a job working for the Circle Diamond outfit that handled nothing but steers, mostly of the long-horned breed. That was the last I ever heard of Bill Cameron, one of the best all-round cowboys that I ever knew and worked with.

During this fall of 1899, Al and I went to the Crow Indian Reservation where there were a lot of Crow ponies rounded up and offered for sale. Preacher Glen and his son, Joe, Al, and I got first choice of these unbroke ponies at five dollars per head. I bought twenty-five geldings. Al bought twenty-five dry mares. The next in line were the Glens'. I don't know what they got. There were other buyers. Some horses sold for three dollars and fifty cents. The Indians begged us to buy the big colts at a dollar per head.

Al shipped his mares to Iowa. Just about broke even on the deal. After breaking my geldings to ride, I sold them anywhere from fifteen dollars up to forty-five dollars per head. The forty-five-dollar horse was raised by Yellow Weasel and Frank Grouard.

OFF FOR CANADA

AT THE TURN OF THE CENTURY, in the spring of 1900, lots of changes were made. Now that I was twenty-one and could vote, I didn't consider that I was a kid any longer. I had about fifty head of cattle of my own and twenty-five or thirty horses, which was mostly tradin' horses. Well, I just got the feeling that I would like to start a little spread of my own. When Bob Wilkerson wrote back down here as to what a wonderful country Alberta, Canada was, Mat Bedsaul, the PK horse wrangler, decided that he would like to see what the Alberta country looked like, especially the High River country where Bob Wilkerson, Nye Barnett, and Bert Pierson were now employed by the Eckford or High River horse outfit.

Along about the first of April, 1900, I broke Brownie and a bay bronc to work on a buckboard. About the tenth of April when the grass started to get green, I loaded on to the buckboard my cowboy outfit, a small camp outfit, a war bag with my clothes, two pair of hobbles. I hooked the team to the buckboard and said good-bye to my folks, and headed for Alberta.

At the PK I spent the first night. Here Mat joined me with his roundup bed, teepee tent, and a saddle horse of his own. We had plenty of grub in the grub box that Mother had given me before leaving home. Mat and I were to sleep together in his bed.

After leaving the PK we camped that first night on Pass Creek. Here we had some trouble with the bronc that was Brownie's mate. This bronc I had named Bill, after Bill McBride, the man that I had got him from. Well, Bill was plenty ornery about being hitched onto the buckboard. He had a habit of kicking at a fellow when he was bein' unhitched from the rig. There on Pass Creek, Bill took a kick at me when I started to unhitch the outside tug or trace. He came near getting away from us when the buckboard tongue came loose from the neckyoke. The next night when we pulled in on Rotten Grass Creek on the Crow Reservation, I decided on tying the bronc to a tree before unhitching him from the rig. Everything went O.K. 'till I started to unfasten the outside tug, then Bill took a kick at me, sat down on the tongue of the buckboard, and broke it in two. After we got Brownie free from the outfit, Bill started to buck and kick with that neckyoke and piece of tongue wired to it hard and fast. He broke the halter rope that was tied to the tree. Out across the little flat he went bucking. Didn't see the ten-foot cut bank on Rotten Grass Creek. Right over the bank went Bill. We couldn't see what happened to him. When I peeked over the bank, there he was standing belly-deep in water.

At the rear of the buckboard Mat had been leadin' his sorrel saddle horse, so he mounts his horse and goes after Bill, who was plenty wet but wasn't hurt any. Now we had some problem on our hands. The next morning we cut down a green sapling and were tryin' to splice the broken tongue, when along comes an immigrant outfit. I gave them five dollars to trail the buckboard into St. Xavier where there was a blacksmith shop.

Mat then rode his horse Will. I rode Brownie and led this outlaw Bill, who was a six-year-old, a beautiful bay, one of the best-built horses that I ever owned. He weighed about eleven hundred pounds, same as Brownie. When I first traded for Bill, I tried to break him to ride. All he wanted to do was to buck. So I broke him to work—or did I. While the blacksmith was mending the broken tongue, a big buck Indian came riding into St. Xavier on a brown work horse a little bigger than Brownie. I hit this Crow up for a trade. He looked Bill all over, then he said, "Is him a race horse?"

"Don't know," says I. "never did race him."

We made the swap even up, no boot. I rode Brownie and led Bill two miles out to where the Crow was living. There I gave the Crow a bill of sale. I took the Indian's horse, which I named Crow, and beat it back. By now the tongue was mended. We hitched the team on to the buckboard and left in a hurry before the Crow Indian either got killed or bucked off by Bill.

Over on Pryor Creek, as I remember, we came to the forks

of the road. Here we didn't know which road to take to Billings, Montana. About fifty yards over to one side there was a new tent. It wasn't an Indian tecpee. There was a few Indian ponies saddled and standing nearby. Here I gave Mat the lines while I headed for the tent to try and find out as to what was the Billings road. It was a cold, windy day. I had my six-shooter buckled on under the tail of my sheep-lined coat. At the tent I opened the flap of the tent door and stepped inside. Seated at a table there was a white man, probably a trapper, and five young bucks playing poker. Settin' on the trapper's rolled-up bed there was a big breed. Right from the start these young bucks began to say, "You go. You get out of here."

Before the trapper had time to tell me the way to Billings, the big breed got up off the bed and made as if he was going out of the tent door. Instead of that, he grabbed my shoulder and spun me half-way round, hurting my shoulder.

It was then that I came out with my gun and pointed it at the breed's belly. He fell right over backwards onto the bed and stayed there until I told those young bucks if they batted an eye, I would shoot it out. I was plenty mad, and they were scared until they were about the color of the trapper. I didn't take any chances on those young bucks, just held the gun on them 'till the trapper told me which road to take. Then I backed out of the tent door and beat it for the buckboard. From there we made fast time into Billings. Here we made camp on the north edge of town and stayed over a day on account of rain.

We spent most of our time up town where we took our meals. From Billings to the Marias River we had no trouble. But when we reached the bank of the river, it was running nearly bank full. There at the crossing was a sheep herder on a pony, bareback. He was afraid to try and cross over the river and wanted to ride on the tail end of the buckboard and lead his pony. I told him that his chances were better on the pony. Mat had already sold his horse to a sheep herder for thirty-five dollars. The crossing didn't look none too good. There was nothin' to do but try crossing. Our grub box we put on the seat of our rig and tied almost everything fast to the floor of the buckboard, so that it couldn't float away. Mat was sitting astride of his bed. I was sittin' on top of the grub box, with the sheep herder on the tail end of the rig. We didn't drive far out until the water was well over belly-deep to the team. The herder was now in water up above his waist line.

A little farther on the team began to swim toward shore, which was only a distance probably of fifteen or twenty feet, when the tail end of the rig started to swing around downstream. I began to think that we were going to lose the outfit, but the team pulled the outfit ashore. The sheep herder was wet up to his armpits. Mat was wet to his waist line. With me sitting on top of the grub box, I didn't get much wet.

The herder headed off for some sheep camp, while Mat and I made camp near some brush. Everything was wet except our grub box, where most of our food was. Our bed we took apart and put on the brush heaps to dry. That afternoon while we were drying our wet things, a fellow came riding down the road to our camp. I thought he looked familiar to me. It was Little Benny of the TL outfit. He stayed about two hours and visited with me. He told me about Sam Miller and Lulu Miltz getting married; that Agnes Miltz had married Mr. McNamara. When I asked him about the N Bar freak, Bob Roberts, Benny says, "Didn't you hear about him killing two of those YT cowboys, and how he was sent to the pen for the rest of his life?"

I don't remember where Benny was working at this time.

When we got to the Canadian line, we were held up by the Canadian customs officer, who said that we didn't have equipment enough to enter Alberta as immigrants. He said that we would have to pay thirty-five dollars duty on our outfit. Well, I didn't have that much cash left, as I had been footin' the bills most of the time. Mat had the cash but hesitated about loaning it to me, so I sold my outfit to a sheepman for a hundred dollars, which was about half what it was worth. Here at Sweetgrass we waited a couple of days getting things fixed up before going on to Coults and into Alberta. The customs house was a frame building, one hundred feet long, painted red. It had a porch full length of the building. On the east side there was a walk with a yellow stripe painted across the center of the walk. This was the dividing line between the United States and Canada.

On the Canada side there was nothing much, only a few out buildings. The Canadian side was named Coults. On the U.S. side it was Sweetgrass.

In the U.S. Custom House there was an eatin' place run by a Welshman, a small, very busy man. One evening while we were sitting on the porch, the little narrow-gauge train pulled into Sweetgrass. On this train there were several large sacks of spuds for the eatin' place. When I saw that the spud sacks were a little too heavy for the Welshman, I helped him with them. Meals were thirty-five cents. That night when I handed the Welshman fifty cents, he gave me in change two quarters. At the next meal it was the same thing. When I asked him why he was doing this, he says, "You done me a favor and I like you, and would like you as a partner. There is more work here than I can do. I already have a license for a saloon. Down there in that little frame building I am starting up a grocery store."

When I asked him how much it would take for a half-interest, he said, "Four hundred dollars." When I told him that I only had one hundred, he says, "I'll let you in for that."

When I told Mat that I was at the end of my journey, he

185

began to belly ache, saying that he was going back to Sheridan.

I thanked the Welshman for the wonderful offer but told him that we would be moving on, that we wanted to find a location where we could build up a ranch. This is what he said, "I've got 160 acres over on the Milk River, all fenced. No use for it. I'll give that to you if you'll stay with me."

When I told Mat about it, he blew up and called me a piker because I wasn't going to High River with him. Once again, I told the Welshman how things were with Mat and me.

He says, "You're passin' up a wonderful opportunity here."

And that's what I did, and I knew it. Nine years later when I made a trip to Alberta, the Welshman owned most of the town of Sweetgrass. He had a grocery store, a hotel, livery stable, and a lumber yard. Don't remember what else. It was then I thought of what the fortune teller told me. She said, "You are an ornery devil. You have good judgment, but you let other people influence you too much. Someday there is going to cross your path a blonde lady." I don't remember nothing about any blonde woman. I never saw one.

When we left Sweetgrass on the narrow-gauge railroad, with the dinky engines and small cars and coaches, the speed was none too good. At High River we left our baggage in the baggage room at the depot. All the baggage I had was a war bag with my clothes and my cowboy outfit in a gunny sack. Mat's was the same except for his roundup bed.

High River was a nice little town near the stream called High River. There near the depot were some Indians that had several ponies. At a hitch rail there was a good-looking gray bronc, quite a bit better than the average Indian pony. This pony I bought for fifteen dollars. Mat bought an old white pony that had glass-colored eyes for eleven dollars. Right off, the Indians and some whites began to ask when I would ride the horse that

I had bought. "Tomorrow morning," says I. "My cowboy's outfit is in my war bag."

Probably I did look something like a cow*poke* or tenderfoot. The next morning when we went for our ponies at the stable, we had on our cowboy outfits, chaps and spurs and our saddles. Already I was a little suspicious about the pony that I had bought so cheap. At the livery stable, on the corral fence there were Indians and whites to see me ride the pony. It was halter broke and easy to saddle. When I mounted the pony, he shot up like a skyrocket, came down a bucking high jumps, and a little crooked. But not hard to ride out there for about fifty yards, when he quit buckin'.

After I got the pony back to the corral, I just sat on him till he got his wind. Then I hooked him with my spurs. Away we went again for another bucking spree. Just thought I'd give the crowd their money's worth. After the show was over, we headed up the High River some four miles to the Eckford horse ranch. Here we met Bert Pierson, who was the bronc rider for the outfit. We stopped over night with Bert, whom we both knew as an OW cowboy of the J. B. Kendrick Cattle Company, fifty miles out from Sheridan on Hanging Woman Creek.

After leaving the Eckford ranch on our two Indian ponies, we traveled some twenty-five miles up High River to the Bar U cow ranch. We saw a lot of beautiful rangeland, with very few fences. At the Bar U we met the foreman of the outfit, McKennon, who informed us that he wasn't in need of any more cowboys until the roundup wagon pulled out onto the range.

From here we rode to the Oxley outfit on Mosquito Creek. Here Scotty Henderson, the foreman, gave us the same answer as we got at the Bar U. These were real cow outfits where we were made welcome. At the Lane outfit where Herb Miller was the boss, it was the same answer. We were now twenty-five or thirty miles out east of the town of High River.

On the Little Bow River, where the Lane outfit was located, everything was new. Only two years previous, the outfit shipped or trailed in from Oregon. They had both horses and cattle.

After five days looking for a job of riding, I was back in High River town. I tied my Indian bronc to the hitch rail, and was inside the general store and post office, when in came Herbert Eckford. Herb says, "Bob Wilkerson is leaving my Little Bow horse camp and recommended you to take his place. He is in charge of the camp. The wages will be forty per month, with everything furnished. You and Nye Barnett will have to batch. There will be about seven hundred mixed horses in the herd that you and Nye will be range herding on the big, open prairie during the daytime. At night there is a two-hundred-acre pasture to hold them in."

When I told Herb that I would take the job, he said, "Ride your bronc on up to the ranch. Then in the morning I'll take you down to the Little Bow River camp. After finishing a letter to my folks, I saw a man lookin' at my bronc tied to the hitch rail. He says, "Would you want to trade that bronc for a nice, old gentle horse?"

This man had a ranch about halfway out to the Eckford place. At this place we made a horse swap. About this time the fellow's sister showed up and says, "What have you done? Did you trade off my saddle horse?"

There was quite an argument about this old brown saddle horse. When the young lady, who was about eighteen, went back to the house, she was about half-crying. I sure felt bad about the old horse that I wouldn't have any use for. When I mounted the horse and started headin' for the Double Oar Lock ⊃―⊂ horse ranch of Eckford, every little way that old horse would stop and look back at his old home. The old fellow was surely homesick, and didn't want to leave the young lady who seemed so fond of him. And I didn't blame him for that. Out about a half a mile, he didn't want to go any farther, so I got off and turned the old fellow loose to see what he would do. He sure high tailed it for home, with me following along on foot. It was only a few minutes 'till the young lady came leading the horse back to me with tears in her eyes.

I says, "You and that old horse seem to be pretty good pals." She said, "Yes, sir. We were raised together, and just to think that my brother would trade my old pal to a stranger!"

I didn't have any further use for the horse, and I told Jenny if she would ride with me to the Eckford ranch, I would give the horse to her and the bill of sale that her brother had given to me. At the Eckford place when I handed the lead rope to the young lady, her eyes filled with tears of gratitude. At first I thought she was going to kiss me, but she didn't. Just said, "Thank you." Then she headed for home with the old horse and a bill of sale for him. I never talked with her again, but her brother told me later that he didn't consider the horse safe for his sister to ride. He was getting stiff in the knees.

The following morning, which was now about the tenth of May, Herbert hitched his driving team on to the "Democrat," just an ordinary spring wagon. Then we headed down the Little Bow River to the horse camp. It was about eleven o'clock when we got to the camp. The horse herd were going into the river for water about as fast as they could run, with Bob Wilkerson in the lead trying to slow them up some. Nye was following up with the drags at a slower pace. This was out on the big open range. The nearest ranch was the Arnold ranch, six miles down the river. Four miles farther down the river the Lane outfit had a ranch fenced in.

Bob rode with us on to the cabin of the camp, where he cooked up some dinner. After dinner he and Herb headed for High River, where Bob took the train for Sheridan.

After they left, I went out to relieve Nye so that he could come for his dinner. After Nye had ate and washed up the dishes, he came back out to the herd. These horses were the Hunter herd that had been trailed to Alberta the previous year. In our little cavvy were twenty-five good saddle horses. A part of them were raised by George Brewster at Birney, Montana. The cavvy wasn't kept in the pasture. It grazed along the Little Bow, not far from our cabin. We took turns at cooking and wrangling the cavvy in before breakfast. At five-thirty the horse herd were most always at the gate ready for the outside. One of us would hold back the horses while they opened the long wire gate. Then we had to get away from the gate while the horses were passing through to the big open range, where the country was mostly level, with just a few knolls here and there.

After the herd were through the gate, it usually was about an hour before they settled down to grazing. The herd scattered out over a territory about half to a mile square. Nye would get upon a knoll and watch one side while I watched the other side. On the east side there was our pasture fence. At first we had no trouble with the herd, not until the mosquitoes began to show up. We would take a novel from the stack of books at the cabin. Up on the knoll sometimes we would sit until time for dinner. Then one of us would ride to the cabin, cook and eat dinner, then come back to the herd and let the other one go for his dinner. Some days when I would get tired of reading, I would go to one of the pot holes or small lakes where the range cattle were watering and do some calf roping just for practice. In my string of saddle horses there were two top rope horses, a smoky buckskin and a sorrel with plenty of speed. This horse I named

Socks on account of his white legs, up to his hocks. The other I called Smoky. There were animals on the range that I never could rope called skip foxes, only about half the size of a red fox. Had a large bushy tail. Didn't have speed enough to out-run a horse, but plenty of speed to out-dodge a loop. Up here in Alberta, with plenty of pot holes scattered over the range, Mallard ducks nested and raised their young. A young Mallard is almost grown before it has wing feathers enough to start flying. These pot holes were usually about belly-deep to a horse. The water was clear. Out in these pot holes I would ride my horse and kill some of the young Mallards with my quirt. These young ducks were very good either fried or roasted, much better than bacon, which we had three times a day. Later on when the pot holes started drying up and the ducks were nearly grown but could not yet fly, when they saw us on horseback, they would leave the pot holes and take to grass and hide. We would get off our horses, tramp through the grass until we had killed enough ducks for a meal or two. This lasted about thirty days, then we had to go back to bacon again.

One morning when we rolled out of bed, it was stormy look-ing, so foggy that we couldn't see anywhere. While I was cook-ing breakfast, Nye tried to find our cavvy. It was eleven o'clock before we had our cavvy in the corral, so we decided on some lunch before taking the herd to the outside. While we were having our lunch, there came an awful lightning and thunder storm. After lunch when we went to turn the horse herd to the outside, there wasn't any herd to be found. They had stam-peded, ran through a three-wire fence, knockin' down about three hundred yards of the fence. The only horses left were a few cripples—ones that got hurt during the stampede. Nye and I rode in a gallop most of the time before we got to the lead of the herd, which were now at the Lane place, ten miles down

the Little Bow from our camp. It was about three in the afternoon. Nye was for turning the herd into the Lane pasture for
the night. When I said that we would take the herd back to
camp, Nye didn't like the idea, until I had the herd a headin'
for camp. Then he got in and helped me. With our ropes we
whipped every horse over the tail end that we got close to. We
took the herd back on high. Every little way, one would drop
out of the herd all in. We just left them, went on with the herd,
and got back to camp about five. To the outside of the pasture
we left the herd for a couple of hours while we mended the
fence, before putting them into the pasture. About eight miles
from our camp along the railroad there was a station or section
house called Nanton. Here is where we went for our mail. One
day when I went for the mail, there was a man with three horses
and a prairie-breaker, a walking plow, plowing fire guard along
near the railroad tracks. This fire-guard plower told me that
his base or main camp was down the line about four miles. Of a
morning after breakfast he would hitch the three horses on to
the walking plow and plow a furrow until noon overtook him,
which was usually at his temporary camp. There he would eat
his lunch, feed and water his team, then plow a furrow back
to his base camp that afternoon.

These fire guards were let out on contract at so much per
mile. On both sides of the track out about a hundred feet there
was a twenty-foot fire guard plowed. With all that heavy grass
there was danger of prairie fires.

About this time, Nye got homesick and headed back for
Wyoming. The mosquitoes were so bad at night that we had
to build a smudge for the herd. From the main ranch Eckford
sent down to our camp a couple of men with a team and wagon.
Out in the center of the horse pasture these two young men dug
a pit ten foot square and four foot deep. Down near the stable

where there was an old haystack partly rotted, they hauled enough to fill the pit, tramped it down good and solid. There was a regulation in regards to this, as it had to be fenced to keep the horses from pawing into the pit of fire. It was surprising to see how fast this herd learned about the smoke of that smudge. The herd sometimes would be strung out for a quarter of a mile standing in line of the smoke. When the wind would change, the smoke line moved over a little. The horses would follow the smoke.

After Nye left, two young men stayed on and helped me with the herd. It wasn't long 'till Eckford sold the yearling colts. From the main ranch came Eckford, Bert Pierson, a husky young Scotchman, and the two Bond brothers, Art and Jim, to help take the herd to the big stock yards at Nanton, where they were corralled and the yearling colts taken out. This was sure some job, with every pen jam full of horses. Hadn't much more than started to cutting out the yearlings 'till a big fat colt got its hind leg broke. The colt was butchered; a hind quarter was taken to our camp, where Art Bond was cooking some dinner. At noon Art had some colt steaks fried and some bacon, along with other food. I didn't want to be a piker, so I took a colt steak along with the bacon. The more I chewed on the steak, the bigger it got. I couldn't swallow it at all, just spit it out and went for the bacon, which sure looked good to me.

There was a hundred head of these yearlings to be separated from the other horses. As I remember we were the most of two days at Nanton. Here the yearlings were loaded into stock cars and shipped away. A week later, here came Bert Pierson and the two Bond brothers with fourteen draft studs from two to six years of age. They were turned loose into our herd. This was breeding season. During the next two weeks we saw a lot of good stud fights, mostly of evening when we were bunching the herd together before putting it in the pasture. Out on the range each stud had his own little bunch of mares. When we began to bunching the herd, that's when the fun started. At the lead of their little bunch of mares, they would meet each other with their mouths open and squealing. Sometimes they would come together standing on their hind legs. Those stud fights were fast and furious. Some of the studs would have teeth marks all over them. Sometimes they would get crippled 'till they couldn't take care of their little bunch of mares for a few days.

The next important job was the branding of the spring colts. There were a hundred and twenty-three head of them. The night before the branding Eckford came to the camp with some extra provisions; with him came the Bond brothers and the Scotchman with a load of wood for the branding fire. There were three round horse corrals, all in a group on the creek bottom near the stable. The mares and colts and the rest of the herd were upon a flat in the west side of the pasture nearly half a mile from the corral.

When we were all mounted and up to the herd, Eckford says, "Now you boys line up behind me. We'll ride into the herd, cut off enough horses to fill two of those round corrals. The third one will be for branding in. We'll just ease this cut down over the little ridge into the corral."

Each time we tried this, the cut ran out around and back into the herd. After three trys at this, Eckford says, "Bard, I'm stuck. What will we do now?"

When I told Eckford to let me run the outfit for awhile he says, "O.K." I told the boys to "take down your ropes. When we cut off the required amount, just whip every horse over the tail you can and keep them a comin' fast as you can, till we get them down on the creek bottom."

194

Eckford had already told me that it would take two days to do the branding, that he had brought along Jim Bond to do the roping of the colts. After the horses were in the corral and the branding irons were heating, Eckford says, "Did you ever do any roping?"

"Yes, a little," says I.

"Well, then maybe you had better do the roping. Just ride in there and rope a colt around the neck and drag it into the vacant corral, where Jim or the Scotchman will wrastle it down."

The wrastler would go along up the rope, get the colt by the ear and nose, twist the colt's head sideways until it fell on its side. Then a rope was put on its front feet. The colt was held on the ground with someone sitting on its head. By the time the branding was done, I had roped another colt and was waiting at the gate to the branding corral. These colts that I was roping were mixed in with other horses. As soon as the colts were branded, they were turned out on the range and another cut was corralled and the colts branded. At four o'clock the branding was done and the herd turned loose on the range.

The kids, or young men, staying with me were staying at the camp and riding line on the herd to see that they didn't head back for Montana. Eckford took me to the ranch to take over Pierson's job of breaking broncs and getting them in shape to sell as mounted-police horses. Counting Eckford's polo ponies, there were supposed to be a hundred geldings running in a pasture near the buildings and a set of good corrals for handling horses.

Each morning after corralling these geldings, Eckford would tell me which five he wanted rode that day. About the first five that he told me to ride got out and bucked like rodeo horses. The first one was a good, breedy-looking black that bucked with his head up. He was a crooked bucker. With that head up I couldn't pull any on the reins to steady myself. Just had to ride him straight up and on a balance, like a tight-rope walker.

Usually of a morning after these five broncs were tied in the barn, Eckford would go somewhere, then I could do as I damn pleased, which was much better. He was a tough one to work for, even wanted me to ride a bronc to wrangle on. I told him that I would quit rather than to use a bronc for wranglin' horses. We had several arguments over this.

One day after I had caught up the five broncs that I was to ride that day, he says, "Catch Monkus for your wrangling horse. Well, I knew Monkus was probably the worst bucking horse he owned, so I turned Monkus back with the others and and kept up a bronc to wrangle on. The next time, he was at the barn to see me ride Monkus. He says, "Why did you let that Monkus horse loose? He's such a nice, gentle horse."

I says, "Look here, Eckford, that's the worst bucking horse you have. I can tell it by his actions."

"No," says Eckford. "I wouldn't lie to you about a horse."

"Probably not," I answered. "Some day I am going to ride this snaky-looking black, and I'll ride him plenty."

Eckford had bought four hundred head of cattle, of which a part was cows and calves. The other half were big steers which were to be taken over onto Mosquito Creek and turned on the range with range cattle. A ranch hand and I were to do this. This was the kind of ride I wanted for Monkus. After saddling him I run him around the corral 'till I had him pretty well warmed up. He didn't buck when I mounted him, seemed pretty well broke to rein. We rounded up the cattle, cut the steers away from the cows and calves.

Eckford says, "Bard, you had better ride down to the house, where the Chinaman cook will have a lunch ready for you." I had to wait a few minutes for Loue, the Chinaman, to fix the lunch. I rolled the lunch up in my slicker and was going to tie it on the back of my saddle. By now Monkus had rested enough so that I had to tie up a hind foot before he would let me tie on the lunch. When I mounted him, he bucked around the corner of the blacksmith shop, right into Brown, the painter, nearly knocking him over backwards. After he quit bucking and we were drifting right along up the bottom to where the steers were now waiting, Monkus downed his head and came near piling me right into an irrigation ditch. I grabbed the saddle horn just in time to save myself from a duckin' in the ditch.

All that day Monkus kept bucking, 'till we were both played out. It was probably a hundred miles that I run that horse before we were back to the ranch. Several times during that day I would leave the ranch hand to drive the steers while I took Monkus for a run out across the country. Next morning Eckford was down at the corral, as usual, when he saw Monkus limping around all drawed up. He says, "Bard, I wish that you wouldn't take Monkus off on any more of those long rides."

I told him not to worry a damn bit about me ever riding that damn ornery horse again. I told Eckford that I was quitting.

He says, "You can't do that now. It's only a couple of days 'till I'll be leaving for Winnipeg, Manitoba to get married. You will just have to stay on and take care of the stock while I'm away for a month or six weeks. Your job will be to ride two of those horses each day. Sorta ride line on those cows and calves. Then ride out to look for any of my horses that are ranging out west of here. Then when the roundup wagons pull in near, it might be well if you went along for a few days to see what cattle I have on the range."

At the ranch there were only three of us beside the Chinaman cook, Louie; Brown, the painter, who was painting most of the buildings and gates; McLean, the ranch foreman, who had a hay camp out about two miles north of the ranch; and myself. The camp was out on the big open range where there was water for the work stock from the ranch. Water for drinking and cooking had to be hauled. The hay crew had some trouble with the range cattle tearing the hay shocks apart. Sometimes the big steers would start to horning the stacks to pieces. Soon as one hay yard was finished, it was fenced, before another yard was started. This hay was to be hauled by bobsled to the ranch for winter feeding. The grass must have been of good quality, for here were steers that looked like cornfed steers. Most all cattle were of the Durham breed. The country was not much settled as yet. Land was cheap, from a dollar to five dollars per acre. There was lots of choice homestead land to be filed on. To me this High River country was a wonderful-looking country, the best part of Alberta.

Out three miles west of Eckford's there was a small stream where the Bond family lived. Mr. Bond, Art, Jim, and another brother all had homesteads. They wanted that I take a homestead near them. I was very much in love with this little valley. Quite often I would ride over to the Bonds', have lunch, then help Frances Bond with the dishes. Frances was about eighteen and a very nice young lady, at least I thought so. This family was from Nova Scotia.

From here I would gallop out across the country to look for some of the Double Oar Lock horses of Eckford. It was five days that I went along with the Oxley roundup wagon where Scottie Henderson was the wagon boss. Working along with this wagon there was the Bar U wagon and the Lane outfit. During these five days I saw a lot of nice country and learned the ways of the roundup. The country was mostly level or rollin'. No badlands or rough breaks. Among the cowboys there were just about everything: Americans, Canadians, breed Indians, Scotchmen, and Englishmen. No one carried a gun. There was a red coat or mounted police along with the roundup, a stock inspector. The Blood or Blackfoot Indians were keeping pace along with the roundup. Here the big-jawed steers were shot down and given to the Indians as beef. There were times when some of the Indians would go on day herd for some of the cowboys. When the roundup wagons were camped along the High River, the Indians would catch trout for the roundup wagons.

Take it on an average, these Alberta cowboys were not as good as the Wyoming cowboys, where a lot of the range hands had come up from Texas in an early day. I don't remember seeing any mavericks up here. The calves were kept branded up. No outfit had more cattle than they could take care of. While I was with the Oxley wagon, Scottie Henderson told me all about how Jumbo McKenzie came to be drowned while working with his wagon. Here is the story as told to me. "Jumbo and Bill Cuttler were working for the '44' outfit down near Fort McLeod. These two men were reppin' with my wagon. Near Willow Creek we were camped at a spring two or three hundred yards from the creek. We were there five days waiting for other roundup wagons to join us. While we were camped here, Jum took this opportunity to go to Fort McLeod to see his wife and infant son, who he had not yet seen. All the time Jum was away, it had rained. Willow Creek was running bank full. Was dangerous for a horse to swim. On the fifth day when we seen Jum come riding down on the opposite side of Willow Creek, we didn't think much about it until we heard Jum yellin' for help. When we got to the creek, all we seen was Jum's horse washed up against a cut bank. Jum wasn't found 'till forty days later. The only way he was identified was by his big gold front tooth and his spurs."

As I remember, it was several miles down Willow Creek that Jumbo McKenzie was found.

About the time Eckford came to the ranch with his bride, I received a letter from my Mother telling of the hig horse boom down at Sheridan. She told me to come home and look after my horses. That evening I rode over to the Bond homestead and said good-bye to my good friends. The next morning Eckford wrote out my time. A ranch hand hitched a team onto the "Democrat" and took my war bag, saddle, and cowboy outfit into High River to catch the narrow-gauge train back to Great Falls, Montana. From there on to Sheridan it was a standard-gauge railroad.

HORSES FOR THE BOER WAR

I HAD JUST ARRIVED BACK IN Sheridan from my trip to Alberta when I hailed a taxi at the depot and loaded in my outfit and headed for town. I bumped into Sam Bell and Bill Dunning, who were looking for a bronc rider. Over at the Checker Board Feed and Livery Stable they had some broncs that were partly broke to ride. Some of them were spoilt horses from the Quarter L ⌐ cavvy down in the Powder River country. There were three horses in among these horses, two bays and a chestnut sorrel, all good-looking horses, seven or eight years of age.

Bill and Sam offered me seven-fifty to ride these three horses from the Checker Board barn up Main Street to the Willis Peak Livery Stable, where Grant Dunning was buying Boer War horses for the Moncreiffe brothers, who had a large contract to furnish the English government with horses to be used over in South Africa. This looked like easy money to me, so I took on the job. The first horse that I caught in the corral was a good-lookin' bay that had an old saddle mark or two on his back. While I was saddling this horse, there were two fellows sitting on the corral fence talking. One said to the other, "Isn't that the horse that bucked off that rider yesterday."

The other fellow says, "Yes. Shut up you damn fool. They're going to have this twister to ride him."

The horse was well broke to the saddle. No trouble to mount. He just stood there with a hump in his back waiting to be grabbed with the spurs. Instead of grabbing this horse with the spurs, I went to petting him along the neck. Soon the hump was out of his back. He was a well-broke horse, only for his bucking. At the Peak stable, Grant Dunning accepted this horse and the chestnut sorrel, which was very much like the bay. The third one to be ridden was a keen-lookin' bay wild as a rabbit. When I roped him, I had some trouble in saddlin' him. I took him to the outside of the corral in the alley to mount. All the time I was tightening up the cinch of the saddle, this horse was on the move circling around me. Off to one side there were a couple of kids standing. One said to the other, "He'll never mount that bronc."

The other kid says, "Don't you fool yourself. When he gets his foot in the stirrup, he's mounted."

Well, that's about the way it was. By the time I was mounted, that bronc was buckin' and bawlin' right up the alley by the Bucket of Blood Saloon, where Bob's Surplus Supply Store now stands. Right across Main Street he went abuckin', right up to the big glass door of the O'Mare grocery store located in the Cady Building. Quite near the door the bronc stopped buckin' long enough to get his wind.

Somewhere along the route, he hit the bridle bit with a front foot, breaking the bit in two. Now the bridle was useless. All the time this bronc was getting his wind, he kept bouncin' up and down. I was afraid that he would kick out one of those big glass windows which would probably cost me fifty bucks to replace it. Along the sidewalk sat an old foreign woman in a single buggy. When I told the lady that she had better get her rig out of there, that I would be comin' out of here and didn't know which way I would be headin', she says, "Mine God, man, you gone clean crazy?"

It was then I said to three men that were standing nearby, "One of you fellows better drive that apple cart away from here. We're liable to buck right over the top of it."

Soon as the rig was driven away, out we came right down the sidewalk toward the Denio flouring mill. The bronc was buckin' and I was workin' him over with both my quirt and spurs. At the end of the walk, Bill Dunning picked us up. After puttin' on another bridle, Bill rode with me to the Peak stable, where Grant accepted this bronc as a Boer War horse.

At this time Uncle Sam was buying cavalry horses which were the tops of the country. Andy Breckenridge, a rancher from the Tongue River, came to town with a half-broke hot-blood horse and offered me five bucks if I would ride this horse and sell him to the U.S. as a cavalry horse. The horse passed the test, and I got the five bucks for riding him. I now had twelve dollars and fifty cents for my half-day's work.

The town of Sheridan was alive with horsemen, horses, bronc riders, who were pullin' off about the same stunts that I did. Every evening after a day's buyin' some of the Moncreiffe men would trail these horses that had been bought out to the Moncreiffe ranch about three miles south of Big Horn. Here these horses were all rode by some of the Moncreiffe bronc riders.

This afternoon, after I had got the twelve-fifty for the riding of the four horses, I got a bronc and rode out to the Bard ranch to say "Hello" to my folks. Tode was already at the Moncreiffe ranch as one of the bronc riders. The next morning I rode over to the Moncreiffe ranch to say hello to Tode and to learn something about the horse inspections. There in what was called the mountain pasture, just south of the ranch buildings and the big alfalfa meadow, there was a set of branding corrals for branding cattle. Here the Moncreiffe riders were riding out the horses that were bought the day before. There were at least a hundred head of these horses. Among them were the three that I had rode the day before. I hadn't been there long 'till I saw a bay horse that was sure enough buckin' with Walt Tompkins. Walt didn't stay only about four bucks 'till he was bucked off.

It was then Malcolm Moncreiffe says to Archie Tompkins, one of their top riders, "Bring your saddle here and take it out of this bronc."

Arch didn't stay any longer than Walt did. This was the same bay that I had rode the day before, the one that I had talked to or petted out of bucking. John Cover, one of the riders, drew the bay that had bucked with me up one street and down another. John says, "Is this the horse that done all that bucking with you?"

When I told John I didn't think so, he says, "You can't fool me. Your marks are still on him."

John was a good rider. It didn't bother him none to ride this bronc. I spent most all day here at these brandin' corrals where the inspections were held. This wasn't horse-inspection day, so I just stuck around most of the day watchin' the ridin' and visiting with the riders who I already knew: the two Tompkins brothers, Arch and Walt, Frank Wood, Albert Pierce, Luther Dunning, Tode Bard, and another one or two that I don't remember.

That evening I rode back to the Bard ranch where I spent a week's time in getting some of my own horses in shape to sell to the Moncreiffe's as Boer War horses. These I sold to Grant Dunning, who was not so practical as Malcolm Moncreiffe as a horse-buyer. The age limit was five up to nine years. The price was forty dollars per head paid. Grant was a good buyer. Anything above a four-year-old on up Grant would buy, just so the horse had good wind, eyesight, and not too many blemishes.

Grant sure knew horses and how to handle bronc riders. He was Moncreiffes' main stay. Was the corral boss on inspection days. It was the Moncreiffe outfit that started the biggest horse boom that was ever heard of anywhere, which saved many a rancher from going broke.

Prior to 1900, horses were worthless. No sale for them, only a few choice horses as driving teams and some work stock. Some cow outfits were buying a few young geldings as cowponies. Some of the cow outfits were raising their own saddle stock. At this time everything was cheap. The county was hard pressed for money. I remember along in the 1890's when I needed a new saddle and didn't have the cash to buy one, Mother said to gather in enough fat cattle to buy one. From the range, in among our cattle I gathered in two fat, three-year-old dry heifers, a fat dry cow, and a three-year-old steer, which I sold to the Coslett brothers, Joe and Al, who had a butcher shop in Sheridan. These four head of fat cattle I sold for the sum of sixty dollars at the Otto Kettleson hardware store, where he was selling a saddle that was made by a saddle-maker at Fort Collins, Colorado.

After paying Otto fifty dollars for one of these saddles it didn't leave me much cash, only ten bucks, which nowadays would only buy about what a fellow could put in his vest pocket.

During the Moncreiffes' horse-buying and selling nearly every one in the country and in the town were getting Moncreiffe money. Just about every rancher and what horse men that didn't near give their horse herd away prior to this time were selling horses for forty dollars per head. Some of the cow outfits were selling off a part of their cavvy and replacing them with three- and four-year-old geldings. Some of the town people were selling their driving horses. The Moncreiffes were buying most everything that would fill the bill or come near to it. Captain Heygart, the inspector for the English, didn't know too much about the age of a horse. This was left up to his veterinarian, who wasn't the least bit particular about the age of a horse, just so it wasn't too gray up around the ears.

A part of these Boer War horses did live to reach South Africa. Some died on the way across the ocean and were dumped overboard as fish feed. Well, the vet knew just about how things were going, so he wasn't particular about age, which helped many a rancher to dispose of the older horses.

The Moncreiffes' company had horse-buyers out in all ten of the western states, buying war horses. Most of the horses bought within a hundred miles of Sheridan were trailed overland to the Moncreiffe ranch. The railroad was getting a two-way go at this company money. They were freightin' horses into Sheridan and freightin' them out in stock cars. Nearly every concern in the county was profiting from company money. The ranchers were now able to pay off their debts and to buy much-needed new stuff of all kinds. With all these horse men, ranchers, and bronc riders in and out of Sheridan, most of the business men in town were getting their share of the money. The sporting houses with their girls and dance halls down along Grinnell Avenue were out with their mitts gettin' their money from off the bronc riders and whoever else had horse-money to spend.

After a week spent at the Bard ranch selling my horses that would do for war horses, I went into Sheridan and became one of the riders. My work was gentling broncs so that they would pass inspection, at the Peak barn. There were a lot of green-broke or half-bridle-wise horses coming into Sheridan that needed more riding before they could be sold. That was us bronc riders' job—to give these horses a little education. There were some horses that had had too much education and needed a little of it taken out of them. The horses that were trailed into Sheridan were either corralled at the Checker Board barn down near Big Goose Creek in back of where the Crescent Hotel now is located, or at the East Side barn where Lou's Transfer is now located. From these two barns there was no telling which way we would be riding until these broncs were a little better bridle wised. Where these broncs bucked the most was down Grinnell Avenue, where the dance-hall girls could see the fun. I don't know what the other riders were makin'. With me, I was makin' anywhere from five to ten dollars per day. I was spending it just about as fast as I made it, with Sheridan being a wide-open town. Everything was booming, both day and night. Of a night there was a crowd down along Grinnell Avenue where there were a half-dozen sporting house-dance halls. Here at the Castle, the best place along the avenue, there was always a crowd of men from everywhere: rangemen, railroaders, clerks, office men, and a few coal miners. The cowboys and the railroaders didn't get along none too well. There was a sort of rivalry between them. One night some of us riders were at the Castle, just standin' around with our backs to the wall watching the dancing, a rider called Ed was standing not far from me. He was just standing there not sayin' a word to anyone. From a side room off from the dance hall came a blonde-haired railroader stewed up a little. When Blondy came to where Ed was standing, he hauled off and floored Ed for no reason at all. When Ed got back on his feet, he was fighting like a wildcat. He knocked Blondy down and was sitting on his chest, tryin' to twist his boot heel into Blondy's eye, when in walks the night marshal.

When he started to arrest Ed, I told this night bull that he was taking the wrong man. The bull says, "What you got to say about it? I'll arrest you, too."

I told him to go ahead if he thought that would do any good. Soon as he found out his mistake, he took Blondy and left for uptown. I think he took Blondy out around the corner and let him go. In less than half an hour there was a loud pop which sounded like a six-shooter being shot off. From a side room came a man that looked very much like Blondy. He was screamin', "O, my God, I've got something that I'll carry to my grave." There was a big gash across his forehead, and the blood was running down his face.

I thought the fellow had been shot. So did everyone else. As I made a run for the door, I says, "Come on, boys, let's get out of here."

As I was going through the door, a big gal grabbed me around the neck and says, "Take me with you."

Says I, "Turn me loose. I'm leavin' here."

She didn't turn me loose until we were across the road near Little Goose Creek, then she asked what happened.

"Damned if I know. It looked to me as if someone got shot. If so, we don't want to be a witness to any shootin' scrape."

It was then someone came up and said the guy got an empty beer bottle broke over his head. I started to leave for uptown and my room, which was up over the George L. Smith Drugstore, a long, two-story frame building on the corner, where the dime store is now located. This dance-hall gal says, "Haven't you got a room that we can share together for tonight."

"I've got a room, but I'm not sharing it with you. If you get caught in my room, it would probably cost us a hundred bucks each."

When I asked the girl why she didn't want to go back to the

dance hall, she told me that her home was in Iowa, that she was supposed to be working in a candy kitchen while out here on vacation. I told her the best thing she could do was to finish her vacation, then beat it for home. This big, good-lookin' girl says, "The vacation is finished. I'm leaving here soon as my grip is packed. It's too tough a life for me." Well, that's about the way I felt about it.

The soldiers from Fort McKenzie, a troop of infantrymen, weren't allowed down along Grinnell Avenue, probably an order from the commanding officer. Fort McKenzie was about two miles north of Sheridan. These soldier boys usually walked from the fort into Sheridan, where they began making eyes at the town boys' girls. Of course the town boys wasn't standing for nothing like this, so they organized a little gang of about a dozen young men. They were called the Dirty Dozen. One Saturday night when a bunch of soldier boys was walking into town, the Dirty Dozen were waiting for them in the alley back of the Bucket of Blood Saloon. The soldiers were just about to enter Main Street when the town boys attacked them. The fight didn't last long 'till the soldiers were heading up High School Hill with the town boys chasing them out of town.

This troop of infantry was only at the fort from 1899 'till in the fall of 1900 or spring of 1901. They were relieved by a troop of Negro cavalry. It wasn't long 'till some colored gals showed up. The only place for these women to shack up was farther down along Grinnell Avenue to Sheridan Avenue. Here's where the colored cavalrymen spent most of their time while in town.

Among the cavalry horses there were two, a bay and a brown, that would buck off the Negro soldiers as fast as they tried to ride them. When the commanding officer offered to pay a certain price to anyone who could ride these two geldings, it was Harry Brennan, the top bronc rider for the Moncreiffe outfit, who rode the two buckers. As I remember it was a Sunday, the spring of 1901, that the riding took place near the fort. There was quite a crowd to see the show. Harry gave the crowd their money's worth. He did a wonderful job of riding these two hard buckers. This I know for sure, 'cause I was there.

The colored troop was only there a year or two and was then transferred somewhere else. More white soldiers were brought to Fort McKenzie. Soon, however, the fort was abandoned for awhile, then it was made into a mental institution for war veterans.

When the colored troop was transferred, some of their women folks continued to make their homes down along Grinnell and the end of Sheridan Avenue. The stock route through the east side of town was along Sheridan Avenue, across Little Goose Creek Bridge, under the railroad grade, over the viaduct, and continued on down Sheridan Avenue to Eighth Street. From there the stock route continued on north near the railroad track about four hundred yards to the Burlington Stock Yards.

In trailing war horses to and from these yards, we knew quite a lot about Grinnell and Sheridan Avenue. It was only a day or two after the run-in with the candy-kitchen gal that Grant said, "Pistol, don't you want to go along with me out to the Moncreiffe ranch where they are short on riders and go to work for the company."

As I remember, Bill Dunning, Grant's brother, took over the horse-buying at the Peak stable while Grant was away. Grant and I trailed some war horses from the Peak barn out to the Moncreiffe ranch, where Grant took over the job as corral boss and foreman of the bronc riders of which I was one. Some of the riders had already quit the company. Said it was too dangerous riding up there at those branding corrals. There were too many boulders on the outside of the corrals for a horse to buck over.

209

Now the only bronc riders the company had were Grant and Luther Dunning, their nephew Albert Pierce, all from Otter Creek. There was Wild Horse Jerry, who had recently trailed a bunch of horses across the Big Horn Mountains from the basin country, Tode, and myself. With the amount of horses arriving daily at the Moncreiffe ranch, the company needed at least four more riders. We were paid seventy-five dollars per month with board and room at the ranch house and bunkhouse. We were working long hours in riding all horses trailed to the ranch and inspection corrals. The very first job consigned to Tode and me was to put in five days at the Jim Kemp corrals riding about twenty-five spoiled horses. These horses were in a small pasture near the corrals. This Jim Kemp place was owned by Jim Kemp, an Englishman, a horse man who came here along in the early 1880's. In the 1890's, Kemp sold his hundred-and-sixty-acre homestead to the Moncreiffe brothers, Malcolm and William. The morning we corralled these horses, William was there. There were two RL horses in the bunch that we were told not to ride. They were hard-bucking horses. Soon as William left, these were the first two horses that we did ride, thinking that we might buy them cheap. In among these horses there was every-thing: buckers, stampers, fallen-back horses, and one or two corral-balky horses. One of these balky ones was the same brown gelding that we worked on the old bed-wagon stagecoach while working for the RL up on the Musselshell.

I was yet a little peeved at this work horse for the way he used to balk. When I mounted this horse, he began to balk and run over to the corral fence, where he tried to get rid of me. When I began working on him with my spurs and quirting him alongside the head, he soon left there and took across the Kemp flat. One day Tode said he would ride this good-lookin' RL horse, a three-year-old Thoroughbred black gelding that we had named Paddy. Paddy was the one that we were supposed not to ride, which we bought from the company for twenty dollars. When Tode came back from Big Horn, he sure had on a big grin. He says, "Down there at Big Horn, Jake McAdams just got in from the Crow Reservation with some horses. Among them was a buckskin that bucked off everyone that tried to ride him. After taking up a collection of four dollars and sixty-five cents, we led this horse out onto the space in front of the Skinner store, where we took the bronc down, put on my saddle. When he started to get on his feet, I mounted him, and got the easiest money that I ever made."

As I remember, come inspection day these horses that Tode and I had been working on for five days, except the bay RL horse that had curbed himself on one hind leg while jumping the corral fence, were not bought by the company but were put through inspection on approval. If the horse passed inspection, it was paid for by the company. Otherwise the horse was property of the owner.

Wild Horse Jerry trailed in some horses from the basin. Among the bunch there were three ornery ones: a buckskin and a bay, both eight or nine years old, studs that had been caught out of the wild bunch by Jerry. There was a big chestnut gelding that was ornery. Of these three horses, Tode, Jerry, and I drew straws to see which horse we were to ride. Jerry drew the little buckskin stag. Tode drew the bay, which left me with the chestnut. Jerry was the first to ride his buckskin, which bucked around and fell down. When Tode mounted the old bay stag, he bucked for a while then quit bucking, reached around, and grabbed Tode by the leg with his teeth. When Tode quit the stag, he got kicked on the hand good and hard.

Billie Moncreiffe was standing there closeby. He says, "Take the saddle off. We won't fool with that kind."

When I went to take off the saddle, the stag layed back his ears, opened his mouth, and was about to rush me. I started to hit him over the head with a hard-twist rope. Billie yells, "Don't hit him over the head. You might knock out an eye."

At that I hit the horse down across the head, front footed him, threw him down, and we took off the saddle. We three were a little sore about what Billie had said. Grant and the other riders had gone, probably to move some horses from one pasture to another. When my turn came to ride, I mounted the big chestnut sorrel. He started to buck, changed his mind, then tried to jump out of the corral. He landed up on the top rail on his belly and was sorta balancing there. I slid off over his rump and ran back out of his way to where Billie and the other riders were. Tode and Jerry were standing. We three were for quitting, when Billie apologized for what he had said about hitting the stag over the head. Tode's hand was pretty badly swollen. He did quit. Saddled up the Paddy horse that we had bought for twenty bucks, then headed for the Bard ranch. Now we were really short-handed for riders.

Next day or two there were about a hundred head of horses trailed in from the Otter Creek country. Bob Walsh was one of the men with these horses. Grant knew the men and most of the horses. This was the first time that I saw Robert Walsh. Grant said Bob had been working on a ranch at forty dollars per month. He was only at the inspection grounds two or three days, 'till he headed for some of the western states as a horse-buyer. He made a lot of money for himself and the company.

Soon Mr. Wallop, who owned a ranch just to the south and west of the Moncreiffe ranch, went out to Oregon and Washington to buy in war horses. He owned a ranch, a big ranch, that joined the Moncreiffe ranch. Mr. Wallop, an Englishman, was a good friend of the Moncreiffes. During the next two years the

One hog-tied calf.
"With a sharp pocket knife
it didn't take long to freeze off a left ear."

Branding at the Gallatin Ranch, 1918,
with Floyd Bard doing the roping
"The wrastlers said if I roped calves that way the next day,
they would chuck me in the crick."

Mabel Almy Bard.
"For her wedding present from me, I gave Mabel
the beautiful brown seven-year-old gelding, Neri."

four men, the Moncreiffe brothers, Robert Walsh, and Oliver H. Wallop, made a lot of money handling war horses.

Among the Otter Creek horses brought in by Robert Walsh there were several Circle Bar horses owned by Levi Howes. There were three horses that were fairly well broke to buck, as well as to ride. Grant and Luther Dunning and I drew numbers as to what horse we would ride. Luther drew the grey gelding raised by the "21" horse outfit. Grant drew a big dark-chestnut sorrel that had quite a scar on one thigh where he had been bitten by a wolf at some time. I drew old Limber Ass, a big light bay, a limber sort of horse when he bucked. Grant said that old Limber usually piled his rider when he bucked. Luther's "21" grey just bucked straight ahead, Wolf whirled around and around with Grant 'till he fell down. When I mounted old Limber, he just stood there with a humped-up back. After I had petted him awhile, he trotted off like any broke horse. Malcolm said, "You had better ride him to lunch and back to see if there's any buck in him."

It was a mile and a half to the ranch house where we ate. All the way there and back I kept easing old Limber along so that he wouldn't buck me off. Just got back to the corral when Limber blew up. Made one big buck. It was then I said, "Who got off him?" And I pulled off my saddle and turned him into the corral with the other horses.

There was a bunch of horses trailed in from the Tongue River country. Several of the McCarthy horses were in the bunch. Among these McCarthy horses there was a gray gelding, well broke to ride, but he had the habit of fallin' over backwards, breaking the cantle of my saddle. Now I had to have another saddle. Didn't want a new saddle to break in on this kind of a job, so I got a second-hand one.

One inspection day Grant says, "Pistol, guess it's you and me for it. We'll do the riding today."

213

Here's about the way things stood. Just a few feet out from the corral gate there were two big posts set in the ground about fifteen feet apart, with a two-inch rope cable stretched tight from post to post. In the corral there were men roping and bridling horses with snaffle-bit bridles. The horses were led to the outside, where the reins of the bridle were wrapped two or three times around the cable. About forty yards from there was a little frame shed, where there was a bookkeeper. Captain Heygatt and Wall, his vet, were near this shed. When the riding started, Grant and I came out mounted. We trotted our horses out by the captain to a distance of a hundred yards, then we came back on a fast gallop right up to the small shed. Here the captain looked the horses over for blemishes, listening to their breathing, and looked to see if the horse had good eyes. Then the vet would look at the horse's mouth for the age and then the color of the horse. The age was supposed to be from five to nine. Height was from fourteen two on up. The tall ones made good mounts for the officers. With Grant and me, as soon as we rode out one horse there was another one waiting. It didn't take long to change the saddle from one horse to another, just like a relay race. Now and then we would get a bucking horse.

When one of the horses bucked right up to the captain he said, "Ah, Bard, and don't you know I don't mind these high gallopers. They show some spirit."

But when some horse showed a little too much spirit, it was put back in the bronc bunch for more riding. Horses were coming to the Moncreiffe ranch so fast that we were nearly swamped. There were horses in all the pastures of the Moncreiffe and Wallop ranches. Horses that were trailed or shipped in from quite a distance were turned in on the big alfalfa meadow to fill up and rest for a week before inspection. With winter comin' on, the company had a crew of men building corrals and

214

making a new inspection ground, about a quarter of a mile to the east of the Moncreiffe buildings near Little Goose Creek. The corrals were located where the Gallatin ranch barn now stands. This was a good location, well sheltered with brush. Trabing Creek near the corrals was only about a hundred yards from the county road.

Just before the company moved into their new quarters, a horse started bucking with me for an open shed. The buck before it went in the shed, I quit the bronc, hit the ground with most of the weight on my right foot, throwing my ankle out of place or spraining it badly and breaking a bone in my foot. Now I was out of the bronc riding for at least six weeks.

When I went back to the Moncreiffe place, the outfit had moved into their new quarters. Grant was yet corral boss. There were a lot of new bronc riders. Harry Brennen, Bud Lumbeck, Ed Smart (called Goo Coo Eyes 'cause he was always makin' eyes at the girls), a slender-built rider, and a good rider called Turkey Neck 'cause he had a long neck. In later years this man became sheriff at Wheatland, Wyoming. There was Ed Thorp, Willis Cooley, Jim Hackley, Johnnie Kraft, and others.

While the inspection was going on, Malcolm Moncreiffe had the riders on the lookout for ponies that might make good polo ponies. Malcolm had already established a polo field on his Hanna Creek ranch; there training polo ponies were Guy Wood and John Cover, who became a wonderful polo-player. Malcolm at this time was shipping trained polo ponies to England, where he sold them at a good price. Tode and I never went to work for the company. We bought horses which we sold to the company. Then we bought some reject horses that the captain refused to buy. We were living at the Bard ranch with our folks and doing ranch work. The horse business was sort of a side issue. With so many horses at the Moncreiffe ranch, there

215

wasn't much room or feed for their cows. The cows were mostly fed hay on other ranches.

On the first of March, 1901, Moncreiffes' outfit trailed nine hundred cows to the Bard ranch and bought hay for a month's feed for these cows. Along with the cows came Roy Garber with a big, stout team, a hay wagon and rack that would hold about two tons of hay. During the next thirty days we were sure busy hauling hay to these cows, then they were trailed to the Moncreiffes' Dutch Creek ranch and pastures to be pastured for the next eight or nine months, depending on the weather conditions.

Along in May, 1901, I bought a five-year-old half-broke gelding. One day when I went to ride this gelding he started bucking. Bucked off the ear bridle that had no throat latch. When he throwed up his head and began running, I yet had the reins in my hand. This bronc ran for a half-mile or more before he slowed down to a trot. I jumped off but held on to the bridle reins. After putting the bridle back on to the bronc's head and tying it hard and fast, I started back to the house. On a steep hillside I met Tode coming to look for me. All at once this bronc blew up. The fourth buck he lost his footing, and we piled in the bottom of a washout or draw, with the bronc on top. This time I got most of the peelin' scraped off one side of my face when I took a header into the grass, a gash over my left eye that required four stitches, a broken collar bone, and a dislocated left knee.

This laid me up for another six or eight weeks. The bronc I sold to Grant Dunning, who was at the Peak barn buying war horses. Grant paid me forty dollars for this buckin' bronc. The company was yet going strong with horse inspections most every day. The horses were trailed to and from Sheridan, not along the Little Goose Valley where the highway is now located, but on the old dirt road on the bench land just to the north and west of the valley, down by the girls' school, then on into Sheridan. At this time there were no cars to block the traffic or frighten the horses while being trailed to the Burlington Stock Yards.

Late in the fall of 1901, the company moved their inspection outfit to Grand Junction, Colorado. During that winter the company held regular inspections the same as they had held at the Moncreiffe ranch. By the following spring, 1902, the horse business was over. The company shipped their outfit back to Sheridan, then on to their Big Horn ranch. About two hundred reject horses were shipped to Verona, then trailed five or six miles to the Dutch Creek ranch where they were sold to whoever wanted them. The Bards bought several head of the rejects, which were very useful horses.

Come Fourth of July and Sheridan's second big wild west show of three days. The company yet had some of their top riders, along with several horses that had a little too much spirit for the captain and galloped too high and crooked. During this three-day show, it was the Moncreiffe outfit that furnished most of the riders and buckin' horses.

The first day of the show, Harry Brennen won the first new saddle by ridin' a hard-buckin' bay gelding belonging to the company. The second day, Ed Thorp won the new saddle by ridin' Keystone Brownie, a company horse. The third day Johnnie Blocker won the third new saddle, whose horse it was I don't know. The cow roping was won by Jim Carpenter, a Crow Indian. George Gardener, who was riding my rope horse, got second money in the roping.

Walt Granger was driving his four high-spirited bays on the old stagecoach. When the stagecoach was being attacked by the Indians during the sham battle between the cowboys and In-

217

dians, Walt's four-horse outfit ran away, turning over the coach and breaking one passenger's collar bone and spraining another passenger's ankle. The lead team broke loose from the coach and headed off towards Prairie Dog Creek. This show was near the Park Street bridge over Little Goose Creek, east of Sheridan.

There were no chutes to saddle and mount the buckers in. Just had to be snubbed to some cowboy's saddle horn while being saddled and mounted. The little corral on the east side of Little Goose Creek up near the brickyard would hold only about eight or ten of the wild long-horn three- and four-year-old heifers that were used as ropin' stock.

It was a good wild west show that we saw. It was only a few days after the show that a young barber, about my age, and I went over to Buffalo. There we bought a two-chair barber shop from Jim Wright, who was retiring. Mother thought this a good idea, that I should take on something easy until my broken shoulder and knee were sound once more. I left what stock I owned at the Bard ranch and on the range 'till I tried out this venture.

I took one saddle horse with me, a big chestnut sorrel that I named Sandy. Sandy was put out in a pasture at the edge of Buffalo, so that he would be handy in case that I wanted to do some riding. Right from the start Jim, my partner, and I hit it off O.K. We rented a room from Mrs. Weber, a widow lady who I had known since 1890. Her rooming house was just across the street on the opposite corner from where Dad and the Swede cowboy had their restaurant in 1892. This was only about two blocks from where Maggie Jess yet had her dance hall.

With the shop we were doing all right. With me just learning the trade, Jim kept me busy honin' razors. When my right hand played out, I would go it left-handed. Having been a sorta roundup barber during the summer of 1895, it wasn't long 'till

I was doing barber work same as Jim, but not so fast. The shaving was easy. When it came to hair-cutting, that was more difficult, especially when someone came into the shop that hadn't seen a barber shop during the past three or four months, with whiskers and hair four or five inches long. That was a difficult job for me to tackle. But with instructions from Jim, I made out fairly well. There were four or five cases of barber's itch in town. The worst case was a young man who played the piano at Mag Jess's dance hall. These men would wait for my chair, as they said I took plenty of time in shaving them and didn't hurt their faces as much as a regular barber. With some kind of special after-shave face lotion this itch was completely cured up.

A barber named Miller came to Buffalo from the Black Hills of South Dakota. He was looking to set up a barber shop. I told Miller that he needn't look any farther for a location, that I would sell out my half-interest in our shop. This was agreeable with Jim. Well, I wasn't cut out to be a barber. It hadn't taken me long to find this out.

A day of two after selling my interest in the barber shop, I met Mr. Holland on the street. He was the owner of the 4H cow outfit, not far from Buffalo. Mr. Holland, who had known me for years, said that Josh, his top cowboy, was leaving the roundup wagon for a week or two, and that they were already shorthanded. Would I go to the roundup wagon that was now gathering beef down along Clear Creek? He said I could use Josh's bed and ride his string of horses. When I asked about the horses, Mr. Holland says, "Yes. They're all gentle except two, Black Diamond and Jimmie Hicks. You won't have to ride them unless you want to."

I told him that I probably wouldn't want to since my knee wasn't yet healed, and sometimes, with too much weight on it, the knee joint would sorta pop out of place, making me lame for awhile.

Mr. Holland had a good little cow outfit. With me everything was O.K. up to the fifth day, when the wagon boss caught out of the cavvy a good-looking young bay gelding, which he told me was one of Josh's string. All the time I was saddling this horse, he was acting sorta spooky. Just as I was ready to mount him, I heard one of the cowboys say, "Do you suppose that barber can ride Jimmie Hicks."

Well, I was givin' the cowboys no chance to call me yellar by takin' off the saddle. When I mounted Jimmie, he ran about fifty yards before he broke and started buckin'. At the first buck, my knee slipped a little out of place. It was then that I grabbed the saddle horn and rode this fast-buckin' bronc 'till he quit buckin'. When I stepped off onto the ground, I was so lame, and my knee hurt so bad, it was all I could do to hobble back to the bed wagon where the cavvy was yet in the rope corral.

I told the boss what I thought of him for getting me crippled up again. After one of the cowboys had caught and saddled Sandy for me, I headed back for Buffalo. I put Sandy in the feed stable for a few days until my knee was better.

TAKING INVOICE

DURING THE NEXT FEW DAYS, I sorta took invoice of my life from start to finish, up to the present time. It was just about one year previous that I had put a homestead filing on 160 acres of land adjoining the Bard ranch to the north and east. To the south and west there was the Frank Woods homestead, which was fenced. My 160 acres included the forty-acre water gap in between the two ranches. The other 120 acres lay to the east side of Mead

Creek. The more I thought of that homestead, the more I thought of getting married and having a ranch of my very own. As to a wife, I didn't even have a steady girl. In fact, no girl at all. It was then that a family living three miles from the Bard ranch came into Buffalo headin' for the Ten Sleep Creek up in the Big Horns, to the south and west of Buffalo, on a ten-day fishin' trip. In this party there were three young men, brothers, and a sister who had lost her husband. There was J. H. (Joe) Rebman, his wife, Myra, their two young sons, and a Miss Mabel Almy, a sister of Mrs. Rebman. I was asked to join this fishing party.

"O.K.," says I. "If you will drive the wagon over to the grocery store, I'll buy some provisions."

From the feed stable I got Sandy and rode along with Miss Almy and the two neighbor boys. The rest of the party rode in the wagon, which was loaded to the brim. After leaving Buffalo we headed south some ten or twelve miles towards Crazy Woman Creek. At the foot of Charley Sister's Hill, we made camp for the night. Our four-horse team had made a little more than forty miles that day; everyone was tired. The two teams were tired and needed an all-night's rest before pulling that heavily loaded wagon to the top of that steep hill, which would bring us nearly on top of the Big Horn Mountains.

Next morning we moved camp up over the divide to Ten Sleep Creek where the fishing was good. There was a nice place to camp with plenty of grass for the horses. The Rebman family I had never met before this trip. Miss Mabel Almy I had met a couple of times before: first, on the Fourth of July, 1901, when there was quite a celebration at Story; and again in the Messick Dry Goods Store in Sheridan. Several young folks from our community went to Story on horseback for the celebration. On the way home that afternoon, my girl friend, Stella, and I got caught out along the road in a downpour of rain. For shelter we rode in to Dudley Thurmond's ranch home on Mead Creek, about four miles from the Bard ranch. Here visiting Miss Ella Thurmond over the weekend was Miss Almy from Sheridan. While Miss Thurmond was helping Stell off with her wet jacket, Miss Almy helped me off with my wet coat. My shoulder had not yet mended from the break which I received when the bronc landed on top of me two months earlier. We stayed here a couple of hours getting dried out and getting acquainted.

A month later, while in Sheridan, I dropped into the Messick Dry Goods Store to buy a handkerchief and to renew my acquaintance with Miss Almy. After visiting a few minutes, she says, "What was that you wanted? A pair of socks?" She just laughed, went and got the socks, and wrapped them up and handed them to me saying, "Thank you. Come again, some time."

I didn't see Miss Almy again until I was headin' for Buffalo to buy the barber shop. This time about all we said was "Hello" and "Good-bye."

Now here we were together on the Ten Sleep Creek in the same camp with the fishing party. We camped during the next six days. The first day every one went fishing except Mrs. Rebman, who stayed at camp to take care of her two small sons, Harold and Ben. Along Ten Sleep there was some down timber and big boulders to climb over, which was quite a difficult job with my lame knee. That evening while we were headin' for camp with plenty of nice trout, I just about wrecked the seat of my pants on a fallen log. It was the only pair I had with me. When we got into camp, I doubled over a log while Leona, the young widow, took needle and thread and mended the tear. In doing so she sewed my drawers hard and fast to the seat of the pants, but that didn't make any difference, as I went to bed with my pants on.

Four of us men slept out in the big open, where the weather got quite chilly during the night. We were all in one bed, with no room to spare. We slept spoon fashion. When one turned over, we all turned over.

I didn't go fishing any more after that first day. I stayed around camp, looked after the horses, cut up some fire wood for cooking, and did that kind of work while the others went fishing.

One day Mabel stayed in camp to help her sister with some work. Already I was deeply in love with this girl who had big blue eyes and rosy cheeks. We sat together on the big log in back of the campfire. Mabel told me about herself. She had been born in Aurora, Illinois, and after her parents died, she had lived part of the time with a brother in Chicago and part, with a sister in Aurora. She spent her summers on a farm with an aunt. There she would help milk the cows, take care of the chickens, and was happiest when she drove old Nig on the sulky rake.

Right there on that log we drew up a lot of our future plans. When we rode down off of the Big Horn Mountains, we were two of the happiest persons in the world. So was Mother and Dad when I told them about my future wife. Dad says, "Son, we are happy to know that you are getting married and quitting your wild ways. We'll do all we can, Mother and I, to help you get started on your homestead."

When they met Mabel for the first time, they were more pleased than ever. About all I had to start with was a good bay team that was broke out the year before, which was now at the Bard ranch. Ranging with the Bard cattle there were close to fifty head of cattle, all wearin' the Quarter Circle UE brand, which belonged to me. I also owned about thirty head of horses, of which a part were young broke saddle geldings. I didn't have near enough cash on hand to buy what was needed for my raw homestead, where there was nothing much except a lot of sagebrush.

It was near the first of September that W. F. (Bill) Cody came to Sheridan for the purpose of buying some bucking horses and a few cavalry horses for his wild west show. At this time Cody was buying extra horses and contacting some good riders for his show, which would be sailing for Europe in the early spring of 1903.

When I heard of this, I saddled up Sandy and took another one of my saddle horses and headed for Sheridan and the Sheridan Inn, where Cody made his headquarters while in town. Cody paid me sixty dollars for Sandy, an ideal cavalry horse. My other horse he refused to buy. This horse I sold to a rancher at forty dollars.

By the last of November I had a log cabin and bank barn built on my homestead. And at high noon on December 2, Mabel and I were married in Sheridan by Rev. W. A. Petzoldt, pastor of the First Baptist Church. A snow storm had begun the night before, and by the next noon there was more than fifteen inches of snow on the level. Following the wedding, the Rebman family gave a turkey dinner for us. Many guests had been invited both from the country and the town. Owing to the storm, none came in from the country. Among the town guests there were only a few that I had ever met before.

By the time we had our rig packed and ready to start for home, it was storming hard, with snow now hub-deep. After saying good-bye to the wedding guests, we headed up Prairie Dog Creek, ten miles to Mead Creek. By now there was a wind blowing the snow into drifts. There were places along the Prairie

Dog where the fences were drifted over, with only a few fence posts showing on either side of the county road. It was a hard pull for the team wading through those belly-deep drifts. We weren't in the road more than half the time. Came near turning the rig over a few times. Just before dark we drove into the Bard ranch, where my family had prepared a wedding supper for about fifty guests. Owing to the storm not many guests arrived.

For wedding presents we really did get a lot of useful things. Among them were a dozen hens and a rooster, which started us off in the chicken business.

For her wedding present from me, I gave Mabel the beautiful brown seven-year-old gelding, Neri, that I had bought from the Levi Wood ranch over on McCormack Creek. This was the best saddle horse that I ever owned, three-quarters Thoroughbred, about fifteen hands high, weighing one thousand pounds.

HOMESTEADING YEARS

AFTER WE WERE SETTLED IN OUR LITTLE HOMESTEAD with our little bunch of cattle, plenty of hay hauled from the Bard ranch, and with fresh beef, milk, and eggs, we were sitting pretty.

The only thing we were bothered with were some grub-line riders. These were mostly cowboys that were out of work. They just rode the grub line from one ranch to another, stopping and staying at a ranch until they thought their welcome was running out, then they would move on.

Mabel wasn't used to this kind of doings. She didn't like it, not at all. One fellow came and stayed for five days. He was

225

too lazy to take care of his own saddle horse. Jest set in the cabin and read most of the time, while Mabel went with me to do the feeding. I could have done the feeding by myself all right, but this was an excuse for her to be away from the cabin while I wasn't there.

After this, when one of those line-riders showed up, we just didn't have room for them to spend the night. They were welcome to a meal. Then they had to move on, 'cause we had no room to spare in our little cabin.

One day a neighbor came to our place and wanted to do some horse-swapping. He wanted to trade for my good bay team. He said that he would give me five coming-yearling Durham heifers and three sorrel broncs for the team. This neighbor only lived about two miles from our place. Mabel and I went home with Al to see what the swapping stuff looked like. Two of the broncs were a matched team of sorrel geldings, only halter broke. There was a halter-broke sorrel mare of saddle stock. One of the geldings had a wire cut in the hock joint. In the feed lot there were about fifty head of yearling heifers. Al says, "Just ride in there and cut out the five that you want."

Well, that's what Mabel and I did. Up Mead Creek we headed with the five red heifers and the three broncs. Al went along with us to get the bay team. Then I had to go to where some of my horses were ranging out in the hills for another broke team. I had named them Jake and Brownie. The bronc with the wire-cut hock I tied up in the barn. Every day I would bathe that wire cut with hot water and a little turpentine in the water. Come spring time that bronc was all healed up. He had only a little scar.

Those five red heifers were the starter of our milk stock. That winter Mabel and I broke out several head of broncs, both to work in harness and as saddle horses. Once a week we went somewhere to a dance, usually in a sled. All that winter there was plenty of snow for good sledding. There were times when the snow was most too deep for one team. We would hitch four horses to the sled, and a crowd of us young married folks would head off for some dance. There were times on some side hills we would turn the sled over. That didn't make any difference. We just shook the snow from off the robes and quilts, then piled back into the sled again. That was during our first winter.

Three winters later it was a little different when the babies began to arrive, but it didn't stop us young married folks from goin' to the dances. We just bundled up the babies and took them along.

The spring of 1903 was an exceptionally early spring. By the first of April, I was out breaking prairie sod with Jake and the team of sorrel geldings. I didn't have a riding plow, just one of those old foot-warmers, where you walked behind that prairie-breaker and held on to the handles. The two lines were tied together and hung around the plowman's neck. Jake was a good furrow horse, didn't need much reining.

Down near the cabin where the roundup wagons had camped so often, the ground was packed down 'till it was tough plowing. A quarter-mile to the east where the roundups were held and the herd was bedded down for night guarding, the plowing was tough. It was all three horses could do to pull the twelve-inch breaking plow through this tough sod. It was tough to work up into a seed bed.

Out from around our cabin near the spring, there were yet some picket stakes where the cowboys used to stake out their night horses. About where our cabin stood was where Rattlesnake Jack, the wolfer, was camped the first time I met him. This was the favorite spot of the PK outfit to camp on while rounding up the Mead Creek country.

All that summer when I had riding to do out on the range, Mabel rode Neri and went along. We usually took along a lunch. When it came noon, we would ride up some draw or ravine to a spring where cattle were watering. There at the little spring I would lay down on my belly and drink like most rangemen. Mabel couldn't get used to that way of drinking, so she tied a tin cup onto her saddle.

One day when we were coming from the Dutch Creek Hills with some cattle, we jumped two wild mares and a wild gelding that I wanted to break to ride. Mabel, with the best saddle horse in the country, took in after the horses, while I brought along the cattle. The last I saw of her was when she went over a divide in a fog of dust, heading for Prairie Dog Creek. Some three hours later when I got to our little homestead, Mabel was there. She had corralled the horses and had cooked some lunch for the two of us. Right then I knew that Mabel was going to make good as a rancher's wife, even if she was only eighteen and weighed only one hundred and ten pounds.

That summer we raised a wonderful garden on the new land that had never been cropped before. We raised four varieties of spuds and so many cabbages we didn't know what to do with them. There was not much market for cabbage. From town we got two fifty-gallon barrels, which we filled with sauerkraut. This we sold in Sheridan at fifty cents per gallon. With the kraut and spud money we bought most of our winter's groceries.

By now we had our homestead all fenced, the grain crop harvested, and our little bunch of cattle in from the range. When spring came, we sold our range cattle. With the dry farmers coming in on the range and filing homesteads and leasing state land, the free range would soon be gone. The Old West was changing fast. The nester was not talked of any more. Seldom

William Moncreiffe and Floyd Bard
on the horse Red Wing, 1916.
"A tall, lanky Englishman with a lot of freckles
on his face . . . asked me to come with him
and be the foreman of his ranch."

Bard at the old Burgess cabin, scene of a snowy tragedy.
"The last that I saw of Roy and Mel, they had crossed over
Little Goose Creek and were pointing at the knob or knoll."

"Pistol" on Snip, working cattle in the stockyards.
"Every pen was jam full of horses. As I remember,
separating a hundred head of yearlings from the other
horses took most of two days."

"The Sunflowers" on the polo field (left to right):
Floyd Bard, Harold Hilman, Doc Spear, and John Cover.
  "With time running out, one of the cowboys
  jolted Wilson's pony from the ball . . . ."

was the granger mentioned. Now it was ranchers and dry farmers. The latter were referred to at times as "Honyockers."

What we claimed as our home range in between Mead Creek and McCormack Creek nearly over to Little Goose we had lost. Old man Whitney had slipped in and leased all of this range land and had it fenced. Dad had already made application for a part of this land, but his application with the required amount of money was returned with a statement that the land was being leased by E. A. Whitney, who owned a ranch on Mead Creek. With the dry farmers homesteadin' all the land in between the Bard ranch and Little Goose Creek, the range was all gone.

There yet was some range over in the Cat Creek country, little patches of range land here and there, where stock yet had free range. There's where my thirty or forty head of range horses were wintering. They would die there of old age. It wouldn't be too long until this land would either be homesteaded or leased.

In this year of 1904, the dude business was getting under way. Teepee Lodge was already founded, with a few log buildings being built near Teepee Creek up in the Big Horns. There was the Hilman ranch near the mouth of Little Goose Canyon that was catering to a few dudes or eastern people. There were the Eaton brothers, who came this year from the Dakotas. They established a dude ranch on Wolf Creek at the foot of the Big Horn Mountains.

This is probably the year that the "cowpokes" first came west. Up to this time we only had our cowhands, the cowboy or cowpuncher. There was no such a thing as a cowpoke or cowpoker. Where they came from, we old cow hands don't know. All we know is what we read about them in books and newspapers.

This was the spring that Buffalo Bill came to our neighborhood. He hired George Gardener and his wife, Jim Jennings and his wife, Tode Bard, and Paul Case. These men were hired as bucking-horse riders and to do other stunts in the wild west show. Their wives were to ride in parades, help put on the quadrille on horseback. Mabel and I were offered the same kind of jobs at a hundred per month, with expenses paid. We would have liked to have gone to Europe with Cody, but we were now tied down on our homestead. By spring we were churning about fifty pounds of butter a week.

One day at our homestead there came a man looking for a horse trade. With him he had nearly a new shotgun, a twelve-gauge pump gun. After I had my trading horses corralled, he picked out the one he wanted, which was a half-broke bronc. When I tried to tell the Iowa farmer that he'd better take a more gentle horse, he said, "I know what I want."

There was no more argument. The farmer took the bronc, leaving the gun. This was the only gun I had. My forty-five six-shooter I had loaned to George Gardener when he left for the Cody show. With this shotgun I kept our table well supplied with meat such as prairie chickens, sage chicks or hens, and wild ducks.

All summer long I worked like a beaver trying to improve our homestead. One day while I was making the regular trip through the town of Big Horn to the sawmill for some lumber, I met Jack Walsh, who was now Malcolm Moncreiffe's foreman at the polo ranch. Jack was looking for a calf roper. This was the first time I had met Jack Walsh. He was a brother of Bob. Jack asked one or two of the old-timers if they wanted the job of roping out about 175 calves at Malcolm Moncreiffe's Mead Creek ranch. They refused the job. He then asked me if I was a calf roper. I told Jack I would try the job.

He says, "The wages will be five dollars per day. You furnish one rope horse and I'll furnish one. Tomorrow morning we'll start rounding up the cows with calves. Right after noon we'll start branding."

By noon the cows and calves were all in a big lot at the old Charley White ranch, near the head of Mead Creek. These calves to be branded were big, husky calves. Some were fall or winter calves. It was all hind-foot roping that I had to do, with the cows and calves in one lot together. When one of the first calves was roped by a hind foot, Jack was going to show the calf wrastlers how to tail down a husky calf. Somehow the calf tripped Jack, and he went through the branding fire head first. It didn't hurt him any, only blacked him up a bit. It was then that Frank Sprahlen, caretaker of the Mead Creek ranch, showed the Big Horn kids how to tail down a calf.

At about there o'clock Jack's rope horse was about played out dragging calves up near the branding fire. I changed on to my rope horse. By supper time the calves in the lot were all branded, a hundred and fifty of them. Well, I didn't consider this much of a branding, but the wrastlers said if I roped calves that way tomorrow, they would chuck me in the crick.

The next morning there were only twenty-three calves rounded up to brand. For a rope horse Jack told me to use one of Malcolm's polo ponies. Without a doubt this was the best roping pony that I ever used in a branding corral. The pony was good, and I was doing my best. A time keeper that I knew nothing about made the statement that I had roped by the hind foot or feet twenty-two calves and dragged them to the branding fire in fifteen minutes. Fifty years ago that was considered good average time. Nowadays that kind of time wouldn't win much money.

The twenty-third and final calf to rope was a big, husky bull, near a yearling, that was roped by both hind feet. In dragging this young bull near the fire it was a heavy pull for the pony, and the short latigo of my saddle broke in two. The saddle and I went off over the rear end of the polo pony. I lit on my feet. The rope came off the bull's hind feet, but no serious damage was done. The second time the bull was roped, I only had him by one hind foot; when John Cover went to tail him down, he got horned in the belly. His wind was knocked out, but only for a minute. Those kind of things can be expected at most any branding bee.

For the two days of branding I was paid ten dollars and had a bushel of fun. Not long after this I was out along the county road on the east side of the homestead fixing some fence, when Dick Case and Henry Sickler came along with about fifty head of Indian ponies that they had trailed in from the basin country. I knew these two men quite well. Right off Dick says, "What you got you want to trade for that Arapahoe Indian stud. The one with the bald face and the stocking legs. He's a nuisance to this herd."

After rounding up my trading horses, for this stud I swapped a four-year-old unbroke gelding with a bad shoulder. This turned out to be a good trade for me. This little stud only weighed eight hundred pounds, but was all horse. We named him Baldy. Right off I started to riding him. He wasn't even halter broke when we made the swap. He was five years old and never did buck. After a month's riding of Baldy, I took the little stud down and made a gelding of him. After that, Baldy became the family saddle pony. We all rode him. Mabel's Neri horse came in one morning with a crippled shoulder. We never did know for sure how he got sort of crippled. When a sheep herder came looking for a horse to buy, we sold him Neri for fifty dollars. Neri probably got a good home. Most of the sheep herders

232

were good to their saddle horses. Seldom ever rode them off a walk. Their dog done most of the work.

On July 20, 1904, the stork flew over our cabin leaving a baby girl on our door step. She was a cute little tike with brown eyes and a turned-up nose like a big button. We named this little girl Rhoda Irene Bard. Now it seemed as if we had everything we ever wished for.

After our harvesting was done, one of the last jobs before the ground became frozen was to dig some post holes for a corral, then build a round corral that no bronc could jump out of. When the corral was finished, the bronc riding was to take place among my little bunch of range horses. There was a red sorrel that I had named Red. He was quite gentle and well halter broke. It was the winter of 1901 that I brought a little tough-looking colt in from the hills. The colt's mother was an old black mare that didn't give much milk. With the snow deep, the colt was having a tough time of it. To save the little fellow from starvation, I dropped a loop over his head and took him to the Bard ranch. All that winter the colt was kept around the barn where he had plenty of oats and hay. Now Red was a beautiful four-year-old gelding. He weighed about a thousand pounds. Of good build and well muscled. One day I decided to ride Red for the first ride or two. I always rode a bronc inside of a corral if one was handy. My new round corral was plenty handy, not far from our cabin. Mabel left the baby asleep in the cabin while she came to see me ride Red. I didn't suppose that gentle horse would buck, so I didn't put on my chaps or spurs. After I mounted Red, he went to bucking, fast and furious. Sometimes he nearly fell over backwards. Mabel began to scream, "Get off that horse before you get killed."

Red was bucking so fast and swapping ends so that I couldn't get off without being bucked off. I didn't want this to happen. A rider never knows what end he might land on, so I just grabbed the horn of the saddle and rode Red 'till he found out he couldn't buck me off. Then he tried to rub me off on the corral fence. That's when I quit him. By now Mabel was crying and wringing her hands.

When I went and put my arms around her she said, "I thought you were going to get killed. Promise me you'll never ride that bronc again. You've already been crippled up enough by riding broncs."

Well, I gave her that promise. This was late fall of 1904. Tode Bard had only been back a day or two from Buffalo Bill's Wild West Show, where he had spent the season in Europe. When Tode rode up from the Bard ranch to make us a little visit, Red was in the corral with the saddle on, waiting for someone to ride him, not me. I was through with that horse.

When Tode saw Red in the corral ready for someone to ride him, he asked, "Have you rode him today?"

I told him, "No. You'd better try him out. He's a pretty good bucker."

Tode mounted Red, and the horse began to buck and swap ends, and nearly fell over backwards. "What kind of a damn bronc is this? Will he fall over backwards?" Tode yelled.

"No. All you need to do is keep on ridin'," I told him.

Later Tode said that he rode nearly every bucking horse in Cody's show. None bucked as hard as Red. He says, "What you going to do with that bronc? Are you goin' to ride him?"

"No," says I, "that horse is yours if you want him."

Tode took Red and finally broke him of bucking. My experience with horses has been the wilder they are, the easier they are to break. Fifty years later I asked Tode who was the best rider and showman that he ever knew. He says, "George Gardener." When I asked him what was the hardest buckin' horse he ever rode, his answer was, "Red."

From the time I rode Red up to the present time (1957), I never rode many broncs, probably ten head all together. Among them was one of those cotton mules that we didn't ship south at weaning time. They were called cotton mules, as they were to be worked on a cultivator by the Negroes in the South. During several years of raising cotton mules, there were only three that we ever tried breaking: one matched team of four-year-olds that were used as a buckboard team and a mule colt. From a gray Indian mare and the Spanish jack there was raised a mule colt that I broke to ride as a four-year-old. This mule was neat and trim as a deer. No trouble to break to ride. Would neck rein like a cowpony. This mule I named Gray Eagle. As to color, he was a dark gray, only weighed about eight hundred pounds. I didn't have this mule long 'till he was sold at a good figure.

Mabel and I worked hard with our crops, chickens, and livestock. By 1908, the homestead was pretty well under cultivation. I was planting most of the plowed land to wheat. On the grain drill with Jake and Brownie there were two four-year-old broncs that I was breaking. It was the end of the day. I had been drilling in wheat all day. There was only a little more drilling to do, then I would be finished with the wheat. When I went to dump another sack of wheat into the seeder box, one of the broncs got the bridle caught on Brownie's harness. When I went to unfasten the bridle, the bronc pawed or struck me in the face with one front foot, cutting a hole in my lip and breaking my nose. By the time the four horses were unhitched from the drill and drove to the barn, my shirt was covered with blood, and the nose was yet bleeding. At the hitch rail the four horses were tied while I went to the cabin door.

There Mabel says, "Sweetheart, what happened to you?"

235

When I told her, she says, "I wish you would quit fooling with those damn broncs."

After the nose quit bleeding and Mabel had me washed and bathed, there were the two broncs to take the harness from. While I did this, Mabel took the harness off Jake and Brownie. Then she did the chores while I kept hot packs on my face. It was two days before the lip and nose were down to near their natural size. I didn't know the nose had been broke 'till I started to have a little hay fever. The doctor told me that the nose had been broken and was probably causing the hay fever.

That winter of 1908 and that of 1909 were no different than the preceding one. Not too much to do, only dances and parties. No broncs to break. The spring of 1909, we went ahead with our work as usual. When the summer began to get drouthy, we sold out almost everything, the homestead included. We had made final proof. We were wanting a location where there was yet free range with plenty of grass and water, where we could start up in the cattle business. Red Deer, Alberta, Canada was the place we selected for our new adventure.

We were taking a gambler's chance in going there. The only thing I knew of Alberta was the summer of 1900 near High River, where the country was now pretty well settled up. By going two hundred miles farther north, we expected to find what we were looking for.

At Sheridan, Tode and I chartered a Burlington emigrant car and headed for Alberta. Tode was now married. Had a sweet little wife and two small children. They both were willing to take a gambler's chance, same as Mabel and I.

We set up housekeeping in Red Deer in a big two-story house. Here our families lived while we men with a team, spring wagon, and camp outfit spent nearly two months trying to find homestead land suitable for a small cow ranch.

In the Turtle Back area we found that quite a few of the ranchers were using oxen instead of horses. One day while out in the country, I came on to a farmer that was mowing hay with a span of oxen. When I asked the man how he liked oxen as a mower team, he says, "Pretty damn slow at times and too damn fast at other times. Just the other day when the heel flies hit this team, there was no holding them. Just took off across country with their tails over their backs. Never stopped 'till they were belly-deep in that pot hole of water down yonder."

I didn't want any ox whackin' in mine! With the coming of winter, we stayed in Red Deer and did all kinds of hauling with our teams. When we first came to Red Deer, there was only one automobile in town, an old high-wheeler that looked just the same as the one Norm Gaston brought into Sheridan during the year 1894 or 1895.

When spring began to come on, and the grass turned green, both Mabel and I were sure missing the ranch that we were so fond of. We decided to go on to Salmon Arm, on Shuswap Lake, in British Columbia. This was a pioneer country on the boom. The land had been logged off, the stumps being dynamited and blown to pieces. This was a fruit country, probably not more than ten years old.

While I was looking around for ranch land, Mabel was taken sick with typhoid fever. As soon as I returned, the doctor said, "Young man, I'm going to give it to you straight from the shoulder. Your wife is a sick woman, not only physically ill, but homesick as well. She's not going to do any good here. The best thing for you to do is to take her back home to Wyoming."

He didn't need to say any more.

When we arrived back at Sheridan, Wyoming from our Canadian trip, the only things we owned were two suit cases and two trunks. One trunk had some wearing apparel and a few old pictures; the other was jammed full of bedding. For some reason or other, Mabel and I never did like city life. We were determined to go back to ranching. Whether we could rent, buy, or steal one, we were going to get a ranch.

CHANGING SCENES

BY APRIL FIRST, WE WERE COMFORTABLY LOCATED at the old Wagnor place, on the north edge of the town of Big Horn. This season we not only farmed on this ranch, but a mile east of Big Horn I leased a small ranch that didn't have much of a water right for irrigation. Just leased the place to have more pasture for our stock.

There were Sunday afternoons when I had an invitation to go to the Moncreiffe polo field for a game of polo. At these times Mabel and our two children usually went along. (Little Freddie had been born on June 10.) While I was in the game, Mabel would visit with the women and see the game, which was quite exciting at times. I didn't have any polo ponies of my own, just rode whatever pony Malcolm told me to.

During one period or chukker, the pony I was riding was tripped by another player's horse, causing my pony to take a tumble, with no damage done. One Sunday afternoon when a Mr. Forbes from the Beckton stock farm came for a game of polo, his bay polo mare somehow took a header into the ground and rolled over Mr. W. Cameron Forbes, hurting him quite badly. At first we thought he was dead. I just can't remember whether this was before or after that Mr. Forbes became governor of the Philippine Islands.

That fall we were one of the first to get our grain crop threshed. In one part of the barn in grain bins, all of our threshed grain was stored. One day while I was helping a neighbor with a threshing with a team and bundle wagon, a man who was pitching bundles onto my rack says, "Look down yonder. Someone's barn is on fire."

It was my barn that was burning. Leaving the team with the bundle-pitcher, I took off fast as I could run to where we lived, which was more than a quarter of a mile away. I had left my team, as it would have been impossible to take the short cut with them because of a wire fence and a large irrigation ditch. Ahead of me there was a bucket brigade formed at the well, throwing water on the house and out buildings, trying to save them from burning. In a lean-to shed back of the barn there were two horses and three hogs that were plenty warm. The hogs already had the hair burned off their backs. We didn't lose any livestock in this fire, but we lost all of our grain, harness, saddles, and tools that were in the saddle room of the barn. In the barn loft there were several tons of hay that added fuel to the fire. With no insurance this was a total loss. We never knew for sure how the barn caught fire, probably from a spark from a threshing machine engine that had just passed along the road not far from the barn.

With winter coming on we had no place to house our stock. The man who owned the Wagnor place lived in Iowa. He would only furnish enough lumber for a temporary shed in a bank down near Little Goose Creek, some fifty yards from where the barn burned down. This was a mighty poor substitute for the barn that had burned. We got by all right 'till the first of March. Then with two four-horse teams and hayracks we moved our household goods to a ranch on lower Tongue River, twenty miles north of Sheridan. This ranch was known as the old Christian Dick place. It was owned by E. A. Whitney or the Whitney estate. This ranch I rented of J. D. Thorn, who was sorta ram-rodding the First National Bank at this time. Here we moved into a new five-room cottage. There was a new barn, not yet finished. Everything about the place was new except the old log house used as a cow shed. In making this thirty miles from Big Horn to the Whitney ranch at the mouth of Young's Creek where it emptied into Tongue River, there was snow hub-deep to the wagons at times.

Feed for our stock we bought from a neighbor living just across the Tongue River. We hauled the hay by bobsled on the ice across the river, enough hay to fill the barn loft, which would feed our stock 'till grass came. It was a good thing that I had hauled the hay across the river before the ice broke up that spring. There was no fording the river during the next month or two.

As I remember, it was along about the first of April there came a big snow storm, with the weather bitter cold. The snow piled three to five feet deep there in the Wolf Mountains. A lot of big steers in trying to wade through the drifts became ex-hausted and in a weakened condition froze to death, standing in the drifts. There was a big loss in cattle during that storm. One or two big cow outfits with range on the Crow Reservation nearly went broke or did go broke. When the snow melted away and the grass was showing up some on the south and east side of the ridges, about the only range cattle left were dead ones. They were skinned by the cowboys, Crow Indians, or whoever wanted to make a few dollars by skinning dead cattle that were yet partly frozen. That's when the coyotes and wolves were getting their living mighty cheap.

With this old Christian Dick place there was a 320-acre pas-ture that I had leased along with the ranch. A county road divided the two places. The pasture lay up on Young's Creek. The pasture fence was good, four barbed wires and good posts all the way round. When we moved to the Tongue River Valley, our near neighbor said, "You won't get any good out of that pasture. There are some mighty ornery range cattle down here; 'bout the time your grass is good, they will open the gate, go in, and eat your pasture."

He was right about this. But the cattle didn't eat much of the pasture. One day when a hundred head or more cattle were in there, I drove them back out on the range, closed the gate good and tight, and rode on home. The next day those cattle were back in the pasture with the gate wide open. I just left them 'till I rode home where I gathered up all the tin cans I could, including one or two five-gallon coal-oil cans. I strung them all on a wire and twisted the two ends of the wire together. Back to the pasture I rode.

With my throw rope I tied onto the wire. When that bunch of cans was dropped on the ground, I headed into those cattle with my saddle horse on a run and me screaming like a wild Indian. Those cattle sure left there in a hurry. Some didn't go back through the gate that was wide open, just run through the wire fence. Some were scratched up a bit. One cow got fastened in the fence. I didn't quit running those cattle 'till they were a mile or two away from the pasture. The next day there were only four head of cattle back in the pasture. When I went to drive them out, a big steer got on the fight and charged my horse. After outrunning the steer, I rode on to the house, got the shotgun. The next time that steer made a run for the horse, I gave him one charge of shot in the face. He turned, headin' for the gate. He got another charge of shot in the rear end. Never was bothered by those gate-opening cattle that probably got a little help from somewhere.

Most all that summer there were Indians going and coming from the Cheyenne Reservation to Sheridan. We most always camped here on Young's Creek. We were doing quite a bit of horse-swapping back and forth. One day when some Indians had camped at the creek, I thought I would ride to the camp to see what they had to swap. In among my trading horses there was a good-looking sorrel gelding that wasn't worth a lead nickel. When Curtis Red Neck offered to swap a horse that he caught out of a wild bunch, I told him, "No. Have to have two ponies for my pony."

Curtis pointed to a pinto pony. I says, "Yes. We swap if you ride the pinto for me."

Curtis put his saddle on the pinto and rode home with me. The pinto was a four-year-old that had only been rode a few times. Was yet pretty spooky. Down at our house when Mabel came out to see the swapping horses. Curtis says, "You want to see a horse buck."

She said, "Sure I do."

At that Curtis grabbed the bronc with his spurs. That bronc sure did buck. When Mabel asked Curtis if the bronc was a hard bucker, he said, "Not too bad."

The pinto I never did ride, only had him a few days 'till he died. The brown six-year-old gelding that was caught out of the wild bunch turned out to be the best horse that I ever owned as a saddle or driving horse, as soon as he put some flesh on his bones and the saddle sore on his back was healed. He was good anywhere.

One day I bought from a white man a four-year-old work horse that was only half-broke. He was pretty spooky about the harness. At times the horse would blow up and start bucking while hitched to a rig. One day I hitched him in with a black four-year-old that was pretty well broke. I hitched them on to our light buckboard and was going to one of our neighbors'. Mabel went along holding our baby on her lap. While we were driving along down the county road, the bronc blew up, started to bucking and running. Mabel jumped out of the buckboard with the baby in her arms. They both got quite a jolt when they hit the ground. Sorta knocked the baby out for a few minutes. When the bronc quit running and bucking, he had a tug in between the hind legs.

While I was trying to get the outfit straightened out, two men with a driving team and a light buggy drove out around my team and buckboard. They stopped just in front of me. One of the men came back to help me with the bronc. The bronc blew up again, knocking me down, jerking the lines out of my hand. When my team came to the rig in front, they just sorta spread apart, scooping up the outfit. Down the road the whole works went, fast as they could run. The man in the buggy tumbled out and got run over. Down the road a hundred yards the buggy team broke loose from the buggy and run through a four-wire fence. My team broke loose from the buckboard and ran on down the road, stopping in a neighbor's barnyard. In a way this could be considered a lucky runaway, with no one getting hurt much. The team that run through the wire fence got scratched up some. The two rigs were a total wreck. When I offered to pay the man for his outfit, he says, "No. I had no business stopping in front of your rig."

When we moved into the Tongue River Valley, our neighbor told us that nearly every season someone got hailed out in this locality, that we should have our crop insured. Well, we just kept putting it off from day to day 'till we had up most of the hay crop, enough for winter feeding of our stock. There was yet about eight acres of choice blue joint or native hay to be mowed. I intended selling this hay to the Dietz coal mine as horse feed.

243

The next day after mowing this hay and raking it into windrows, somewhere up along Young's Creek there came a heavy rain or cloudburst. On our ranch there was an awful hail storm which beat our crop into the ground. Young's Creek went out of its banks, flooding most of the hay that was raked into windrows, washing away part of the hay. What was left in the field was so muddy it was worthless. To get the hay off the meadow, it was put in a stack just off the meadow.

With our hay in the stack and the grain all threshed out, I had nothing to do except to trap some beaver here on the place and a few on our neighbor's ranch. I had to do something to make a few dollars, now that our bank roll was pretty well shot. The beaver down here were all bank beaver. They lived in holes or dens along the river bank. These dens were usually dug or made in the bank near where there was an eddy with deep water. Here the beaver had its winter supply of food, called a cache. Beaver all work upstream from this cache. After cutting down a tree with its teeth, the beaver then cuts the tree into short lengths and either drags, pushes, or rolls it to the stream and floats the pieces to the cache near its home. Here the green bark is peeled from the trees, mostly small cottonwoods. This is what the beaver lives on. Most of the beaver trapped by me were along the river bank where they had fallen a small tree into the river. On either side of the tree I would set a beaver trap. When the beaver came to trim the branches from the tree, it was sure to step a foot in one of the traps.

There were times when I trapped them on their slides, where they slid from the river bank into the water. Too, I trapped them in their runway. There are a lot of methods used in beaver-trapping. I don't remember how many beaver I trapped that fall and early winter, but it was better than a hundred dollars worth of skins that was sold. That would pay for the winter's coal, buy the groceries. Our taxes didn't amount to much. They were a small item at that time.

From our eight milk cows we were getting a cream check of fifteen dollars per week. Take it all the way round, we were making out O.K. Why worry over a little tough luck from a hail storm.

In the spring of 1913, Mother and Dad wanted us to move to the Bard ranch on Mead Creek so that they could have a little vacation away from the ranch. They were now running a small dairy there. Mother was much in need of a vacation. She had been the main spoke in the wheel during all those years since 1882 when she and Dad filed claims on Mead Creek.

In the fore part of April, we moved all of our belongings from Tongue Valley to the Bard ranch. Soon Mother and Dad headed for the West Coast and Alaska. Two years they were away from the ranch. During those two years my younger brother, J. R. Bard, and I kept the dairy running. We milked thirty-five cows during the summer months; twenty cows during the winter months. The cows were milked by hand. The cream separator was turned by hand.

During the summer season, three times a week there was sweet cream delivered to the Sheridan Creamery. During the winter time, the trip was only once a week. Fred Geise was the manager of the creamery. One day Fred told me that we were furnishing more sweet cream to the creamery than any other dairyman in Sheridan County.

There was sure plenty of work to be done on this Bard ranch, even with the two hired hands and a girl to help Mabel with the housework. We were putting in long hours, usually from daylight to dark.

We made enough money out of the dairy business that fall of 1914 so that we were able to buy a Model T Ford car, one of

245

the first to be bought in the county. This Model T was worse than a bronc to handle and get broke in. At a gate it wouldn't whoa like a team. It would run right through the gate. Old Lizzie would kick like a mule when a fellow went to crank her. On cold mornings Lizzie and a half-broke bronc were alike. Had to jack a hind wheel up on Lizzie, crank her over thirty or forty times before she'd take off. With a bronc on cold mornings, usually had to tie up a hind foot, kick the bronc in the belly a few times before it could be saddled. Not much difference between the two. One was just about as stubborn as the other. Sometimes we would drive Lizzie to a dance, if the snow wasn't a foot deep. Cold nights when she was left standing out in front of a dance hall, we would blanket the head end of Lizzie over with a blanket, sometimes two or three, cause the radiator had nothing but water in it. On real cold nights, I would dance awhile, then go out and crank Lizzie, run the engine for a while sorta warming the old gal up. Even at that, those Model Ts were good cars during all kinds of weather, and over all kinds of dirt roads.

In early spring of 1915, I drove Lizzie over to the Moncreiffe ranch to see about selling some war horses. The Moncreiffes now had a contract to furnish the English government with war horses. The Moncreiffe brothers, Malcolm and William, were rather short-handed as to help. When John Cover, foreman for the Moncreiffes, asked me if I could help them out for a few days, I told him, "O.K."

I was put to roping and bridling war horses for the bronc riders. Each morning during that week I drove Lizzie to and from the Moncreiffe polo grounds, where inspections were held.

One day Bob Walsh called me over to one side and says, "I don't see any reason why you couldn't be one of our horsebuyers."

When I told Bob that I probably could do as good as some of the buyers, he says, "That's the way I thought about it." But he didn't say any more for a couple of days, then he says, "Tomorrow you get ready to go down in Nebraska and start buying horses."

When I told Bob about the dairy, he said if I could make arrangements to take the buying job, to report back as soon as possible. It was during this week that Mother and Dad came back to the ranch from their vacation. When I told them about the horse-buying job offered me, they said, "O.K. We'll take over the ranch and dairy business."

J. R. (Dick) Bard, my kid brother, and I divided up what stock we owned together, both cattle and horses. My part of the cattle were sold. What horses were not sold as war horses, I put in a pasture to hold as trading horses. Now I was free to accept the job as a horse-buyer for the Moncreiffes.

WITH MALCOLM
AND WILLIAM MONCREIFFE

BEFORE GOING TO NEBRASKA AS A HORSE-BUYER, a day was spent at the Moncreiffe polo field, where horse inspections were held. It was Captain Heygatt who was conducting the inspections, the same captain who was the inspector during the Boer War. I was taking particular notice as to what horses were being accepted or rejected. The captain with the aid of his vet, a Mr. Armstrong, was carefully looking each horse over as the horses were being ridden up for inspection. The captain seemed much more particular now about age limit than he had been during the inspections of the Boer War.

There were not many whites or light grays up for inspection. The captain wouldn't even look at one, just passed them by. The captain was now wised up as to how some horse-dealers were working over a smooth mouth by burning a cup in each outside lower tooth to make it appear as if the smooth-mouthed horse was only an eight-year-old. A horse-buyer had to be up on his toes to keep up with those horse-jockeys or dealers, which were sorta turning a horse inside out, or outside in, to cover up blemishes.

When I landed down at Crawford, Nebraska and went out into the country up along the Loup River and over to Snake River to buy horses, I was probably too particular as to what I bought. The grass was late coming. Most horses were in poor condition. Some hadn't yet shed their winter coat. There didn't seem too many horses in this part of the country that would do as war horses. I spent three weeks buying a carload of twenty-five prospective war horses, with only one reject out of the twenty-five. I felt much encouraged about horse-buying.

The next territory assigned to me was the Sundance, Wyoming district. I went from home by train to Moorcroft, Wyoming, then by stage it was forty miles to Sundance, where my headquarters were established. The first two horses bought here were two cavalry horses from the sheriff, John Thomas, a blue roan and a sorrel. They were both top-notch saddle horses. Each day I rode one of these horses out into the country. Among the ranchers and horse men several horses each day were bought, branded with the Mule Shoe A brand. These were put in a pasture at the edge of Sundance.

I had hired as a helper a cowboy-rancher who knew all the stockmen in the country out around Sundance. Before getting married and settling down on a ranch of his own, Ira had worked as cowboy for different cow ranches. From ranch to ranch Ira and I went, buying war horses. Strapped to my saddle was a telescope measuring rod for measuring the height of horses. All horses bought had to stand fifteen hands high, measuring from the ground up along the front leg to the top of the wethers. There were a lot of good horses just under fifteen hands that were not bought. The same was true of four-year-olds. They were rejected for army use; among them were some of the best horses in the county. Just had to pass them up 'cause they didn't yet have a full mouth, still had two baby teeth that would be gone in a few months.

As to cavalry horses, it was a shame to pass up a good horse 'cause he lacked an inch of being tall enough. Didn't have to do much measuring of artillery horses as to height. The horses being bought as war horses were divided into three classes: the cavalry horse which had to be bought under $125; the light-artillery horse of eleven to twelve hundred pounds, for which we could pay up to $150; and the heavy artillery horse, for which we could go as high as $165. Nothing was said as to how cheap we could go on buying a horse, but we were supposed to buy as cheap as possible.

There was only one method that I bought by. First, I would ask a man what price he expected for his horse. If the price was too high for me, there was no argument. I didn't try to Jew the man down on his price, just let him keep his horse. If his price was below where my sights were leveled, just wrote him a check. Always took a bill of sale.

One day over on the Little Missouri River, a rancher, Vent Bloxson, had a good artillery horse for sale. When I asked Vent what he wanted for the horse, he said, "$150."

When I started to write out the check, Vent began to laugh. I says, "What's the joke?"

Vent says, "You're the first man that I ever sold a horse to that didn't try to Jew me down."

On down the river there lived Jim Bloxson, that had a bay artillery horse for sale, the best artillery horse that I ever bought. The horse was perfect in every way as a work horse.

Jim said, "The only reason I am offering this horse for sale, he's afraid of steam engines. Can't do nothing with him. When I meet an engine out on the road, he's liable to run off and kill somebody."

While I was trailing this horse from the Sheridan stock yards to the polo ranch, along with other horses, a steam engine came down the track near the road. The artillery horse was so scared he run through a four-wire fence, cutting a muscle of a front leg. When the horse was healed and brought up for inspection, the captain said it was the best artillery type that he'd ever seen. Jim sure told the truth about the horse. Most always a buyer could rely on what the rancher said. It was the horse-dealers or sharks that needed watching.

One day a fellow sent me word that he had a carload, twenty-five head of war horses for me. These horses were priced plenty high. There were six cavalry horses in the lot that were old grandpa horses, already gray up around the ears, but had perfect eight-year-old mouths. The teeth had been rasped down, and a perfect cup burned into each corner tooth. When I offered to buy a part of the horses, he said, "Take all or none."

I told him just to keep his horses until a white-collar buyer came along in a car and wanted to do business in a big way. Out of the twenty-nine horse-buyers, the Moncreiffes had only two of these kind of buyers, one was an Englishman, the other was a hotel man. One day when Ira and I were out in the country east of Sundance, we had bought four head of war horses, when we came to the store and post office of Horton. Here at the store was this Englishman buying war horses. He asked us if these four horses were for sale. I says, "Sure they're for sale."

After looking these horses over, he says, "Can't use them." And he went to finding fault with this one and that one. There was a beautiful bay cavalry horse among the four. When I asked him why he couldn't use that kind of horse, he says, "Not built right. Too much daylight under him."

When this horse was inspected by the captain, he pronounced him perfect as an officer's mount. The other horses all passed inspection by the captain. It's probably a good thing that everybody doesn't see alike. After three weeks of buying I had seventy-five head of prospective war horses in our little pasture. These horses we trailed forty miles to Moorcroft and loaded them into stock cars. I gave Ira a check covering his wages at five dollars per day and expenses. I never saw Ira again. He was one of the best stockmen that I ever worked with.

To see how the inspections were going, I boarded the caboose and went into Sheridan along with the cars of horses, helped trail them out to the Moncreiffe ranch. During the next two days I loafed most of the time. One day when the captain saw me standing over by the corral fence, he says, "Come over here."

When I walked over to where the captain was making ready for the daily inspection of the horses, he says, "Bard, what you doing today?"

"Nothing but loafing."

"Well, then come here with me and mouth these horses for me," he said.

All day long there was a continual stream of horses being rode out by the bronc riders, then led by corral men or corral dogs, as they were referred to. We were sure busy with the inspection. Then there came riding in on the polo field some six or eight dudes from the Hilman dude ranch. When the captain saw them, he says, "I say, Bard, what kind of people are those?"

251

I answered, "Some dudes from Hilman's."

"Ah, and why do you call them dudes?" he wanted to know.

"I don't know anything about that. Along in the 1890's they were called tenderfeet," I told him.

"And why are they wearing such funny-looking clothes?" he asked.

This one I had no answer for, 'cause this was the first time for me to see men and women alike wear those knee pants with the big baggy rear end, with enough surplus material for two pair of pants. The inspection was held up about thirty minutes while the captain was asking questions about those queer-looking people. All the time I could see those two white-collared horse-buyers standing apart from other horse-buyers who were watching the inspection. These two white-collared buyers were pointing and talking about every horse that was led up for inspection.

Come noon, we roughneck horse-buyers went to the ranch house and had our lunch along with the bronc riders and corral dogs. The white-collared gents went along with the captain and Moncreiffe and had their lunch at the big house where the Moncreiffes were living.

During the forenoon one of the corral dogs had roped a horse that run him out of the corral. This bronc was put into another pen or corral and left there with the rope yet on his neck. Soon as John Cover, the corral boss, and I had finished with our lunch, John says, "Come with me. We'll gallop up to the corrals and take the rope off that bronc before the rest of them get there."

Up at the polo ground, in a pen, stood this man-eating horse. John was the first in the corral. While I was closing the gate, the horse made a run for John. Before John could make it to the corral fence, the bronc pawed him in the back. As John went up the fence, the bronc whirled and kicked at him. By now the gate was closed, and I had picked up a stone about the size of a baseball. When the bronc made a run for me, I let him have it right between the eyes, knocked the bronc down flat as a pancake. While the bronc was sorta knocked out, John pulled off the rope. We took a look at the Lazy Mule Shoe |⊃ brand on the left shoulder to see who had bought such a bronc as this. It was one of the white-collared buyers who had bought him. The horse was turned into the reject bunch and later sold at auction.

The Moncreiffe outfit now had horse-buyers out in all the western states. To my way of thinking, it was Mr. Oliver H. Wallop who was shipping in the best war horses from out in the states of Washington and Oregon. Not many rejects among the horses that Mr. Wallop bought. The cavalry horses were all supposed to have been rode out for the buyer before being bought. The artillery horses were not rode until at the inspection ground. It was the light-artillery horse that did some hard bucks the first time or two that it was rode by one of the Moncreiffe bronc riders. I had seen quite a lot of bucking-horse shows, but nothing any better than was put on here at the polo field. Those twelve-hundred-pound horses could really buck some, hit the ground like pile-drivers, just sorta shaking a feller's eye teeth loose. Some of those cavalry horses were in on the show, too.

There were usually plenty of spectators there to see the bucking-horse show. Some brought along a lunch and stayed most of the day. There were ten or twelve top-notch bronc riders hired by the month to ride these horses. About twenty corral dogs were hired. These men mostly had homes in Big Horn or near by. They were hired by the day, going home every night.

One moonlight night there was quite an amusing thing hap-

pened down at the Moncreiffe bunkhouse where the riders held
out. One of the Moncreiffe ranch hands was keeping company
with a young lady that lived down the road a quarter of a mile.
When Olie went to visit his girl friend, he always took it on foot.
Olie was a powerful-built young man, a young Swede. Just to
frighten Olie, Ed, one of the bronc riders, took a white bed
sheet and went down along the road. He wrapped the sheet
around his body and hid in a brush thicket to give Olie a scare
when he was returning home.

When that ghost run out of the brush thicket, Olie didn't scare.
He took in after that ghost. Up the road they went. Olie says,
"You son of a b——, if I can catch you I'm going to kill you."

At that Ed put on all the speed he had. When they turned
into the little lane that led down to the Moncreiffe ranch buildings, Ed didn't have time to turn in at the bunkhouse. He ran
down around the barn and out through the cowshed, then
doubled back for the bunkhouse. Now Ed was enough in the
lead that he ducked into the bunkhouse, threw the covers back
on his bunk, and jumped into bed with all his clothes on. He
was all covered up and asleep when Olie came in a few minutes
later. Olie suspected Ed and went to Ed's bed, but found him
asleep.

The next day when Olie had cooled down a bit and we had
got the complete story, one of the boys told Olie that wasn't any
decent name to call anyone, let alone a ghost.

Olie said, "I was so damn mad, I was going to work that ghost
over if I had caught up with it."

That's just one of the many pranks that was pulled off by those
bronc riders. John Cover, the Moncreiffe horse foreman and
corral boss, was just the same as the bronc riders when it came
to jokes and scuffling or wrestling with the riders. One day when
we rode down to the ranch house for our lunch and were water-

254

ing our saddle horses at the water trough, John and Bones Taylor, one of the best bronc riders of the outfit, a gangling-built fellow good at scufflin', were with us. John decided to duck Bones in the water trough. It was then that two or three of the other riders came to Bones's rescue. They picked up John and ducked him into the water trough and held him there 'till he was as wet as a drowned rat. This didn't make no difference to John. He crawled out of that trough alaughin', saying, "I'll get even with you damn bronc riders for this." And he probably did. I don't know, as I was only at the ranch a couple of days 'till I was planning on catching the train to Moorcroft to buy more horses.

John says, "Why not wait over till tomorrow morning. Then you can help us into the stock yards with those five hundred war horses. We're going to be short-handed and need your help."

That evening we riders rounded up those five hundred war horses that the captain had bought. These horses were branded what was known as the Turkey Track brand Ⱶ. Why the English government was using this brand I don't know. It was probably just a road brand 'till the horses landed on the other side of the pond, where they probably were rebranded with some army brand.

That night these horses were kept in a small pasture across the road from the polo field. The next morning by light, we eight riders had those war horses heading down the road for Sheridan. The main reason that we were out on the county road so early in the morning was to avoid traffic. Five hundred horses traveling on a fast trot down a dirt road will create such a dust cloud that it nearly blinds the riders. To avoid the dust, on account of hay fever, I was one of the three riders that rode in the lead of the horses to slow them up when they went into a gallop. We sure made good time in traveling those fifteen miles from the polo ranch to the Burlington stock yards at the north edge of Sheridan.

During the next three weeks I bought and shipped to Sheridan three cars of war horses and was starting to buy more in the Sundance country when a message came saying to come to Sheridan at once, that Mother was quite sick. She became sick out at the ranch. A doctor was called, who said it was nothing to worry about, nothing but a light attack of "flu." The next morning when Mother was no better, my only sister, Florence (Dot) Bard, brought Mother to our home in Sheridan, where she was put to bed. Another doctor was called, who said that Mother had blood poisoning caused by a small cut on her hand. We did everything we could. There were two trained nurses. The doctor stayed most of the day and night, but it was too late. Two days later Mother passed away.

Soon after the funeral when I went out to the Moncreiffe ranch, William Moncreiffe informed me that the horse business was about over. The buyers were being called in. Half of the bronc riders were paid off. William Moncreiffe asked me to come with him and be the foreman of his ranch. This was a queer deal. We were to receive eighty dollars per month, with everything furnished, and I was allowed to have ten trading horses at the ranch.

The wages were not so much since Mabel had the cooking to do for our own family and three or four hired men. But with my trading, buying, and selling, which probably would average fifty dollars per month, it was a good deal.

By the first of September, we were comfortably located in the ranch house at the William Moncreiffe ranch. The ranch at this time had been whittled down to about five hundred acres on both sides of Little Goose Creek. On the northeast part of the five hundred acres was a set of nice ranch buildings. Near the ranch house, Mr. William had built a big two-story home, one of the best in the country, with a nice big lawn with plenty of shade trees. The handy man at the big house, where Mr. and Mrs. William Moncreiffe lived, had flowers growing everywhere. Upon Mr. Moncreiffe's retirement from the cattle business in 1912, he sold out all of his land, which included his big ranch south of Big Horn, only retaining the five hundred acres. All of the pasture land in the Dutch Creek country was sold to the Goelet Gallatins, a wealthy family from New York City. They were tourists spending the summer at some dude ranch over near Cody, Wyoming, where they had spent some time out on a pack trip with Roy Snyder as their guide. Upon hearing that the Moncreiffe ranch was for sale, Mr. and Mrs. Gallatin, along with Roy Snyder, came to have a look at the ranch and the surrounding country. After the three of them, Goelet and Edith Gallatin and Roy Snyder, had spent some time sizing the situation up from every angle, they decided this was a good possibility as a cow ranch. The Gallatins bought the outfit from Mr. Moncreiffe and hired Roy Snyder as their foreman. The place was stocked with cattle. A nice ranch home was built for the Gallatins. There were all kinds of ranch buildings built near by, including a home for the Snyders, a bunkhouse for the hired men. All told, the Gallatins spent probably two hundred thousand dollars, maybe more. The ranch alone was $110,000, so Mr. Moncreiffe told me. It was all money well spent. Now the Gallatins' E4 cow ranch was one of the best in the country.

These people were our near neighbors when Mabel and I took on the job at the Moncreiffe ranch. It was about August 20, 1915, when all horse-buyers were called in. The British contract was finished with all hands paid off. The hundred head of reject horses were put in a pasture over at Mead Creek, where

George Webber, a bronc rider from Buffalo, was retained to look after them 'till sold at auction. John Cover, the horse foreman, went back to his job with Malcolm Moncreiffe as horse man and trainer of polo horses. Along with the polo business, Malcolm was handling some of the best sheep, with Joe Gilgorea as his sheep foreman. With the horse contract finished, everything was back to normal.

PLAYING POLO

WE WERE ONCE AGAIN PLAYING SOME POLO. Mr. Moncreiffe, who came to northern Wyoming in 1885, was among the polo enthusiasts who were responsible for starting the sport in this area. One of the first polo teams organized in this area shortly after the turn of the century had on it Frank Woods, Clyde Sackett, John Cover, and Mr. Moncreiffe. Other early-day polo players here included Fred Skinner, Floyd Bard, Harold Hilman, Milton McCoy, J. M. Wilson, Dave White, and Ray Wood. Back in 1914, Mr. Moncreiffe had a top-notch team that he took to Colorado and the Dakotas. In one game played in Denver, the Moncreiffe team downed a Kansas City club, 7–5.

During 1915, when Tommy Hitchcock, one-time champion polo player of the world, was visiting at the Gallatin ranch at Big Horn, a round-robin polo meet was held with four teams taking part. I was a member of the Hitchcock team which won the championship. Mr. Gallatin presented each member of the winning team a silver cup. The games were played on the Gallatin polo field on the old Kemp flats.

In 1918, we played a special polo match at the end of the

season. It was between the cowboys and the Moncreiffe team. Members of the cowboy team included Doc Spear, Harold Hilman, John Cover, and myself. We wore chaps and spurs and used cowboy saddles. On the Moncreiffe team were Mr. Moncreiffe, Bob Walsh, Lee Bullington, and Mr. Wilson. They were known as the Magpies. They wore silk shirts, half-white and half-black. Our cowboys were known as the Sun Flowers. Mrs. John Cover made us shirts of light yellow with a dark-yellow sun flower worked on the front. All through this game between the Magpies and the Sun Flowers the teams were sure even. Then the Sun Flowers were penalized a half-goal for a foul. During the last half of the final period, Wilson pulled his pony up short and stopped on the ball. With time running out, one of the cowboys jolted Wilson's pony from the ball. Just as the final whistle blew, the cowboys or Sun Flowers made a goal, giving them the game by a half-goal.

To go back to 1915—in September, the French government wanted a hundred more war horses. It was Malcolm Moncreiffe who handled this contract. During this time I was over in the Big Horn Basin country buying two- and three-year-old steers for William Moncreiffe, who wanted to get back into the cattle business, more or less as a hobby. He didn't need the money that he made in the cattle business. He already had more money than what he knew how to spend.

One day he told me that it was his foreman who made the money for him. A lot of the stockmen don't give their foremen credit for the good work being done. Mr. Moncreiffe, being a good business man, with the war clouds hovering over us, thought it a good time to invest in steers. He must have had some confidence in me when he gave me a check book and told me to go to the basin country to buy steers and a couple of cars of war horses, that the Italians would be along soon for war horses.

At Thermopolis, Wyoming, I made a deal with a stockman for two hundred coming-three-year-old steers, mostly Black Angus breeding. They were now ranging in the badlands to the south and east of Thermopolis. These steers, when gathered off the range, were to be shipped to Sheridan.

With a driver of a livery team and buggy, I went across country some thirty-five miles to the May brothers' cow ranch on Wood River. After looking at some of the two- and three-year-old steers, I bought 525 steers, the coming threes, at sixty-five dollars per head. For the coming four-year-olds I paid seventy-five dollars per head. While waiting for these steers to be gathered off the range, I made a little trip up Wood River to Sunshine post office to visit Josh Dean, an old friend. While there I bought a team which were good prospects as light-artillery horses. One of them was a good, gentle saddle horse. Now I had something to ride. While we were trailing the steers across country to Cody, which was a two-day drive, after the steers were gathered and tallied out, I handed to Ernest May a check for thirty-seven thousand dollars for the steers. I received a bill of sale.

I had only trailed the steers a short distance when an old man with a gray beard came galloping up to the tail end of the herd where I was driving the drags. He wanted to know if I wanted to buy a cow horse. When asked how old the cow horse was, the old man says, "Here he is. Look for yourself. The horse was pure white, a six-year-old of about ten-fifty or a thousand and fifty pounds. A well-built horse, gentle, well broke, with plenty of speed, but a little nervous.

The old man says, "I'll show you that Snip is some cow hoss." After a steer or two had been cut from the herd, the old man says, "He's yours for eighty bucks."

We rode back together to Wood River, where the man had

a small outfit of his own. He knew how to handle a good cow hoss, and I gave him a check for eighty dollars for Snip.

At Cody, the Josh Dean team and Snip were loaded in with a car of steers and shipped to Sheridan. The steers were trailed out to the Moncreiffe ranch. When Billie Moncreiffe found out that the E4 were intending to buy these steers, they were divided at the branding chutes. The first steer was branded with E4 brand, the second steer, with Billie Moncreiffe's Pipe brand ⌐ . The Pipe steers were cut away from the E4 steers and were located on Billie Moncreiffe's Wolf Creek ranch, the old Netherly place, of several hundred acres.

We just got these steers located when here came the two hundred Black Angus steers, which were plenty spooky to handle. When we started headin' these steers up Sheridan Avenue, one big black steer on the fight wouldn't stay with the others. He kept running across lawns to the east of the avenue. When a husky, good-looking Irish gal came out of her home with a broom to keep the steer off her lawn, the steer headed for her. The gal headed for the kitchen porch, which was about three feet up off the ground. Here the gal landed on her belly, kicking the steer in the face and screaming for help. I run Snip in between the Irish gal and the steer and turned the steer away. With that Irish brogue that gal was sure tellin' me what was what, that I was no gentleman to let such a thing happen to her! There trying to kick the steer in the face and screaming, I could see that she was no gentleman. Never saw that gal any more while trailing stock up and down Sheridan Avenue.

Just before entering the town of Big Horn, a man with a tin Lizzie tried his luck in driving through these steers. One steer got on the prod and butted in the front of the man's radiator. Billie Moncreiffe bought the man a new radiator for his Model T.

These steers were wintered at the Jack Moore ranch near

Lake DeSmet. Later after buying two hundred steers at Sheridan, Montana, we had all the steers we wanted. These steers were mostly Durhams, both red and roan Durham. After branding with the Pipe brand they were kept at home and fed hay during the winter months.

About the time winter set in, the Italians came along for some war horses. Malcolm Moncreiffe and Mr. Wallop yet had some war horses on hand. Owing to bad weather, the inspection was held inside of Malcolm Moncreiffe's big polo barn. Here is where I sold the Josh Dean team at $250, making $130. This was the last of the horse inspections.

It was only a few days 'till Mr. and Mrs. William Moncreiffe sailed for England to spend the winter months. During the time while I was away buying the steers, Mabel discovered that there were a few bed bugs, both in the ranch house and in the bunkhouse, which all were under the same roof. When Mabel told Mr. Moncreiffe about this, he says, "We just can't have that. We've got to get rid of those bugs."

Out from Sheridan there came some painters. After fumigating the ranch house and bunkhouse, they painted the two buildings both inside and outside. All of the ranch buildings were painted white. Everything was painted white, even to all the gates and board fences. The painters were here for a month or more before the paint job was finished. The ranch now looked like a million dollars.

With the Moncreiffes away for the winter, there was a lot of work to be done. There was hay to be bought, with the hay stacks to be measured and figured as to how many ton to each stack. Hay was selling at four to five dollars per ton, depending mostly on where there was open water and some shelter near feed grounds. Over on Piney Creek, from Jim Van Metz, a renter of the lower old Flying E cow ranch, I bought 205 tons of good hay. It was well stacked and the stack yards were well fenced with four strands of barbed wire. Near Piney Creek there were two springs that never froze over, open water for the stock. This hay was bought at five dollars per ton, with the field pasture and a straw pile thrown in. Jim was to do the feeding of the steers.

Along early winter, Roy Neal, a cowboy ranch hand at the Pipe ranch, and I trailed the two hundred steers from Wolf Creek to the Pipe ranch at Big Horn, then over to Jim's place the following day.

That night Jim and his wife, Roy Neal and I sat up playing high five 'till eleven o'clock. Then Mrs. Jim made coffee, fixed a nice lunch, and about midnight we went to bed. The stars were all shining nice and bright. Roy and I were sleeping in the northwest bedroom of this old Flying E house. Right at the foot of our bed there was a small crack in the wall. Some time before morning there was a young blizzard. When we woke up, there was a little snowdrift on the foot of our bed. Those blizzards sure have a way of finding all the cracks on the north and west side of an old house.

This spring of 1916, when we went to move the steers from Jim's place to pasture, we, Mr. Moncreiffe and I, bought Jim a new suit of clothes for taking such good care of the steers. When Jim offered to contract this year's hay crop to us the same as the hay that we had bought at five dollars per ton, we drew up a contract, paying Jim two hundred dollars down on the contract. That fall when we went to measure the haystacks, there were two hundred tons of hay. Hay was now selling at ten dollars per ton. Mr. Moncreiffe says, "What will we do about this?"

I told Billie, "Why not meet Jim half way and pay him $7.50 per ton for the hay."

When Mr. Moncreiffe wrote out the check, he made a mistake and only paid Jim seven dollars per ton for the hay. Jim was satisfied, saying that he was too hasty in contracting the hay. After we had left the place in Mr. Moncreiffe's car and got out about a mile, Mr. Moncreiffe discovered the mistake about the check. He said to Fred McCloud, the chauffeur, "Turn the car around. We're going back to Jim's."

When Mr. Moncreiffe asked Jim for the check back, Jim looked at him in a puzzled sort of way but didn't say anything 'till he received the check for one hundred dollars more, then he said, "Thank you. You gentlemen have been mighty white to me."

That summer all the Pipe steers were pastured in Jack Moore's large pasture over in the Box Elder country, near Lake DeSmet. Earl Harper boarded at the Moore home and looked after the steers, keeping the pasture fence repaired and keeping the strays out of the pasture and the Pipe steers in.

When it came time to ship the steers to the Omaha market, Roy Neal, Steve Harper, Luther Bocker, and a couple of other cowboys took our little cavvy of saddle horses to the Moore place. Billie Moncreiffe and I took the Model T with our beds and camp outfit. There near Box Elder inside the Moore pasture we made camp. During the next couple of days we were busy rounding up steers, putting them in a smaller pasture where they would be handy to round up the morning we headed for the railroad that was built between Clearmont and Buffalo.

About half way between these towns there was a place called Watt. Nothing there but some good stock yards and a section house fenced in with a two- or three-acre pasture, where the section foreman or station agent kept four red milk cows. We had no trouble in trailing the steers from Box Elder to within a quarter of a mile of Watt. Here they balked, refused to go any farther. The only thing to do now was to try and borrow or rent those milk cows from the station agent, which we did. When we put the cows in the lead of the steers, the cows headed for home with the lead steers following them, spooking at everything seen. When they went through that pasture gate, they were in high gear. When a hundred or more of the steers were through the gate, Mr. Moncreiffe rode to the gate trying to slow the steers up a bit. This didn't work worth a damn. The steers became spooked and back to the hills they went, with us cowboys trying our best to hold them up. The steers crowded us back nearly half a mile before we got them to milling in a circle. Then it was a half-hour before they quieted down. The whole thing was to do over again.

This time I told Mr. Moncreiffe to keep away from the gate. What little fat they lost in the gate was nothing compared to what they lost in that little stampede. Once inside of the stock yards those wild steers handled much easier than gentle ones. We didn't have to prod them up the chute into the stock car doorways. When they saw the chute door open, up the chute they went into the stock cars. A cowboy had to be fast in closing the car door before they started back out.

The only hindrance we had was that the switch engine didn't show up to spot the cars. From the section house we got a pinch bar. As I remember there were two loading chutes at the loading platform, where two cars of stock could be loaded. After two cars of steers were loaded, Steve Harper, the only brakeman among the cowboys, climbed to the top of a stock car and released the hand brake. Then by the use of the pinch bar we got the car to rolling with a slight down grade in our favor. Soon as the two cars were loaded, they rolled away from the chute door, and two empty cars were spotted at the chutes.

With every cowboy up on his toes and having his part of the work to do, we were not long in loading those six hundred steers.

Mr. Duffy, the superintendent of this forty-mile railroad from Buffalo to Clearmont where it connected with the Burlington, was there on the platform taking it all in from the time the steers were corralled or penned 'till the last steer was loaded. When we had finished, he said, "Boys, during my time I've seen lots of cattle loaded. Considering how you were handicapped, that's the fastest work I've ever seen done."

There was one thing about it, those Pipe cowboys were no greenhorns or tenderfeet, or cowpokes, when it came to handling cattle. They were all hard-working cowboys.

With the expenses figured up against the steers, Mr. Moncreiffe said, "Why didn't we make more money on those steers?"

When I informed him that he had shipped a part of the steers before they were ready for market, he says, "What would you have done?"

"Well, I just wouldn't ship any steers 'till they were ready for market, if it took two or three shipments," I answered.

He says, "Next year I am letting you do it." And he did.

RANCH LIFE AT MONCREIFFE'S

THAT FALL OF 1916, MR. AND MRS. MONCREIFFE did not go to their old home in England as early as usual, not 'till the steers that I had bought were located in their winter quarters, with enough hay bought to winter them on.

During this winter at the ranch house there was Mabel and I and our five-year-old son, Fred. (Irene, our daughter, was now at St. Agnes Academy in Kearney, Nebraska.) There also were Roy Neal and Andy Lind, a big Swede, who were hauling hay from Garber's ranch to the Moncreiffe ranch, feeding two hundred steers. There also were: George Hooper, an English lad, who was handy man at the big house; Mrs. Moncreiffe's German maid, Miss Emily, who was not allowed to enter England, due to the war.

About the last thing William said to me before leaving was, "The outfit's yours 'till some time in May. You have the check book. Pay the wages and keep the expenses paid."

Well, that's an easy thing to do when you're writin' checks on someone who has a big bank roll. Here I managed the outfit as if it was my own, kept the expenses down as much as possible, and never rode any of the ranch horses. I was always mounted on a trading horse of my own, just in case I should meet some fellow that wanted to swap horses or buy my horse. I was always on the lookout for a good-looking bronc that would make a good saddle horse.

Riding from one place to another looking after the steers was a good place to ride these half-broke broncs. I bought one good six-year-old bronc out of the reject bunch at thirty-five dollars, gave a bronc twister five dollars to ride the bronc a week. I rode him six weeks and sold him for $125. There were some horses that I only made a profit of twenty-five dollars on. This was nothing to brag about, but it all helped out. I did quite a bit of horse-trading with Malcolm Moncreiffe, with polo ponies. Nearly every Sunday afternoon for five years I went either to the Moncreiffe or Gallatin polo field for a game of polo.

In the summer of 1917, we played quite a lot of jokes on the handy men, as we called them. They were men hired to take care of the lawns at the big house, water the flowers, shine the shoes, take the dog out for a little exercise, and do a lot of other things around the big house.

One time Roy Snyder of the E4 ranch phoned up and said

they had a flunky that wanted to go snipe hunting. It was just about dark that Roy Snyder and George Gentry and one or two others arrived with the snipe hunter, a German kid, about twenty, named Fred. We walked Fred to the backside of the Moncreiffe place. In a little draw Fred was left to hold the sack while we went up the draw to drive the snipes into the sack. Fred says, "Roy, dood the snipes fly into the sack, or dood they walk in?" Roy says, "They dood not fly, just walk in. Hold the sack close to the ground so you won't miss any. Whistle once in a while so we'll know where you are at."

Then we headed back for the ranch. Fred was bent over, holding the sack and whistling. The flunky got lost, didn't come back to the E4 'till along sometime the following morning.

One time when Mr. Moncreiffe got a new flunky that claimed to be a foot racer, we were all anxious to see how fast this young man could run. Dick Bard, who was spending a day or two with me at the ranch, ribbed this new flunky up to go chicken stealing down at the E4. When they asked me to go along, I told them that I had some book work to do. While Dick was hunting up a couple of grain sacks for the chickens, I beats it for the E4 where the stage was all set. The gate opening on to the county road was wired shut with barbed wire. Next to the chicken house was a blacksmith shop where Roy Snyder was hiding with our shotguns. Soon Dick and the flunky stepped into the chicken house, where they started putting chickens in their sacks. Dick says, "Listen, I believe someone is coming. We'd better make a run for it. Whatever you do, don't drop the sack with the chickens. The sack is branded." When Dick and the flunky made a run for the gate, we began shooting over them. At the gate Dick crawled under, while the flunky was trying to open the gate. He finally made it, leaving a part of one pant leg on the barbed wire. In doing this he had dropped the sack.

Dick says, "Grab up your sack. We've got some running to do. Down the road they went as fast as they could run, with Roy and I smoking them up with our shotguns. Dick fell as if shot and says, "Run faster if you can."

Down the county road the flunky went. I don't know how far. He didn't get back to the ranch house 'till nearly breakfast time. A sorry-looking sight he was with one pant leg nearly torn off. He had lost his hat and the chicken sack. His shoes were pretty badly wrecked. When I asked him what happened, he told all about it. He wanted to know how Dick was, if he got badly wounded.

When the foot racer found out it was a joke, he quit his job. Another flunky was hired. It wasn't long 'till he was courting one of the girls at the E4. There was a foot path down across country, where there was a foot log across Trabing Creek, a small stream, about half way between the E4 and the Moncreiffe ranch house. One night while the flunky was courtin' his lady friend, a bunch of us went to the foot log and put a roller under each end, tied a rope to one end of the foot log. George Gentry hid in a weed patch with the end of the rope. Roy Snyder, his wife Pearl, myself, and one or two others (Mabel didn't happen to be along this time) hid in the willows. It was moonlight. Trabing Creek was waist-deep. About ten o'clock the flunky came along the trail singing something about the Blue Ridge Mountains of Virginia. But the flunky didn't finish the song. The foot log rolled out from under him, and he took a header into the water.

He says, "Gosh damn the luck anyhow." Then he heard someone laugh. "I can whip the son of a gun that did that," he announced.

But when Gentry raised up from the weed patch, the flunky changed his mind and beat it on up the foot path. The next morning he quit his job. Mr. Moncreiffe says, "You boys will have to quit playing those kind of pranks. Soon as I hire a handy man you run him off with your pranks."

It was now September and time to round up steers and start shipping them to market. When the last of the 560 steers were sold as beef and all expenses were figured up, Mr. Moncreiffe had made a profit of eight thousand dollars off the 560 steers. Out of this money I was to receive $300; Roy Neal, $150; and Fred McCloud, $50.

I said, "Why not make a jackpot of this, and we three share alike."

Mr. Moncreiffe says, "No, sir. You're the man that made this money and you're to have the $300 dollars. The rest of the profit we'll store away as a nest egg, as expense money. We'll buy more steers of which you'll receive half the profit, plus your wages. You might just as well start buying or contracting hay. Then later on you can go to the Big Horn Basin for more steers."

TRAGEDY STALKS
THE DEER-HUNTERS

I WAS THIRTY-EIGHT YEARS OLD when I went on my first deer hunt with Roy Snyder of the E4 ranch and Mel Sutton, a ranch hand at the William Moncreiffe ranch, where I was foreman. We three had an early breakfast at the ranch house. While we were eating breakfast, Mabel had fixed up a nice big lunch for each of us.

It was near six o'clock the morning of October 28, 1917, that we three rode away from the William Moncreiffe house. Each of us was mounted on a good saddle horse with our rifles strapped to our saddles. From the Moncreiffe ranch we headed up through the Wallop ranch, then to the west where we crossed Little Goose Creek, not far from the head gate of the Last Chance. There was a huge pile of drift wood. On up the Little Goose Canyon a half-mile, we tied our saddle horses in a small clump of jack pines. Roy said, "Look over there across the creek at the top of that knob. Do you see that big buck deer standing there? Two of us had better circle the knob from the lower side. The other circle the knob and come in from the upper side. We'll meet in back of the knob."

We were about five miles from the Moncreiffe ranch. The snow was about eight inches deep. It was a warm day, so we took off our top coats and hung them in the jack pines. Then we drew straws to see who should go alone and circle the knob from the upper side. From out of the snow we pulled up a long stem of grass, which was broken into three lengths, two short ones and one long one.

I said, "The two short ones hunt together. The long one goes alone."

Roy drew a short one. Mel drew a short one. That left me with the long one. The last that I saw of Roy and Mel, they had crossed over Little Goose Creek and were pointing at the knob or knoll. On the upper side of the knob it was rough and steep. I had some trouble in making it halfway to the top. There I slipped down and slid a hundred feet back down the knob. Then I made quite a detour in coming up back of the knob. It had been snowing for the past thirty minutes. Now the snow was coming down in big flakes and piling up fast. I couldn't see no distance at all. Snow now was somewhere around fifteen inches deep. I didn't see or hear anything of Roy and Mel. Snow was piling up so fast that it was impossible to locate their tracks. I stayed here at the knob most onto two hours, then I walked on south and west a couple of miles nearly up to the Edleman Trail that led over into the Piney country. I found no tracks nor any sign of the boys. The snow now was about twenty inches.

Coming down Kenny Wood Creek towards Little Goose Creek, there were tracks of two men. After following the tracks down along Kenny Wood, I thought for sure it was Roy and Mel 'till a dog cut in on the tracks, then headed off towards Teepee Lodge. Then I knew it wasn't Roy and Mel, so I continued on down Kenny Wood Creek. Now it was getting dark, yet snowing.

I had quite a lot of trouble during the next half-mile on down the creek to where it emptied into Little Goose. It was so dark, but with a full moon shining behind those clouds, I could easily find my way down Little Goose Canyon. This canyon is mighty rough in places. I had to cross the stream several times on thin ice to avoid a little bluff. Now the snow was nearly two foot deep. The going was tough. I got soaking wet up to the seat of my pants. At first I was terribly cold. When the clothing began to freeze, I warmed up a lot. When I saw some long stems of grass on the north side of the canyon, I realized it was time to leave the canyon and head for higher country. I had quite a lot of trouble in climbing out of the canyon to what was known as Fawntine Ridge. From here to where we had left our horses it was at least a mile. Here the going was much better. I thought best that I should fire the rifle a couple of times to let the boys know that I was on my way. With no answering shots, I knew that Roy and Mel had not yet arrived where the horses were, or that they had arrived and gone on, thinking that I was lost. Just before arriving to where the horses were tied, one of the horses whinnied to me. Then I knew that they had not yet arrived. After putting on my warm coat, I didn't mind the cold too much. After tying the boys' coats to the saddle, I turned the horses loose to break trail. It was no trouble for my horse to follow the new-made trail. Here in the canyon the snow was belly-deep to the horses. Once out of the canyon it was about twenty inches. I made good time from here to the ranch. From the waist down my outside clothing was frozen as stiff as a board. While I was changing into some dry, warm clothing and eating a hot lunch, Roy Neal had saddled up two fresh horses, one for Mel and one for me. An E4 ranch hand had arrived with a fresh horse for Roy Snyder. With plenty of lunch and a pint bottle of coal oil and one of whiskey, the E4 ranch hand and I headed for the drift-wood pile at the mouth of the canyon. While passing through the Wallop place it was snowing so hard that we lost the trail for a few minutes. Near the driftwood pile, we tied the four horses in a clump of trees. By the use of the coal oil we were able to fire the pile of driftwood. It wasn't long 'till we had a fire that lighted up the whole face of the mountain. We figured that Mel and Roy would see the fire and come to it.

With the snow yet coming down and with the wind blowing, it was a young blizzard that we were up against sitting there by the fire 'till four o'clock in the morning. When we took our trail back down to the ranch, I told Mabel to let me sleep two hours, then to call me, which she did. By the time I had a good breakfast, three cowboys from the E4 were waiting for me. It was near eight o'clock that we four headed for the Little Goose Canyon.

We were nearly five hours in following along the east side of the canyon to the Jack Burgess cabin near the head of the can-yon. In some places where the snow was too deep for the horses to wade through, we broke trail on foot. We were wet to the

273

waist and cold. Our lunches were frozen. The cabin door was locked with a padlock.

By looking through the window we could see that the cabin was all set up for housekeeping. A woodbox was filled with cook-stove wood. The only way to enter the cabin was to shoot the Yale lock off the padlock, which I did with my rifle.

After spending a couple of hours here at the cabin, where we built a fire in the cook stove, dried our wet clothing, and thawed our frozen lunch, we went on with our search. Our saddle horses had had some rest after that steady climb up through the canyon. We went back into the valley by way of Red Grade, the old stage road. We didn't see or meet anyone all day long. We sure hated to ride into the E4 with those two empty saddles, with Mrs. Snyder looking out of the ranch-house window to see if we had found her husband.

Now things began to look serious. The next morning soon after breakfast about twenty-five men came to the William Moncreiffe ranch, as a man-hunt was organized with E. C. Bowman, a rancher, in command. Among the party there were two men who knew the Little Goose area of the Big Horns like a man knows his own back yard. One was a Swede trapper, a husky young man. The other man was the U.S. forest ranger with a forestry map of the Little Goose area and the North Piney country. While these three men were mapping out the territory to be covered, other men were doing various things. Some were helping Roy Neal load a bobsled with beds and provisions. Roy hitched two teams to the bobsled and headed for the Jack Burgess cabin by way of the Red Grade, following our horses' trail that was made yesterday.

Someone had brought from Sheridan all the bread the bakers had on hand, plus lunch meat and other things that helped to make up lunches. Miss Maude Skinner from Big Horn helped

Mabel with the making of lunches. They were really two busy women making sandwiches and feeding men who were arriving from the Banner country, from Prairie Dog Creek. They just came from everywhere.

The E4 cavvy of saddle horses, as well as the Moncreiffe saddle horses, were corralled. The first two men mounted were the forest ranger and Lew, the trapper. They headed for the North Piney Creek and the Whedon cabin near North Piney where there was a phone. Other men, mostly ranchers, were mounted on saddle horses, and headed off to the area that was assigned to them. No one went alone. Eight of us rode to the mouth of Little Goose Canyon. From here we took it on foot headin' for the Burgess cabin. The snow was about three feet deep. We each took our turn at breaking trail. Just before starting to climb Fawntine Ridge, a young man and I stopped to examine some tracks in the snow while the other men continued on. They were near the top of the ridge before Frank and I discovered the tracks we were following were made by elk. This being my third day at buckin' snow, I was feeling the effects of it. I was just too tired to climb to the top of Fawntine Ridge, then two miles to the Burgess cabin, so Frank and I backtracked down the canyon.

Most of us searchers had been provided with a small bottle of Scotch whiskey, as well as lunches. Feelin' just about all in, I thought maybe a little Scotch might perk me up a bit. I didn't want to take a drink without offering Frank one. He had never tasted Scotch whiskey before. After taking a big drink, he says, "What kind of damn stuff is that, it tastes sort of oily."

When we came to the creek where we ate our lunch, to sorta pep me up, I took another little nip of Scotch, hoping that Frank would refuse. To my surprise he finished the whiskey that had been put up in a sewing-machine-oil bottle! While eating our

275

lunch we used the empty bottle as a drinking cup. Frank was getting drowsy and wanted to sleep a bit before going on. I told him, "Nothing doing. Better hit that trail and keep going."

When we came to a big log, he says, "Just got to rest and sleep a bit."

I told him that it was getting late and that we'd better be moving on, but he refused to go any farther. I was tired and out of sorts, and knowin' there is no use in arguin' with a half-drunk man, I jerked Frank off the log, gave him a kick in the seat of the pants. I told him to keep headin' down the trail and not to stop 'till we came to the Hilman ranch.

It wasn't long 'till the Scotch started wearin' off, and Frank was O.K. We came to the Hilman ranch about eleven o'clock at night. The Hilmans were making hot coffee and fixing some lunch. As I went into the bathroom, the phone rang. Harold Hilman answered the phone, talked for several minutes, then he said, "They have found Roy Snyder over on North Piney Creek frozen to death. It was Lew Lawson and Y. Z. David, the forest ranger, who found him. That's all that came over the 'phone."

It was about midnight when Harold said, "Mother has some hot lunch made for you men."

That's the first time during my life that I was too tired to eat. Just drank some hot coffee. I borrowed two saddle horses off Harold to ride to the Moncreiffe ranch house. It was now one o'clock or a little later. Lew and Y. were there, or came a few minutes later. Mabel and Maude Skinner were up cooking some supper for these two men. Here we got a part of the story.

That morning while Lew and Y. Z. Davis (just Y., as he was named) were near an old abandoned wagon near Rocky Grade that had been used during the time the Keanny Reservoir was constructed, they met four other men: Fred Skinner, A. R. Crandall, Wes Spracklin', just a boy, Norman Custis, and Allen Harbison. All headed for the Whedon cabin on North Piney. Before arriving at the cabin, Y. and Lew noticed some tracks in the snow. They told the other men to go on to the cabin while they examined the tracks. After carefully removing loose snow from the tracks, they found the footprints of a man. These tracks in the snow were followed down into the North Piney Canyon. Here the going was impossible for a horse. The two men took it on foot, followed on down stream walkin' on thin ice. They didn't see any more tracks. Down near the North Piney water-falls, it was impossible to go any farther. There they found Roy Snyder lying near a jack pine as if asleep. He was lying on his side with one arm as a pillow. When Y. turned Roy over, he sorta doubled up. He hadn't been dead long. Around the tree and on a place thirty foot square, Roy had walked 'till the snow was packed down hard. That was proof to show that Roy was still alive when the storm had ceased. It was getting dark when Y. and Lew found Roy, and they had to leave him where they found him. Roy had traveled about fifteen miles to reach the falls.

After notifying the men at the Whedon cabin, they then rode down off the mountain and notified the E4 ranch, then rode on up to the Moncreiffe ranch, where they met with me.

A tragedy like this spread over the country like wildfire. It's probable that someone at the E4 had phoned to the Hilman ranch, where I first heard of it. It was two or two-thirty when we three men, Y., Lew, and I, retired for a little nap. Y. and Lew slept in the bunkhouse, and I, in the ranch house in a little room to myself. That morning when Mabel started to call me for breakfast, Mr. Moncreiffe, said, "No. Let the poor man sleep. He's all in."

It was near eleven o'clock before I woke. Lew and Y. left the ranch soon after breakfast heading back up the mountain to the cabin where the other men, including Fred Skinner, had spent the night. It was a tough job to bring Roy Snyder's body up from the canyon. It was wrapped up in a canvas used as a toboggan. With the corpse frozen stiff and bound up in the tarpaulin, it was mighty hard to get it the three hundred yards to where they had left their saddle horses.

From here the toboggan was pulled by a saddle horse to the foot of Rocky Grade. Here the corpse was loaded onto a bob-sled and taken to the Gallatin ranch home at the E4.

From the Whedon cabin or near by there was a big pine tree on the north bank of the stream. Attached to this tree there were strands of barbed wire leading about fifty yards to the Whedon stable. With the terrible snowstorm and the wind blowing, in the darkness of night Roy didn't see the stable nor the fence. He was traveling on the south side of Piney Creek. If he had been on the north side, then he would have walked into the wire.

Y. and Lew backtracked Roy a mile or more. Their saddle horses shied out around something buried underneath the snow. Here they found Mel Sutton, with just a tiny bit of Mel's elbow showing above the snow. Just then two more men rode up.

After digging the snow away, they found Mel lying face down, with his rifle yet in one hand or arm. Mel was loaded onto one of the horses and tied there with a rope. From here the horse was led off the mountain to the E4 ranch. Roy and Mel were laid out in the same room. After the two bodies were prepared for burial, the coffins were brought into the big living room of the Gallatin ranch home, where the funeral services were held. Roy Snyder was buried at Cody, Wyoming. Mel Sutton was buried in the Big Horn Cemetery.

Mel was a heavy-set man, with some kind of foot trouble, probably broken arches. He was a fine fellow, didn't talk much, and kept his own business to himself. There was no one knew anything about Mel's relatives 'till a woman wrote to me stating that probably Mel was her brother, who had come west several years before. When this was proven true, we shipped to this sister all of Mel's belongings.

It was a couple of days after the funeral that Allen Harbison and A. R. Crandle went to where Mel was found. From here they started backtracking. They followed the tracks a mile or so to where a fire had been out in front of a small shelf rock. There they found Roy's buckskin gloves hanging on a limb of a small pine tree near by. Roy's 30-30 rifle was standing against a pine tree. The snow was melting fast, and more backtracking was impossible.

Here's the way I have the whole thing sized up. After leaving our saddle horses in the clump of pines up in Little Goose Canyon, Roy and Mel made it to the back of the knob probably thirty minutes ahead of me. It is probable that one of them shot and wounded the big buck deer that we had seen. This wounded buck headed off towards the Piney country, with Mel and Roy trailing him. Mel with bad feet just simply gave up the tracking, couldn't go any farther. After Roy got Mel to the shelf rock, Roy gathered wood, built a fire, and then headed on down North Piney Creek to the Whedon cabin where there was a phone. But he was on the wrong side of the creek and missed the pine tree at the edge of the stream where the wire was attached that led to the Whedon barn. Roy knew this country. Knew of the Whedon cabin and the phone. No doubt he was heading for the cabin to phone to the E4 for help when the blizzard came up so suddenly.

When Roy missed the Whedon place and became lost, Mel started to follow him, became exhausted, fell on his face and died. Or he could have had a heart attack. This was just one old-time ranch funeral. It was the largest one that I ever saw.

At the Gallatin ranch home, where the services were conducted, every room was packed with women folks. The men stood out in the yard in little groups. They were yet speculating as to how a tragedy like this could ever have happened.

Miss Maude Skinner of Big Horn, a real pioneer young lady, was yet at the Moncreiffe ranch house helping Mabel with work. They were serving meals at all hours, both day and night, while the searching crew was going and coming to the ranch. They were near exhaustion when it came time for the funeral, and Miss Skinner said to Mabel, "You go with Floyd to the funeral; I'll stay and take care of little Freddie (our young son)."

When we arrived back from the funeral, Maude had a nice dinner cooked for Mabel and me and all the ranch hands, which showed there was yet true western spirit to be found here in Wyoming.

IN CHARGE
OF THE GALLATIN E4 OUTFIT

THE NEXT DAY AFTER THE FUNERAL, William Moncreiffe asked me if I would take the cowboys of the E4, go to the Dutch Creek ranch, round up the cattle, and wean the calves. We were at the Dutch Creek ranch three days, rounding up something like twelve hundred cattle. We cut away from the cows about 450 calves, which we trailed to the E4 ranch.

In the meantime, Mr. Goelet Gallatin had arrived from the West Coast where he was in officers' training camp. When he asked me if I would come and take charge of the E4 outfit 'till after the war, I told him I would, if he would allow me a ton of hay for every head of cattle the E4 owned. Mr. Gallatin says, "Here's the check book, buy what you need to put the cattle through the winter."

Then Mr. Gallatin went back to the coast and the officers' training camp. Soon he was shipped overseas to France, where he was commissioned captain. Now it was up to Mrs. Edith Gallatin and I to manage the E4 outfit 'till after World War I. Mabel and I were to continue on living at the Moncreiffe ranch house from where I managed the E4, while Mrs. Pearl Snyder, Roy's widow, continued on at the E4 ranch 'till after her baby was born. About the first of April, Pearl Snyder, with her young daughter and infant son, moved to a ranch on Prairie Dog Creek that she had bought. With Mrs. Snyder was Perry Snyder, a brother of Roy, and his wife. It was then that my family and I moved to the E4 ranch house taking with us Roy Neal, who I put in charge of the ranch work. During the next eighteen months it was a tough job that Mrs. Gallatin and I were up against. We were short-handed. The army was taking our ranch hands and cowboys just about as fast as we could hire them. The first man we were to lose was George Gentry, one of the best all-round cowboys in the country.

During the next eighteen months we did just about everything to get along. Mabel, having a cook at the ranch house, she was raising chickens. We were eating whole-wheat or brown bread. As a substitute for sugar we were using corn syrup on breakfast food and in our coffee, so that our soldier-boys could have the best.

From the Gallatin residence there came Mrs. Gallatin, her daughter, Beatrice, and a niece of Mrs. Gallatin, when there were cattle to be rounded up and changed from one pasture to another. They were my cowboys, and three good cowhands they proved to be.

Along in August, when it came time to ship the beef to market, we four went to the Dutch Creek ranch. Here we stayed with the man and wife who were employed to look after the place. With the aid of this man we four rounded up the cattle, cut out two hundred three-year-old beef steers, trailed them some five or six miles to Verona where the steers were loaded into stock cars and shipped to market. By having those three volunteer women to help with the roundup work the E4 didn't need any cowboys. These women not only helped with the roundup work, but they helped with the ranch work.

When it came threshing time of the grain, it was Mary Post, Mrs. Gallatin's niece, who made a hand out in the grain field. She pitched bundles or sheaves of grain onto the bundle wagon. When it came to branding of the calves, it was the ranch hands who did most of the wrastling.

In the fall of 1918, we rounded up the cattle of the Dutch Creek pastures and trailed them to the E4 ranch. There was a half-way stop at the George Harper ranch. Here was a ten-acre lot fenced in with woven wire, a tight fence, where we put the cattle during the night. This night, a couple of E4 ranch hands and I spent the night with Harpers. Mrs. Gallatin and Mary Post rode on to the E4 ranch. The next morning when they returned to the Harper ranch, the Harper boys, Earl and Steve, helped to round up the cattle, while I was cutting out old cows, light-bone cows, and some off-color cows. We wanted to raise straight Hereford cattle. Culling out the cows would leave us a better herd of cows.

When Mrs. Gallatin arrived, she asked, "Mr. Floyd Bard, may I ask why you are working those cattle that way?"

When I informed Mrs. Gallatin what I was doing, she says, "That's a good idea."

After cutting out 160 head of cows from the herd, we put

them in a small rented pasture just above my old homestead on Mead Creek. Mrs. Gallatin said, "What price shall we ask for those cows, a hundred a head?"

"Not that much," I told her. "If we can sell out at eighty dollars per head, we're doing well."

In Sheridan there was a cattle-dealer, a speculator. When he heard of the cows for sale, he came to the E4 ranch offering around seventy-eight dollars for the cows. The next day he came offering seventy-nine dollars. Mrs. Gallatin says, "What do you think?"

I said, "Hold tight. He's coming along nicely."

The following day when he came to the E4 ready to pay the eighty dollars if we would pasture the cows for another three weeks, Mrs. Gallatin looked at me, and I nodded my head.

"Yes," Mrs. Gallatin says, "the cows are yours."

These cows the speculator didn't make a dime on. Sold them to a small cowman. In a year's time when the bottom dropped out of the cattle business, it was the buying of these E4 cows that broke this cowman.

Here is something that amused me. At the E4 we had eleven bulls that we had no more use for. When the Sheridan cattle-dealer found out about the bulls for sale, here he comes out to the E4 with his wife and a friend and wife. He had talked the price over before the arrival of the speculator. Mrs. Gallatin says, "What price shall we ask? $150?"

I said, "It will do no harm to ask it. Choice bulls are only bringing one hundred dollars on the Omaha market."

Mrs. Gallatin said, "When he arrives, I'd like it if you will be at the house."

I was there all right. Upon entering the living room of the house, Mr. Speculator proceeded to introduce his wife and his friends to Mrs. Gallatin. Then he took cigars from his pocket, gave one to his friend. The other he stuck in his own mouth. After lighting the cigar he sat down in one chair, cocking his feet upon another chair and pulling up his trouser legs to show his silk socks. Then he says, "Mrs. Gallatin, what are you asking for those bulls."

"One hundred and fifty dollars," she says.

"Why, my goodness, Mrs. Gallatin, I couldn't pay that much. But I'll give you $125 per head."

By now I was so tickled that I beat it from the room where I could have a good laugh. That cattle-dealer was sure a sucker to fall for a bait like this. It was all his own doings. No one asked him to come and buy these bulls. Mrs. Gallatin was a wonderful lady with a wonderful personality, always was doing a kind deed for someone. Never forgot to send some kind of Christmas greeting to her many friends. She was a perfect lady, loved by all who knew her.

It was about the first of June that Mr. Gallatin arrived back at the E4 ranch. When I informed him that I was leaving the E4, he wanted to know what was the trouble. When I told him that my hay fever was so bad during August and a part of September that I would have to spend this up in the Big Horn Mountains, Mr. Gallatin said, "We knew that when you came to us. When it comes time for you to go to the mountains, you just go. That will be your vacataion."

Mabel and I sure didn't want to leave the E4. Having to be away from a cow ranch during the busiest part of the season wouldn't work out satisfactorily. When we left the E4, the Gallatins said, "If there is anything that we can do for you, just let us know."

That's how we left the E4 and started in the dude business. I switched then from bein' a horse wrangler and wrangled dudes instead. But that's another story.

INDEX

Alger, H. C.: 46 n.
Allison, Al: v, 18, 21, 22
Almy, Mabel: see Mabel Bard
American Restaurant, Buffalo, Wyo.: 28, 29
Amusements: 174, 227; dances and card games, 136–37; a dance in Montana, 162; Fourth of July, 165–66
Anderson, Ralph (assistant professor at Institute): 171
Angus, Red: 17, 40
Arno, Wyo., shipping pens: 88
Arnott, Monie (Boncs): on hay crew, 121
Austin, Preacher: 171, 173
Averill, Jim: 25, 26

Backus, Johnnie (cowboy): 146–47
Baldy Buck (Indian): 159
Banner School: 17
Bar C Ranch: 31
Bar N: 67, 76, 96 f., 139
Bar U (horse ranch): 65, 79, 187
Barber, Gov. Amos: v
Bard, Mrs. Charles (mother of Floyd): 4, 10, 11, 43, 49; cooked for Canton, 5; rents Big Horn Hotel, 14; on Mead Creek, 28;

has new son, 48; moves back to ranch, 105, 137; takes vacation, 245; dies, 256
Bard, Charles Albert: see Tode Bard
Bard, Charles Warren (father of Floyd): 3, 12, 13, 14, 61, 98 ff., 103, 123; hires out to cow outfit, 4; marries Minerva Emily Goodrich, 4; moves to Buffalo, Wyo., 5; invests in livestock, 15; sells out, 16; restaurant, 17–28, 38; buys horses, 48–49; moves into Sheridan, 51; ranch house burns, 53; builds rock house, 53, 57; sells for Loverin and Brown, 175; goes to Alaska, 245
Bard, Florence (Dot): 105, 256
Bard, Floyd: 11, 21, 22, 28, 29, 30–31, 53, 55, 60–61, 102 ff., 146–47, 148, 149, 152, 156 ff., 161, 165, 250, 251–53; on roundup, v; begins to write experiences, vi; called "Kid" or "Pistol," vii; birth, 4; scared of Canton, 5; family moves, 12; had burro, 13; attends school, 13; moves to Big Horn, Wyo., 14; to Buffalo, Wyo., 17; to Powder River with Jack Flagg, 18; becomes horse

285